Communication
and
High-Speed Management

SUNY Series, Human Communication Processes
Donald P. Cushman and Ted J. Smith III, Editors

Communication
and
High-Speed Management

Donald P. Cushman and Sarah Sanderson King

STATE UNIVERSITY OF NEW YORK PRESS

Published by
State University of New York Press, Albany

For information, address the State University of New York Press,
State University Plaza, Albany, NY 12246

Production by Marilyn Semerad • Marketing by Dana Yanulavich

Library of Congress Cataloging-in-Publication Data

Cushman, Donald P.
      Communication and high-speed management / Donald P. Cushman and
  Sarah Sanderson King.
          p.   cm. — (SUNY series, human communication processes)
      Includes bibliographical references and index.
      ISBN 0-7914-2535-5. — ISBN 0-7914-2536-3 (pbk.)
      1. Communication in organizations.   2. Communication in
  management.   3. Competition, International.   I. King, Sarah Sanderson,
  1932– . II. Title.   III. Series: SUNY series in human
  communication processes.
  HD30.3.C87   1995
  658.4'5—dc20   94-41034
                                                                          CIP

1 2 3 4 5 6 7 8 9 10

There is an excitement, a learning and maturing experience that comes from confronting deep and rich ideas. Equally there is an excitement, a learning and maturing experience that comes from forming a deep and rich relationship with another person. High-speed management is such an idea. Exploring this idea together was such a relational experience for us. We dedicate this book to each other in recognition of these two types of productive relationships which formed the sustaining factor in these long but stimulating years of giving birth to this book.

Contents

Preface   ix

Introduction

1. The Economic Environment Which Gave Rise to High-Speed Management   1

2. High-Speed Management: A Theoretic and Practical Communication Framework   21

Part I. Organizational Integration Processes

3. High-Speed Management Leadership: A Global Perspective   55

4. High-Speed Management Corporate Climate   89

5. High-Speed Management Teamwork   119

Part II. Organizational Coordination Processes

6. The R & D and Marketing Interface   153

7. The R & D, Marketing, and Manufacturing Interface   177

8. The R & D, Marketing, Manufacturing, and Management Information System Interface   195

Part III. Organizational Control Processes

9. Auditing the Speed of a Firm's Information and Communication Flow   217

10. Information and Communication in a Strategic Linking Program   235

References   255

Index   275

Preface

This book has been ten years in the making. It all started in 1984 at the time when the second author was a research associate at the Information Resources Policy Center at Harvard University. Assisted by grants from the East-West Center Communication Institute and the University of Hawaii, she was researching the whys and wherefores of location decisions made by business and industry. Not only did she conduct a nationwide survey of all of the States involved in attracting such business and industry, but both authors visited the major high-tech centers in the country and were able to interview many of the political and business leaders in these high-tech companies. This research resulted in the publication of numerous journal articles, book chapters, books, and the presentation of conference papers on location decision making and the emergence of high-speed management.

The first draft of all the book chapters was completed by 1988 and was being tested in courses on high-speed management, communication auditing, and organizational communication theory at both of our universities and by colleagues at other institutions intrigued by the richness of high-speed management theory. We kept tinkering with the chapters and, as new information and developments emerged, we rewrote the chapters considerably. Our students in particular helped us to reframe and refocus, to be more specific in our case studies and at times broader in our conceptualizations.

We want to thank our institutions—The State University of New York at Albany and Central Connecticut State University—for their continued support; the East-West Center Communication Institute, the University of Hawaii, and the Information Resources Policy Center at Harvard University for their financial support at the beginning of this project; the many State and government officials and business and industry professionals who participated in the original survey; S. Laurie Sanderson, Patricia Police, and Regina Dardzienski for their assistance in producing the final copy of the charts; and most of all our students and colleagues who have tested our book in their classes and contributed to its evolution since the first draft was completed six years ago.

Donald P. Cushman
Sarah Sanderson King
March 1994

1

The Economic Environment which Gave Rise to High-Speed Management

> *Being a successful business executive in the 1990s will be very difficult and require a new management orientation. Rapidly changing technologies, the globalization of economic forces, unexpected competition, and quick market saturation are creating an increasingly complex and volatile business climate. As environmental turbulence increases, the rate of organizational change necessary for survival also increases. To compete successfully in such an environment requires that executives employ new management assumptions and practices which emphasize organizational innovation, flexibility, efficiency, and speed of response.*
>
> *To build such an organizational capability, management must reframe and sharpen their information and communication capabilities. In the final analysis, it is the innovative, adaptable, flexible, efficient and rapid use of information and communication which allows an organization to reorient rapidly and successfully in a volatile business environment. The information and communication principles, strategies, and techniques which underlie such an organizational capability are termed* high-speed management *and their explication, illustration, and evaluation are the subject matter of this book.*
>
> (King and Cushman, 1993:1)

Regardless of which corporation or corporations, which nation or nations emerge as leaders in the high-technology race, the world high-technology market has given rise to a new system of management which is revolutionizing the way work gets done in all other markets.

Portions of this chapter are taken from Cushman and King, "The Role of Communication in High Technology Organizations: The Emergence of High Speed Management." In S. S. King (ed.), *Human Communications as a Field of Study.* Albany: State University of New York Press, 1989. Also from Cushman and King, "The Role of Mass Media in World Community." *Informatologia Yugoslavica* 20 (1988): 131–151.

This new *high-speed management system* is a set of information and communication principles, strategies, and tools for coming up with a steady flow of new products, making sure they are what the customer wants, designing and manufacturing them with speed and precision, getting them to the market quickly, and servicing them easily in order to make large profits and satisfy consumer needs. This high-speed management system has been the primary source of *sustainable competitive advantage* first for high-technology and now for other types of firms participating in the emerging global economy.

Fortune magazine each year surveys the CEOs of the two thousand largest U.S. corporations along with selected members of the investment community in order to determine which American corporations have the most admired management teams. For ten successive years the top-ranked management team has come from the high-technology sector. More importantly, at least three and sometimes as many as nine of the top ten management teams have been from high-technology firms (Makin, 1983; Sellers, 1985; Baig, 1987; Scheen, 1988; Davenport, 1989; Smith, 1990; Sprout, 1991; Ballen, 1992; Reese, 1993; Fornham, 1994). *Any attempt to assess excellence in corporate management throughout the world in the last decade would have to give a prominent place to the performance of high-technology firms and to the role high-speed management systems play in generating that performance.*

High-speed management, which began in the high-technology sector, is now diffusing to all sectors of the world economy with promising results. High-speed management is based upon the revolution taking place in information and communication technology and on the emerging global economy. What is high-speed management? Why is it based on the revolution in information and communication technology? What role does the emerging global economy play in this process? How has high-speed management revolutionized organizational information and communication systems? The answers to these and other questions are the subject of this book.

Prior to entering into the main body of our analysis, we shall explore four trends which are restructuring the global economic environment, placing new demands on corporate management, and which gave rise to high-speed management systems. We will then be in a position in chapter 2 to overview the role information and communication principles, strategies, and tools will play in high-speed management and the structure their exploration will take in the remaining chapters of the book.

We have, as Manuel Castells (1986:297) points out, "the privilege and responsibility of living through one of the greatest technological revolutions in the history of humankind." This revolution is rooted in the convergence of four trends.

First, a series of technological breakthroughs have taken place which make possible the generation, processing, and instant delivery of information and communication throughout the world, creating a revolution in organizational manufacturing, marketing, and management.

Second, this revolution is restructuring international and national economies in favor of regions with a large core market, a strong scientific and technological workforce, and a private economic sector which can attract capital in order to provide the infrastructure necessary for increased growth and rapid technological change.

Third, this information and communication revolution and the economic restructuring it induces create a business climate characterized by rapidly changing technology, quick market saturation, and unexpected competition, making succeeding in business very difficult.

Fourth, to compete successfully in such an environment requires that executives employ management assumptions and practices that emphasize organizational change—assumptions and practices that are innovative, adaptive, flexible, efficient, and rapid in response.

The convergence of these four trends has led to the emergence of high-speed management—a set of information and communication principles, strategies, and techniques for responding to rapid change in a turbulent global economic environment.

The Revolution in Information and Communication Technologies

It is hard to overestimate the strategic significance of the new information technology. This technology is transforming the nature of products, processes, companies, industries, and even competition itself. Until recently most managers treated information technology as a support service and delegated it to EDP departments. Now, however, every company must understand the broad effects and implications of the new technology and how it can create substantial and sustainable competitive advantage.
(Porter and Miller, 1985:149)

The information and communications revolution began in the 1950s and has proceeded to change every aspect of corporate life. At the center of this revolution is a constellation of new management tools based on *computers* and *telecommunications* and classified as *new manufacturing, marketing, and management technologies.* Taken collectively, these tools provide a new way of thinking and acting in regard to all the problems that confront management in dealing with a rapidly changing economic environment. Let us briefly examine each in turn.

Computer technologies allow managers to store, search, analyze, and evaluate massive amounts of information at increasing rates of speed and accuracy, making a greater quantity and quality of knowledge available to expert and nonexpert workers. Computer technologies continue to advance. Intel Corp.'s new 80486 microprocessor—"a kind of chip that acts as a computer brain—makes it possible for desk top computers to scan *The Encyclopedia Britannica*—its 29 volumes of 29,000 plus pages—and pluck out a single bit of information you want in just two seconds" (Rebello, 1988:B1). America's Digital Equipment Corp. has developed the Alpha chip. This chip has the same peak performance capability as a Cray-1 system—a small supercomputer. An Alpha chip will run at a clock speed of 200 megahertz and deliver peak power of 400 MIPS, or a million instructions per second (Wilke, 1992). This chip will once again revolutionize computing by allowing portable computers to have the capabilities formerly reserved for supercomputers to store 16 million pieces of information per memory chip and to process that information at breathtaking speeds. *Computers are thus creating decentralized and diversified information processing power.*

Telecommunication technologies combine the power of computers with the power of the telephone, fiber optic, microwave, satellite, or broadcast networks in order to deliver information instantly anywhere on the globe. Such technologies also allow management to access 6,245 major databases and 822 information services and to interact via audio, voice, or print with experts and coworkers in major population centers throughout the world (*Directory of On Line Data Bases,* 1992). Telecommunication technologies allow corporations who have facilities and customers throughout the world to tie their services together into interactive networks. Through telecommunications, investors can gain access to the New York, London, and Tokyo stock exchanges, creating twenty-four-hour access to stock markets. Large international banks such as Fuji, Citicorp, and Deutsche Bank can transfer assets to and from subsidiaries twenty-four hours a day throughout the world (Bartmess and Cerry, 1993). Telecommunication interconnects at decreasing cost and with increasing speed and carrying capacity all human and mechanical information systems. *Telecommunication thus allows for greater integration, coordination, and control of organizational activities throughout the world, creating network power* (Young, 1990).

New manufacturing technologies employ computer-aided and tele-communication-linked engineering, manufacturing, and resource-planning processes to create a sustainable competitive advantage. New manufacturing technologies allow for the development, production, sales, and service of customized new products at low cost, high quality, and easy service throughout the world. Allen-Bradley, a Milwaukee manufacturer of industrial controls, opened one of the world's most modern computer-aided and telecommunication-linked manufacturing facilities. This facility can produce one of a product or 100,000 of the product at the same per unit cost. This plant can receive the specifications for an order one day and deliver the product at its destination the next, cutting the average turnaround time on orders from four weeks to two days. Manufacturing costs decreased by 40 percent while profits increased by 32 percent and product quality control by 200 percent (Port, 1986:100–108). *New manufacturing technologies employ computer-aided and telecommunication-linked manufacturing processes in order to create competitive advantage* (Young, 1990).

New marketing information technologies employ computer-aided and telecommunication-linked environmental scanning, electronic test marketing, and real-time merchandising for speed in providing customers with world-class products when and where they want them in order to increase market shares. Campbell Soup Company, for example, can scan the environment to determine the need for a new soup; model its contents; simulate its production; calibrate its cost, price, profit, and sales potential; develop an artificial intelligence system to control the rate and quality of production; pretest its name, taste, shelf placement, and the type and content of its advertising; and determine its test markets—reducing a management decision process which used to take years to a matter of days. Management information technologies cut the cost of this process by 30 percent while increasing product success rates by 80 percent (Russell, Adams, and Boundy, 1986). *New marketing information technologies allow for the delivery of world-class products which meet customers' needs and delivery when and where customers want them, thereby creating increased market shares* (Young, 1990).

New management information technologies employ computer-aided and telecommunication-linked decision support, operational research, artificial intelligence, and group technology systems to integrate, coordinate, and control management processes in order to create competitive advantage. American Express recently implemented an artificial intelligence system which provides decision support for managers making authorization decisions on individual purchases from 400,000 shops and restaurants throughout the world. This expert system reduced by 20 percent the turnaround time per transaction and reduced by 50 percent the number of authorizations in trouble ninety days later, while providing annual savings of $27 million (Feigenbaum, McCorduck, and Nii, 1988). *New management information technologies allow for more effective integration, coordination, and control of all organizational processes, creating competitive advantage* (Young, 1990).

These then are the new information and communication tools which, when taken collectively, are creating a new way of thinking and acting in regard to all management problems, creating the need for a new high-speed management system.

The Restructuring of the International Economy

Despite occasional setbacks, the world is moving towards global markets. The number of industries that are globalizing and the pace at which they are doing so is accelerating. This can only mean a continuing series of strategic and organizational readjustments for corporations who compete in these businesses. In the future the reward for each success will be the opportunity to make more changes.
(Gluck, 1983:15)

Driven by significant advances in information and communication technology, the global economy is currently undergoing rapid change. New market forces are emerging as the world's economic center of gravity continues moving westward toward the Orient. The economies of most nations are becoming more open to international influence and their relative economic importance is shifting in favor of regions with large core markets, a strong scientific and technological base, and a private economic sector which can attract capital to fuel the change. In order to understand why this economic restructuring is taking place, we must: (a) explore the economic trends of the past four decades, (b) examine how the high-technology revolution intersects these trends, and (c) explore the changes this intersection is creating in the international economy.

Economic Trends of the Past Decade

The international economy is facing an extended period of rapid change, driven at one end by the newly emerging information and communication technologies and at the other end by the rise of powerful multinational corporations throughout the world. Four trends effectively characterize these changes: a rapid increase in international trade, the emergence of regional core markets, the emergence of a single model of economic development, and a shift in global economic power towards the nations located on the Pacific Rim.

First, driven by information and communication technologies and the comparative advantage they create, world trade over the past four decades has grown much faster than the world's gross national product. International exports and imports were about one-fifth the world gross national product (GNP) in 1962, one-fourth in 1972, one-third in 1982, and are projected to approach one-half the world GNP by 1993 (*Wall Street Journal,* 1992:A10).

Second, this internationalization of world trade is leading to the emergence of three regional core markets. In 1994 the United States, Canada, and Mexico signed the North American Free Trade Agreement aimed at lowering trade barriers over ten years between the three nations forming a regional core market of 275 million people, with a GNP of $4.7 trillion and 21.5 percent of world trade (*The Economist,* 1994). By 1992, the *European Economic Community* (EEC), consisting of twelve nations—West Germany, France, Italy, Belgium, Luxembourg, the Netherlands, Britain, Ireland, Denmark, Greece, Portugal, and Spain—began to lower trade barriers between these nations, creating a regional core market of 320 million people, a GNP of $4.1 trillion, and 21.5 percent of world trade (Hillkirk, 1989:4B). In addition, twelve other European nations have applied for admission to the European Economic Community. By early 1992, Japan had taken steps to unify the Asian development corridor consisting of Japan, South Korea, Thailand, Malaysia, Indonesia, and the Philippines into a regional core market of 1 billion people with a GNP of $6 trillion and 38 percent of world trade (Pura, 1992).

Third, over the past decade a single model of economic development has emerged which is influencing economic policies throughout the nations involved in the emerging global economy. As Castells (1986:300) argues:

> Such a model is not necessarily linked to a particular political party or administration, or even to a country, even though the Reagan or Thatcher governments seem to be the closest examples

of the fulfillment of these policies. But very similar policies have developed in most West European countries, in those governed by Socialists, and even in Communist-led regions (Italy) or Communist-participating governments (France, for a certain period). At the same time, in most Third World countries, austerity policies, inspired or dictated by the International Monetary Fund and world financial institutions, have also developed along the same lines, establishing not without contradictions and conflicts (Walton, 1985) a new economic logic that is not only capitalistic but a very specific kind of capitalism.

The generalization of such a model does not imply all governments nor all economies are alike; it merely suggests broad central tendencies in the economic policies of most nations as they begin to participate in the global economy. This model includes seven general features:

1. Control of inflation through fiscal austerity and monetary restrictions
2. Reduction of labor costs as percentage of product cost
3. Increased productivity and profitability through use of information technology
4. Restructuring of industrial and service sectors by disinvesting from low-profit areas and investing in high-growth, high-profit areas
5. Privatization and deregulation of the economy by withdrawing from state ownership and control in favor of open market forces
6. Relative control over the pricing of raw materials and energy, assuring the stability of pricing systems and exchange flows
7. Opening up to world markets and increased internationalization of economies

This general model for effective participation in the global economy arose during the 1970s and 1980s just as the information technology revolution was getting underway, encouraging the growth of multinational corporations and the participation of nation states in the world marketplace. Recently signs are surfacing that even such bastions of socialism as the former nations of the USSR, China, and the countries in Eastern Europe are positioning their economies via this model for entry into the global economic arena.

Fourth, by the late 1980s the economic center of gravity for the global economy began to shift away from the United States and the EEC toward the nations of the Pacific Rim. Japan, Australia, New Zealand, Hong Kong, Singapore, Taiwan, South Korea, Thailand, Malaysia, China, India, the Philippines, Indonesia, Canada, Latin America, and the United States accounted for a higher share of world trade (38 percent) than the countries of Western Europe (21.5 percent). U.S. trade with the nations of the Pacific Rim had by 1981 exceeded its trade with Europe and is estimated to double that of Europe by the early 1990s. The Pacific Rim nations represent a potential regional core market of 3 billion people and represent a $9 trillion-a-year market growing at a rate of $3 billion a week (*Facts on the Pacific,* 1992).

In addition, table 1.1 reveals a similar shift over the past four decades in the world's largest 100 industrial corporations, with the U.S. total declining from 70 to 33, Western Europe's growing from 28 to 41, and the Pacific Rim nations' increasing from 2 to 19. Japan has 16 such companies and South Korea 2. Whether the Pacific Rim nations become a regional core market or not, we are witnessing the attempt by the major trading nations of the world—the United States, West Germany, and Japan—to develop regionalized core markets in which their national products receive preferential treatment. At the same time, the world's multinational corporations are attempting to establish major subsidiaries in each of these core markets, guaranteeing them a global base of economic power.

While the restructuring of the global economy has led to (1) a rapid increase in world trade, (2) the emergence of two regional core markets, and (3) a shift in the center of economic gravity towards the nations of the Pacific Rim, *each change has in turn increased the demand for more effective organizational information and communication systems.* Organizations seek new information and communication systems capable of more quickly integrating, coordinating, and controlling a firm's global activities in response to this restructuring of the global economy.

How High-Technology Intersects These Economic Trends

The *maturing* of the information technology revolution at the beginning of the 1990s is both furthering and significantly modifying these 1980s economic trends. Let us explore how this maturation intersects (a) the global economy and (b) national economies.

First, information technology and increased trade are leading to a realignment of the global economy in several areas. *The integra-*

Table 1.1 WORLD'S LARGEST 100 INDUSTRIALS

AREA	1960	1970	1980	1990
United States	70	64	45	33
Western Europe	28	27	42	41
Pacific Rim	2	9	11	19
Other	0	0	3	7

(Compiled from "The International 500," published annually by *Fortune*, August 1961, 1971, 1981, 1991.)

tion, coordination, and control provided by new information and communication technologies are redefining organizational costs to a point at which comparative advantage is best achieved by locating both production and marketing facilities in these core markets (Dent, 1990; Cohen and Zysman, 1984). This is encouraging both multinationals and small and medium size corporations from the less developed countries to move production facilities to core market areas. *The threat of unemployment in the depressed regions of the United States, Europe, and the Pacific Rim has motivated a new policy of economic incentives by governments, encouraging an* interregional rather than an international division of labor (Rapoport, 1992; Dent, 1990). This is further accelerating the return of production facilities to core market areas.

National and regional governments in the core market areas are beginning to limit or halt market access for multinationals who do not adhere to pricing standards, production quotas, or patent rights. Multinationals are meeting this challenge by relocating in core markets where they conform to or receive preferential legislative exclusion from such governmental actions (Rapoport, 1992; Dumaine, 1990). *National and regional governments are seeking to create favorable conditions for economic expansion within core markets by maintaining low inflation, reasonable wages, access to a highly skilled labor force, low interest, investment capital, and a favorable rate of exchange* between its currencies and others in core markets throughout the world (Cushman and King, 1989).

Second, three factors favor national economic success in the 1990s: the size of domestic markets, technological capabilities, and ability to attract capital to provide the infrastructure for increased technological change. How then do these factors influence the international division of labor emerging in the 1990s?

The group of countries located in core markets with large scientific and technological bases and a private sector with the ability to attract capital includes the United States, Canada, Mexico, Japan, and the countries of the European Economic Community. These countries will experience steady economic growth with a rebirth of production facilities within their boundaries. Further advances in information technology and an increased diffusion of existing technology will substantially increase the quality of life of their citizens.

The group of countries consisting of Australia and the nonmembers of the EEC located in Western Europe have small populations, modest scientific and technical bases, and modest capital accumulation potential. The fortunes of these countries will be tied closely to the core market areas they service. Their growth will be erratic as they benefit from upswings in the core markets but suffer unduly from downswings. Such swings will significantly slow the rate of diffusion of information technology and the corresponding increase in the quality of life they offer.

The group of countries including the newly industrialized nations of South Korea, Taiwan, Hong Kong, Thailand, Malaysia, and Singapore have medium size population bases which collectively could become a new core market, a modest and increasing scientific and technological base, and governments which are capable of significant capital accumulation. These nations will become tied more and more to the core markets they service, with some production shifting offshore, automation at home, and a growing need to invest heavily in upgrading their labor force. Further advances in information and communication technology and the diffusion of existing technology will increase the quality of life of most countries.

The group of countries consisting of the People's Republic of China, India, and Indonesia have very large populations with very low average incomes. For these countries, as their average income rises, they can absorb the world's products and each become a large core market in and of itself, or they can join nearby nations in creating a new Asian core market. If the governments of these countries remain stable, they also may attract outside investment in return for market access. However, it is unlikely that these countries will create an educated and well-trained labor force in the near future, given the size of their current labor force. Further, advances and increases in the acquisition of information and communication technology will increase the quality of life in each of these countries.

The group of countries including Brazil and the nations of the former USSR and Eastern Europe will find the information revolution a mixed blessing as they seek to dramatically upgrade the motivation and quality of their workforce, while experiencing a growing demand by their citizens for capital goods, with insufficient resources to provide for both economic growth and consumer demand. Each of these areas has the potential, if it can maintain political stability, control inflation, and achieve consistent economic growth, to become a core market. All have a growing scientific and technological base. However, Brazil, the former nations of the USSR, and most of the countries of Eastern Europe are huge debtor nations and have only begun the process of moving from a central planned to a market economy. Effective leadership will be the key to their emergence as full participants in the world economy.

The major oil producing countries—Iran, Iraq, Saudi Arabia, Venezuela, and Nigeria—have access to sufficient capital accumulation to begin modernization but lack the scientific and technological base and population base to become a core market. In addition, internal and external political forces are at work creating instability in the form of religious and nonreligious wars in the Middle East, weak political institutions and ethnic cleavages in Nigeria and Indonesia, and weak economies due to large national debts in Venezuela and Nigeria. This suggests that the information revolution will bypass the general population but may intersect certain economic sectors—namely, the military and the elite.

Finally, most of the Third World countries will be bypassed and denied access to the emerging global economy. Some countries, such as *Sri Lanka, Mozambique, Nicaragua, and Peru*, will try to maintain their national integrity by meeting the needs of their countries with domestic production and thus avoid the global economic imperatives of the information and communication revolution. It seems unlikely that such a strategy can isolate these countries from participation in the information and communication revolution and the emerging global economy it is creating.

These then are the economic imperatives which are constraining various nations' differential participation in the information revolution and the emerging global economy.

The Emergence of a New Business Climate

Rapidly changing technology, quick market saturation, unexpected global competition—these all make succeeding in business, particularly a high technology business, harder than ever today.
(Fraker, 1984:66)

The volatile business climate engendered by the information technology revolution and the globalization of economic forces has led to a significant realignment of national economic resources. The emergence of a volatile business climate also has significant implications for the realignment of individual corporations' economic resources. In order to understand this corporate realignment we will (1) explore the unique problem this realignment creates for individual corporations, (2) outline the new corporate perspective for responding to this problem, and (3) examine the new management assumptions that are necessary to compete successfully in a volatile business climate.

The Problem of a Shrinking Product Life Cycle

Most of these environmental forces precipitating the need for rapid change in corporate operations arise from a single problem—namely, the fact that firms are confronted by shrinking product life cycles. The product life cycle is the period of time from the inception of an idea for a product until the market for that product is saturated or disappears due to new product development. A product life cycle normally involves several stages: product conceptualization, design, testing, refinement, mass production, marketing, shipping, selling, and servicing.

Dominique Hanssens, a professor in UCLA's Graduate School of Management, has studied the product life cycle in electrical appliances for years. He reports (Fraker, 1984) that years ago the product life cycle for refrigerators took over thirty years to mature, providing considerable time for each phase of the product life cycle to develop. However, all of this has changed. The market for microwave ovens has taken ten years to mature; CB radios, four years; computer games, three years, and so on. Perhaps the most dramatic example of shrinking product life cycles as a result of rapidly changing technology, quick market saturation, and unexpected competition can be found in the computer industry.

The first commercially successful computer, containing an 8-bit memory chip, came to market in 1977; four years later in 1981 the 16-bit memory chip appeared; two years later in 1983 came the 32-bit memory chip; and one year later in 1984 came the 64-bit memory chip. By 1987 we witnessed the appearance of the 1-megabyte memory chip, by 1989 the 4-megabyte memory chip, and by 1990 the development of a 16-megabyte memory chip was well underway. The industrial shakedown from such rapid changes has taken its toll on Commodore, Atari, Digital, IBM, and Texas Instruments and led to the emergence of Japanese computer companies. Large U.S. companies, once dominant in their respective markets, such as IBM and DEC, who were unable to respond effectively to the end of one product life cycle and the beginning of a new one, lost their market position, with still other firms going out of the computer business.

How can a company manage to avoid these unpleasantries and prosper? What new techniques and skills must managers master to respond to this challenge? Only recently have executives who have responded successfully to this challenge begun to report a consistent pattern of attack which shows promise of providing a foundation for a new corporate perspective on how to respond to rapid environmental change.

A New Corporate Perspective on Rapid Change

Fraker (1984) argues that rapidly changing technology, quick market saturation, and unexpected competition have led to the emergence of a new corporate perspective for coping with a volatile business climate.

- *First, companies must stay close to both their customers and their competitors.* Successful companies always know what the customer needs and attempt to provide it. When products and manufacturing processes change rapidly, it is crucial to keep up with the investment strategies and product costs of rival companies. In order to accomplish this, companies must develop and maintain a rapid and accurate intelligence system capable of preventing surprises.

- *Second, companies must think constantly about new products and then back that thinking with investment fast.* A good new product strategy requires a large, active, and focused research and development team with ready access to and the prudent use of large amounts of capital.

- *Third, rapid and effective delivery requires close coordination among design, manufacturing, testing, marketing, delivery, and servicing systems.* The interdependence of these systems combined with the short lead time in product delivery make certain that any error within, between, or among systems will delay product delivery, endangering market penetration. Close cooperation among these systems requires strong, quick, and responsive integration, coordination, and control systems.

- *Fourth, product quality, user friendliness, ease of service, and competitive pricing are essential for market penetration.* In an environment where consumer and investor representatives compare, rate, and effectively communicate product differences, market penetration depends on quality, utility, and readily serviceable products. This in turn requires the active monitoring, testing, and checking the servicing of one's own and competitive products.

- *Fifth, companies which introduce new products must consider the processes and costs required to cannibalize their own products and to retrench the workers involved.* Companies faced with rapidly changing technology, quick market saturation, and unexpected competition must be prepared to change or withdraw their own products rather than let their reputation and market shares be eroded by a competitor. Corporate planning for new products must include contingencies for shifting, retraining, or retrenching large product sectors rapidly.

- *Sixth, a corporate culture must be developed which emphasizes change, allows for the assimilation of new units with alternative values, and encourages members to learn from mistakes without reprisal.* Corporate cultures which cannot change rapidly will impeded market adaptation. Corporations faced with stiff competition will often acquire other corporations with alternative values which will have to be integrated without delay into their corporate culture. Finally, a certain number of new initiatives are doomed to failure for all the reasons previously cited. Talented members of an organization must learn quickly from their failures and press on to new projects. A corporate culture's responsiveness to these issues will require a strong integration of labor and management interests, group and individual needs, and the values of consumers, investors, and the corporation.

- *Seventh, a corporate strategy must be developed which scans the globe for potential acquisitions, joint ventures, coalitions, value-added partnerships, and tailored trade agreements which can give a corporation a technological edge, market access, market control, and/or rapid response capabilities.* Such a pooling of corporate resources is necessary for survival in a rapidly changing, highly competitive, international economic environment.

Each of these seven issues forms the basis for a new set of corporate assumptions and practices regarding how to effectively reorient an organization to a rapidly changing business climate. This change in corporate orientation has led to the emergence of a new high-speed management perspective aimed at capitalizing on rapid environmental change in order to increase market shares and make large profits.

Executives Must Employ Management Assumptions and Practices that Emphasize Organizational Change

Being an executive in the late 1980s and the 1990s will be like playing basketball with a moving basket. With increasing rates of environmental change as well as the diversified nature of most large firms, continuity and durability of organizational strategy no longer guarantees success. Drafting 5 or 10 year strategic plans becomes an exercise in futility when the organizational environment changes so dramatically that long-term plans fail to adjust for transient targets. To compete in this and the next decade of transformation requires that executives create and maintain organizational assumptions and practices which help clarify and cope with continual environmental change.
(Ulrich and Wiersema, 1989:115)

Rapid environmental change creates organizational problems but also creates organizational opportunities. A high-speed management system is a set of theoretic and practical principles for responding to rapid environmental change. More specifically, high-speed management functions to decrease the response time required to get a desired product and/or service to the customer ahead of one's competitors. It does so by employing three separate theories and sets of practices. *First,* it employs environmental scanning theory to locate the need for new products and/or services and one's competitors' responses to that need. *Second,* it employs value chain theory to identify areas across and within firms where the information and communication processes involved in an organization's integration, coordination, and control systems must be improved. *Third,* it employs a unique continuous improvement theory in order to reengineer an organization's integration, coordination, and control processes, thus increasing the speed-to-market of products, thereby generating a competitive advantage.

An organization's management system, its integration, coordination, and control system, must have certain specifiable characteristics in order to respond to the opportunities created by successive, rapid environmental change. A management system which capitalizes on environmental change must be innovative, adaptive, flexible, efficient, and rapid in response—a high-speed management system.

Innovative management refers not only to product development, but innovation in corporate structure, employee utilization, outsourcing, inventory control, manufacturing, marketing, servicing, and competitive positioning.

Adaptive management refers to an organization's appropriate adjustment to change in employee values, customer tastes, investor interests, government regulations, the availability of global economic resources, and the strategic positioning of competitors.

Flexible management refers to the capacity of an organization to expand, contract, and shift direction on products and competitive strategy; to assimilate acquisitions, joint ventures, and coalitions; and to excise unproductive or underproductive units.

Efficient management refers to maintaining the industry lead in world-class products, productivity, investors' equity, return on investment, employee satisfaction, customer support, product quality, and serviceability.

Rapid response management refers to gaining and maintaining the industry standard in speed of response to environmental change.

Due to a shrinking product life cycle, today's new generation companies compete by decreasing the time required to bring a product to market. Such companies are innovative, adaptive, flexible, efficient, and rapid in response by concentrating on reducing if not eliminating delays and using this response advantage to obtain increased market shares. The organizational benefits which flow from a high-speed management system can be breathtaking.

First, order-of-magnitude changes occur in response time. General Electric reduced from three weeks to three days the amount of time required to deliver a custom-made circuit breaker. Motorola used to turn out electronic pagers three weeks after the factory order arrived; now the process takes two hours (*New York Times,* 1992:C3).

Second, order-of-magnitude changes occur in profits. McKinsey & Company management consulting group demonstrates that high-tech products that come to market six months late earn 33 percent less profit over five years, while coming out with a product on time, but 50 percent over budget, cuts profits only 4 percent. More significantly, IBM obtained a six-month lead over all competitors in the mass production of four-megabyte computer storage chips. This occurred in an industry where the average product life cycle for storage chips is eighteen months (Vesey, 1991:25).

Third, order-of-magnitude changes occur in quality and productivity. In order to increase the speed-to-market of new products, organizations must reengineer and simplify all their production processes. This in turn, according to studies by Clark (1989), Gupta and Wilemon (1990), and McDonough and Barczak (1991), promotes a self-consciousness of organizational functions and processes which leads to improved product quality and increased productivity. Boeing, Intel, Sun Microsystems, and General Electric each achieved 10 percent per year increases in quality and productivity over a ten-year time span after implementing a high-speed management strategy (*Business Week*, 1993:79). A recent survey of fifty major U.S. corporations by Kaiser and Associates, a large consulting firm, found that all listed time-based management strategies at the top of their priority list. Why? Because speed of response tends to improve productivity, profits, and product quality (Dumaine, 1989:54).

Fourth, order-of-magnitude changes occur in investment turnaround and in market shares. A study by Nayak (1990:14) demonstrates that reducing the lead time of new automotive models by 20 percent was Toyota's most effective means of increasing the net present value of its total investment and increasing market shares. A company can thus regulate its exposure to risk by incrementally adjusting the newness of its products in the market and by fine-tuning its innovations with the help of customer feedback (Brown and Karagozoglu, 1993:37).

Fifth, order-of-magnitude changes occur in the diffusion of organizational power and in the flexibility of working modes. Gold (1987) and Millson, Raj, and Wilemon (1992) found that speed-to-market requires the early and participative involvement of all work groups in product and process design, increasing worker responsibility and organizational adaptability.

The implementation of this new corporate strategy and thus *the goal of high-speed management is the use of the new information technologies and human communication process to rapidly develop, test, and produce a steady flow of low-cost, high-quality, easily serviced, high-value products which meet the customers' needs and of quickly getting these products to market before one's competition in an effort to achieve market penetration and large profits.*

In the final analysis, a management system with high-speed characteristics can only be developed, implemented, and maintained by the appropriate use of information technologies within a unique communication environment, which adjusts people to technologies and technologies to people through the appropriate use of three interdependent communication processes—integration, coordination, and control. The uniqueness of these communication processes stems from the parameters placed on communication by the human communication-information technology interface and its effects upon organizational management processes. *It is this relationship which is at the heart of the high-speed management process.*

What are the unique principles, strategies, and techniques of high-speed management for resolving organizations' problems and capitalizing on the opportunities inherent in rapid change? What are the distinctive information and communication issues raised by rapid change? A theoretic and practical framework for resolving these issues and others will be developed in the next chapter, followed by an overview of the principles, strategies, and techniques of high-speed management to be applied in the remaining chapters of the book.

2

High-Speed Management: A Theoretic and Practical Communication Framework

We're in a world that is obsessed with speed. "Time"
has won the race to become our most valued resource. . . .
Time to market . . . that is, the elapsed time between product
definition and availability . . . is becoming a highly competi-
tive issue for U.S. companies, and in the 1990s it may be the
single most critical factor for success across markets. . . .
Speed to market creates opportunities in market shares,
market leadership and profits.
(Vesey, 1991:23–26)

Until recently the search for theoretic principles grounded in human communication processes which can govern and guide all of an organization's significant work activities has been rather barren. The reason has been simple. Organizational strategy, the prime candidate for locating powerful cross-organizational theoretic principles, has had at its core noncommunication activities. For example, if an organization pursues a strategy of *competitive advantage based on product cost,* the central organizational process yielding cross-organizational theoretic activity is production or manufacturing activities. On the other hand, if an organization pursues a strategy of obtaining *competitive advantage based on product differentiation,* then the central organizational process yielding cross-organizational theoretic activity is product uniqueness or research and development (R & D) activities. While human interaction or communication is involved in both organizational manufacturing and R & D activities, the primary cross-organizational theoretic activities are organizational manufacturing and technological innovations. Communication processes function as second-level support activities and are given their regularities based on the primary organizational activities of production and innovation.

21

However, when *speed-to-market or time* becomes the primary source of competitive advantage, this all changes and *effective communication becomes the primary cross-organizational theoretic activity;* other organizational processes such as R & D, manufacturing, sales, and servicing products become support activities to the primary process and are adjusted accordingly (Stalk, 1988).

More specifically, *sustainable competitive advantage in the 1990s* will depend upon a corporation's capacity to monitor accurately changes in external economic forces and then to reorder a firm's *internal and external resources* more rapidly than one's competitors. In order to accurately monitor changes in external economic forces, and to rapidly orient and reorient a firm's internal and external resources, an organization must have a world-class information and communication capability. This capability must provide for a rapid coalignment among product development, purchasing, manufacturing, distribution, sales, and service systems in response to environmental change.

In addition, a world-class information and communication capability must allow an organization to track and respond in real time to international changes in the cost of capital, labor, and raw materials as well as changes in consumer taste and competitor response. In some parts of the world, developing such a real-time tracking and response capability will be impossible due to political, social, and/or economic unrest, which prevents the development of an appropriate information and communication infrastructure. However, in the U.S.-Canadian core market, the emerging European Economic Community core market, and the Asian development corridor, such real-time tracking and response capabilities are already a reality. *In such areas, international trade is expanding more rapidly than GNP, and high-speed management is a chief source of sustainable competitive advantage.*

What distinguishes the top fifty international corporations from their competitors is that they (a) are located in these core markets, (b) have developed such a real-time external and internal information and communication capability, and (c) have continually improved those processes, employing high-speed management principles. To understand how to systematically employ a high-speed management system, we are in need of a theoretic framework to guide the development and maintenance of such a world-class information and communication capability.

More specifically, high-speed management functions to decrease the response time required to get a desired product and/or service to the customers ahead of one's competitors. It does so by employing three separate but interdependent theories and sets of practices. *First,* it employs environmental scanning theory to locate the need for new products and/or services and one's competitors' responses to that need. *Second,* it employs value chain theory to identify areas across firms and within the firm where the information and communication processes involved in an organization's integration, coordination, and control system must be improved. *Third,* it employs a unique information and communication continuous improvement theory in order to reengineer a firm's integration, coordination, and control processes, thus increasing the speed-to-market of products, thereby generating a competitive advantage. It is the purpose of this chapter to explicate these theoretic frameworks. Our explication of these frameworks will proceed in four stages.

First, we shall explore environmental scanning as an information and communication framework for monitoring and evaluating rapid changes in an organization's external economic forces.

Second, we shall explore value chain theory as an information and communication framework for rapidly orienting and reorienting an organization's internal and external resources in response to changing external environmental forces.

Third, we shall investigate the nature, function, and scope of an organization's information and communication system and the role this system plays in continually improving the coalignment of necessary organizational activities.

Finally, we shall overview the theory of organizational integration, coordination, and control or high-speed management to be presented in the remaining chapters of the book.

Environmental Scanning

One suspects that the main profit generator in international business lies increasingly in an efficient and accurate international information system which has the capacity to ascertain almost instantaneously and on a 24-hour-a-day basis where the cheapest capital is to be found, where the most appropriate technology is available, where skilled people can be hired, where the lowest priced goods are or can be produced—and on the demand side, where the opportunities to employ these resources most profitably are to be located and how to do so.
(Robinson, 1981:16)

The Center for Information Systems Research at the MIT Sloan School of Management in 1989 stated that an organization's ability to continuously improve its effectiveness in managing organizational interdependencies will be the critical element in successfully responding to the competitive forces of the 1990s (Rockart and Short, 1989). Effectiveness in managing organizational interdependencies refers to an organization's ability to achieve *coalignment* among its internal and external resources in a manner which is equal to or greater than existing world-class benchmarks in their markets.

Coalignment is a unique form of organizational interdependence in which each of a firm's stakeholders and subunits clearly articulates its needs, concerns, and potential contributions to the organization's functioning in such a manner that management can forge an appropriate value-added configuration and linkage between units. *An appropriate value-added configuration and linkage between units is one which integrates, coordinates, and controls each unit's needs, concerns, and contributions so that the outcome is mutually satisfying to the units involved and optimizing in value-added activities to the organizational functioning as a whole,* thus creating a sustainable competitive advantage.

World-class benchmarking refers to the standards one holds in setting goals for improvement. These benchmarks or goals to be met in improving an organization's innovation, adaptation, flexibility, efficiency, and rapid response to environmental change must be set at world-class levels. They must reflect the highest standards of the best companies in the world. Only then will improvement in an organization's coalignment process provide for the value-added gains necessary for sustainable competitive advantage.

Environments create both problems and opportunities for organizations. Organizations must cope with changes in the cost of capital, labor, and raw materials; shifts in consumer taste, governmental regulations, and political stability; and unexpected competition. Similarly, organizations depend upon the environment for scarce and valued resources, for market growth, and for acquisitions, joint ventures, coalitions, value-added partnerships, and tailored trade agreements. *An organization's environment, perhaps more than any other factor, affects organizational strategy, structure, and performance. However, whether such changes in organizational strategy, structure, and performance lead to positive or negative consequences rests almost entirely upon the speed, accuracy, and interpretation of the information and communication regarding the significance of various environmental changes and the rapid reorientation of an organization's strategy, structure, and resources in order to take advantage of such changes.* This process is termed *environmental scanning.* Our analysis of environmental scanning will be explored in two stages: an explication of an environmental scanning framework and an example of environmental scanning by a high-performance firm.

An Explication of an Environmental Scanning Framework

If environmental scanning is an essential information and communication process for reorienting organizational strategy, structure, and resources, then who is responsible for establishing, monitoring, and utilizing such a capability?

Each industry and market in which a firm operates will contain its own unique underlying competitive dynamic based upon what the firms in the market are doing to influence sales and the influences to which one's customers are responding when buying products. Thus environmental scanning of industrial and market forces must track the organizational strategies, structures, and resources employed by one's competitors and the inclinations, products, and potential products which one's customers will want or demand. This information and communication analysis is normally performed by the product divisions or businesses operating within the industry and/or market.

Once the competitive dynamics of an industry and/or market are understood, then top management normally scans the economic, technical, political, and social forces at work in the global economy which might be employed to influence these competitive dynamics. For example, capital can frequently be borrowed from Japanese banks at 3 to 5 percent less than other sources; skilled labor can be obtained in Singapore, Taiwan, and Korea at 30 to 60 percent less than in the U.S.-Canadian and EEC core markets; some parts and manufacturing processes can frequently be subcontracted from other firms less expensively than provided in-house. These economic forces can significantly influence the competitive dynamics of an industry and/or market and are central to reorienting one's own firm to achieve a competitive advantage. Each of the globe's core market areas has unique political and social forces at work. For example, local distribution and service channels may be required to get products to market. The use of these distribution and service networks may depend on meeting local political demands or employing local organizations through acquisitions, joint ventures, coalitions, value-added partnerships, and/or tailored trade in order to reorient one's own firm to achieve a competitive advantage. An understanding of the competitive dynamics of a firm's industry and markets allows top management to focus an organization's environmental scanning capabilities so as to conserve resources.

Environmental Scanning in a High-Performance Organization

Environmental scanning is at once a simple and complex process. It is *simple* in that the critical information required to analyze the underlying dynamics of an industry and/or market are frequently shared by all the competitors. It is *complex* in that the number of areas monitored to effect this dynamic may be large, and determining the meaning of information to each area and the implications of information from these diverse areas on each other may be very complex. Let us explore the simple and complex elements in this process in a concrete example.

Jack Welch, CEO of General Electric, a very successful global competitor, described the two stages of environmental scanning and its effect on corporate alignment in his firm in an interview. *First,* once a year at the annual meeting of GE's top one hundred executives, each of the firm's fourteen business leaders is required to present an environmental scanning analysis of his or her respective businesses. Each business leader is asked to present one-page answers to five questions:

1. What are your business's global market dynamics today and where are they going over the next several years?
2. What actions have your competitors taken in the last three years to upset those global dynamics?
3. What have you done in the last three years to affect those dynamics?
4. What are the most dangerous things your competitors could do in the next three years to upset those dynamics?
5. What are the most effective things you could do to bring about your desired impact on those dynamics? (Tichy and Charon, 1989:115).

Second, after getting the answers to these questions, it is top management's task to do something to help business leaders influence those dynamics. Welch concluded by saying:

> Five simple charts. After these initial reviews, which we update regularly, we could assume that everyone at the top

knew the plays and had the same playbook. It doesn't take a genius. Fourteen businesses each with a playbook of five charts. So when Larry Bossidy is with a potential partner in Europe, or I'm with a company in the Far East, we're always there with a competitive understanding based on our playbooks. We know exactly what makes sense; we don't need a big staff to do endless analysis. That means we should be able to act with speed.

Probably the most important thing we promise our business leaders is fast action. Our job in the executive office is to facilitate, to go out and negotiate a deal, to make the acquisition, or get our businesses the partners they need. When our business leaders call, they don't expect studies—they expect answers.

Take the deal with Thomson, where we swapped our consumer electronics business for their medical equipment business. We were presented with an opportunity, a great solution to a serious strategic problem and we were able to act quickly. We didn't need to go back to headquarters for a strategic analysis and a bunch of reporters. Conceptually, it took us about 30 minutes to decide that the deal made sense and then maybe two hours with the Thomson products to work out the basic terms. (Tichy and Charon, 1989:115)

Thus, environmental scanning allows us to analyze and act on the forces external to an organization which significantly influence its internal relationships.

Next, value chain theory will allow us the opportunity to focus on the internal relationships which influence an organization's reorientation to external forces.

Value Chain Theory

The distinctive issue in international, as contrasted to domestic, strategy can be summarized in two key dimensions of how a firm competes internationally. The first is what I term the configuration of a firm's activities worldwide, or where in the world each activity in the value chain is performed, including in how many places. The second dimension is what is termed coordination, which refers to how like activities performed in different countries are coordinated with each other.
(Porter, 1986:17)

To begin, we are in need of a theoretic framework for analyzing the kinds of international markets, the types of competitive advantage, and the issues involved in configuring and linking a firm's activities relative to one's competitors so as to obtain a sustainable competitive advantage. Particularly useful in this regard is *value chain theory*. We shall therefore: (a) explicate value chain theory, (b) apply value chain theory to analyze competitive advantage in the international auto industry, and (c) draw out the implications of this analysis for the theory of high-speed management.

An Explication of Value Chain Theory

The basic unit of analysis in understanding international competition is the industry, because it is in the industry that market shares are won or lost. In order to analyze how international competition functions, we must explore various international organizational market strategies, the various types of competitive advantage which can be exploited with a given market strategy, and value chain theory as a theoretic approach to locating the sources of competitive advantage within an organization's functioning.

The *forms of international competition* within an industry range from multidomestic to global. A *multidomestic approach* to markets treats each country or core market as a unique arena and adjusts a firm's strategy for obtaining a competitive advantage to the specific issue in that market. A multidomestic firm views its industry as a collection of individual markets. In such instance, a firm normally operates relatively autonomous subsidiaries in each market.

A *global approach* to markets is one in which a firm's competitive position in one country or core market is significantly affected by the firm's competitive position in other countries or core markets. International competition in a global industry is more than a collection of independent subsidiaries located in individual markets. A global approach rests on a series of interdependent activities that are integrated, coordinated, and controlled so that competitive advantage in one part of the world can be leveraged to obtain competitive advantage throughout the linked system.

Competitive advantage can be conceptually viewed as emanating from four sources:

First, a product or service which provides customers with comparable value at lower cost than one's competitors creates *low cost competitive advantage.* Japanese automakers have consistently produced cars at a cost $750 to $950 per unit lower than comparable American manufacturers, leading to low-cost competitive advantage (Treece and Hower, 1989:75).

Second, a product or service which is comparable in cost but contains some unique quality, styling, service, or functional features relative to one's competitors creates *differentiation competitive advantage.* Toyota and Honda automobiles require fewer repairs, are easier to service, and have more standard features included in the product price, such as air conditioning, power brakes and steering, and AM-FM radios; thus they create higher customer satisfaction than similar U.S. and European cars and a product differentiation competitive advantage.

Third, a firm may provide a broader range of products or services than one's competitors, thus creating *scope competitive advantage.* The Ford Motor Corporation provides its customers with small, medium, large, luxury, sport, and station wagon cars to select from, as well as a broad range of trucks and minivans, creating competitive advantage based on product scope.

Fourth, due to the high demand for certain products or services, the first company into the market with a quality product can dominate the market, obtaining high-end pricing and maximized profits based on speed of response, creating a *time competitive advantage.*

Speed-to-market or time as a controlling strategy or source of competitive advantage has several unique features that other sources of competitive advantage do not produce. In order to reduce the time it takes to get a product customers desire to market before a competitor, a firm must understand what a customer wants and then simplify and reengineer its value chain in order to rapidly respond to change. Such a strategy *first* creates a *customer focus* on pent-up and measurable demand in product design, production, and delivery to a well-defined market. *Second,* such a strategy places product quality within a time frame with a customer focus, creating *affordable quality. Third,* speed-to-market seeks to increase productivity but within a price frame that will allow the market to absorb the product, quickly leading to *marketable productivity,* leading other firms to want to benchmark or buy the productivity system (Carnevale, 1992:34–38). Speed to market thus invokes a cluster of variables affecting competitive advantage, a customer focus, affordable quality, and marketable productivity, while keeping these sources of competitive advantage within their most effective and efficient range, thus avoiding the problem of providing too little or too much of these qualities.

The Chrysler Corporation's development, production, and marketing of the first minivans beat its competitors to market by one year, allowing Chrysler to capture all of the market for minivans for one year, to get high-end pricing for maximum profits, and to hold a majority of the market (51 percent) after its competitors entered the market due to its *time competitive advantage.*

Most top international firms seek to exploit competitive advantage from all four sources. To diagnose where the sources of a firm's competitive advantage are, we need a theoretic framework for disaggregating a firm's discrete activities. Particularly useful in this regard is value chain theory. Organizations term the discrete activities involved in bringing a product or service to market a *value chain.* A value chain arrays an organization's activities into *functional unit* and *business processes* (see figure 2.1).

In examining an organization's *functional unit level* of the value chain, notice that the two circles which denote suppliers and customers are normally found *outside* the organizational structure, while the square boxes denote functional activities performed *within* an organization's structure. In examining an organization's business process level, note how each process includes some activities unique to each business process and some activities which overlap with other business processes.

Functional units and business processes may be located anywhere on the globe where they can gain competitive advantage from their location. *Product development processes are normally* located in regions where firms have access to a steady supply of state-of-the-art engineers such as Silicon Valley in California near the University of California-Berkeley, Stanford University and California Technological University, or Route 128 in Massachusetts near Harvard, MIT, etc. where competitive advantage can be obtained from product differentiation. *Product delivery processes* are normally located near sources of inexpensive and skilled labor and automated production facilities such as Korea, Singapore, and Taiwan, where competitive advantage can be obtained from low cost production. *Customer service and management* processes are normally located in the core markets a firm services in order to obtain competitive advantage from rapid response time.

A firm may obtain competitive advantage from one or more of these sources. Competitive advantage gained from product development or product delivery processes alone tends to yield a *global strategy* based on the platforming of a product from a single country into all core markets, like VCRs. Competitive advantage based on

Figure 2.1   AN ORGANIZATION'S VALUE CHAIN

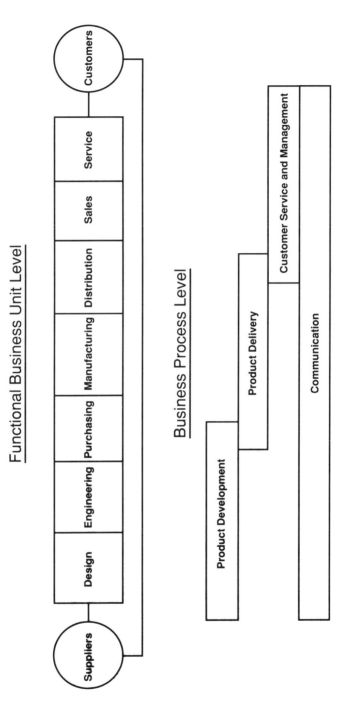

Functional Business Unit Level

Business Process Level

(Revised from J. Rockart & J. Short, IT in the 1990's, *Sloan Management Review*, 1989, 30:12)

customer service and management alone tends to yield a *multi domestic strategy* in which a firm's products are uniquely grounded on a market by market basis, e.g. insurance.

However, competitive advantage gained in one functional unit or business process can be added to or cancelled out by an organization's performance in other functional units or business processes. This is what is meant by value-added or value diminishing chains of activities. When those various sources of competitive advantage are cumulative in force, then a firm's entire range of functional units and business processes must be linked and configured effectively through the appropriate use of information and communication systems or high-speed management. Once again the appropriate analysis of location, linking, and configuration of a firm's internal resources is the responsibility of top management, as is its reorientation in response to environmental changes.

A firm may obtain a competitive advantage in a product or service without necessarily obtaining *large profits.* Large profits result only when the price a customer is willing to pay for these products or services exceed the collective cost of producing them by a wide margin.

An Application of Value Chain Theory to the Global Auto Industry

The international auto market is a multibillion-dollar industry. Ten firms account for approximately 78 percent of world sales. Table 2.1 provides a profile of their 1989 performance.

The top three firms—General Motors, Ford, and Toyota— account for over 38 percent of the world auto market. We shall, for reasons of space, limit our analysis to the international competition among the top three firms in the U.S. core market. The central competitive dynamics operating in the global automobile industry, according to Harold Poling, CEO of Ford, are "vehicle attributes, customer satisfaction and value for money" (Poling, 1989). *Vehicle attributes* refer to styling, power train performance, and road handling. *Customer satisfaction* refers to vehicle comfort, safety, quality, and ease of maintenance. *Value for money* refers to cost, standard features, gas mileage, and insurance costs.

Table 2.2 provides the relevant high-speed management data upon which our analysis for the U.S. market is based.

The General Motors Corporation is the world's largest producer of automobiles. Its U.S. market shares have fallen from 45 percent in 1980 to 35 percent in 1993. A 1-percentage-point drop amounts to

Table 2.1   WORLD AUTO MARKET, SEPTEMBER 1988–SEPTEMBER 1989

	World % of Market Shares	Auto Revenues U.S. $ Billions	Net Earnings U.S. $ Thousands	Vehicles Thousands	World Wide Productions	
					Autos %	Trucks %
1. GM	17.7	99.7	$3,831	7,946	74	26
2. Ford	14.6	76.8	4,259	6,336	70	30
3. Toyota	9.4	53.8	2,836	4,115	76	24
4. Volkswagon	6.6	34.4	921	2,948	93	7
5. Nissan	6.4	36.4	945	2,930	77	23
6. Chrysler	5.4	30.8	629	2,382	48	52
7. FIAT	5.4	26.4	2,453	2,436	90	10
8. Peugeot	4.6	22.8	1,518	2,216	88	12
9. Renault	4.2	26.4	1,451	2,053	80	20
10. Honda	4.0	25.2	945	1,960	86	14

(Adapted from A. Borrus, "Japanese Streak Ahead in Asia," *Business Week*, May 7, 1990, 31:54–55.)

Table 2.2   HIGH SPEED MANAGEMENT DATA FOR U.S. MARKET 1992

	GM	Ford	Toyota
% Market Shares 1980	45	20	6
% Market Shares 1992	35	23	8
Productivity 1992 (Worker Hours Per Car)	20	12	12
Av Replacement Time 1992 (Years Per Model)	5	3	2.5
Factory Utilization (% 1992 Capacity)	60	72	80
Productivity Increase 1992 (%)	4.8	8.2	8.2
Recalls (25% of total sales)	60	78	3
Labor costs (on dollars per car)	$2,358	$1,563	$1,023

(Compiled from *Automotive News* 1980–1993)

114,526 cars or $1 billion. GM's market shares at the lower-end auto price range have been eroded by Ford Escort and Toyota Tercel; at the middle price range by Ford Taurus and Tempo and the Toyota Corolla; and at the upper price range by Ford Lincoln and Toyota Camry. GM has invested $46 billion in plant modernization (a sum equal to the amount needed to purchase Toyota Motors in 1990) and is still the high cost producer. GM in the past three years cut $15 billion from its operating budget, closed several plants, laid off workers, but still ran its remaining plant at 60 percent compared to 72 and 80 percent for Ford and Toyota. As you can see from the high-speed management data, GM requires more worker hours per car, more model replacement time, and has a lower productivity increase than its two competitors. In addition, GM's Buick cars ranked tenth in quality ratings, while Toyota's Lexus, Camry, Paseo, Corolla, and Tercel ranked in the top ten, with Ford's Crown Victoria appearing sixth in the top ten (Templen, 1993:B1).

The Ford Motor Corporation was one of America's most successful global competitors in the 1980s. Ford's market shares increased from 20 percent in 1980 to 28 percent by 1993. Ford produces vehicles at $1,200 less per unit than GM and $540 less per unit than Toyota. Over the past five years Ford has invested $21 billion in plant modernization and has significantly improved its production capabilities. It is evident from our high-speed management data that Ford outperforms GM in productivity, replacement time, factory utilization, and productivity increases in 1993. However, Ford still trails Toyota in several categories (Lohr, 1992:D2).

Toyota Motors has established itself as the high quality and best value automobile producer among the top three. In addition,

Toyota leads Ford and GM in several high-speed management measures. It costs less, takes fewer worker hours per car, less time to replace a car, and on average, Toyota workers are more productive than Ford and GM. That may be why Toyota has gone from 6 percent of the U.S. market in 1980 to 8 percent in 1993. In 1989, Toyota's market shares increased 3 percent in the United States, 3 percent in the European Economic Community, and 4 percent in Japan, yielding a 10 percent increase worldwide, an increase in sales of over one million cars. A 1-percentage-point gain amounts to 114,526 cars or $1 billion. While GM has lost market shares in the last ten years, Toyota and Ford have gained. Toyota's innovative, adaptive, efficient, and rapid response systems, according to Taylor (1990b), accounted for the firm's competitive advantage in product differentiation, scope, and timing (Woods, 1993).

Implications for High-Speed Management. While environmental scanning and value chain theory appear to be useful as analytic tools for exploring the types and sources of competitive advantage employed in the auto industry, two questions arise regarding the framework's generalizability.

First, can the appropriate use of environmental scanning and value chain theory to analyze change in the environment and quickly adjust an organization's value chain to meet these changes *separate successful from unsuccessful international competitors based on configuration and linking processes, irrespective of industry?*

Second, can environmental scanning and value chain theory *demonstrate that firms which have a competitive advantage based on time also have improved performance ratings on all forms of competitive advantage?*

Marquise Cvar (1986) attempted to answer the first question when he undertook a study of twelve international corporations in 1984. For his research, Cvar selected eight successful and four unsuccessful firms. Four of the successful firms were American, while one each was Swiss, British, Italian, and French. Three of the four unsuccessful firms were American and one was Swiss. These twelve firms each competed in separate industries. *Successful firms* were distinguished from *unsuccessful firms* by their high investment in information and communication technology and by the effective use of information and communication to analyze and evaluate quickly changes in the external organizational environment and then to reorient rapidly its internal resource in responding to those changes.

Smith, Grimm, Chen, and Gannon (1989) attempted to answer our second question in their study of twenty-two top-level managers from high-technology electronics firms. They explained major portions of the variance in organizational performance or increases in profits and sales from decreases in response time to environmental change. They found that an external orientation by a firm, a rapid response to competitor threat, and the radicalness of the change initiated in the organization were all positively related to increased profits, sales, and the general performance of an organization. Decreases in response time to external change were highly correlated with communication systems improvements in an organization's R & D, manufacturing, and marketing.

Value chain theory does appear to be capable of (1) separating successful from unsuccessful international firms, and (2) revealing how competitive advantage based on integration, coordination, and control improves overall organizational performance. We are now in a position to overview the theories of *organizational integration, coordination, and control or high-speed management* to be presented in the remaining chapters of this book.

The Nature, Function, and Scope of an Organization's Information and Communication Continuous Improvement System

The basic function of management appears to be coalignment, not merely of people in coalitions but of institutional action—of technology and task environment into a viable domain, and of organizational design and structure appropriate to it. Management, when it works well, keeps the organization at the nexus of several necessary streams of action.
(Thompson, 1967:21)

Our analysis of the philosophical rationale for the primary function of communication within its organizational context suggests that communication serves to continuously improve organizational effectiveness in managing a firm's coalignments between its internal and external resources benchmarked against world-class standards in responding to environmental change. Coalignment is a unique communication relationship in which each of a firm's stakeholders clearly articulates its needs, concerns, and contributions in such a manner that management can forge an appropriate value-added configuration and linkage among stakeholders which is mutually satisfying and optimizing to the value-added activities of the organization when benchmarked against world-class standards, thus creating a sustainable competitive advantage.

In order to see how a firm's information and communication capabilities can provide such a new approach to one of management's oldest problems, that of managing interdependencies, we shall (a) provide a conceptualization of an organization's *information and communication system,* (b) explore how an organization's information system can coalign organizational activities so as to create a sustainable *competitive advantage,* and (c) explore how an organization's *information and communication system* can continuously improve organizational coalignment so as to create a *sustainable competitive advantage.*

A Conceptualization of an Organization's Information and Communication System

An organization's information and communication system provides the unique raw materials from which to manage a firm's interdependencies. *Information* can be defined as any observation and/or inference whose utility is of sufficient importance to be recorded and stored in a fixed procedure or menu entry system and standardized by topic for rapid access and manipulation. An *organizational information system* can be conceptualized as any observation and inference central to an organization which is stored in a menu entry rigid topic system for rapid access and manipulation in creating coalignment among stakeholders and units of that organization. *High-speed management* provides the theory, principles, and practices for a manager to determine what standardized topics for rapid access and manufacturing are needed to forge a value-added configuration and linkage among activities.

Communication can be defined as the interactive sharing of symbolic meaning in which the sharing framework has a range of open to fixed entry points and a flexible to rigid interpretive framework capable of revealing both the diverse and common interpretations of interactants. A *communication system* may employ one or more of three types of interpretive systems. *Personal frameworks* are flexible entry systems employed when the shared meaning is an understanding of how the interactants personally differ in regard to their interpretations of shared symbolic meaning. This understanding is rooted in the recognition of each interactant's unique background and experiences. *Interpersonal frameworks* are flexible entry systems employed when the shared meaning is an understanding of how the interactants are similar in regard to their interpretive systems. This understanding is rooted in the recognition of the interactants' common backgrounds and experiences. *Standardized frameworks* are rigid entry systems which appear at the intersection of information and communication processes and are employed when the shared meaning is an understanding of the standardized usage required by a group of interactants to coordinate rapidly human understandings and behavior in regard to a common organizational task. This understanding is rooted in the recognition that common tasks exist in the organization which require the rapid coordination of two or more people through a fixed entry, standardized communication procedure in order to perform the task correctly.

Organizational communication systems thus can be conceptualized as a multiple-entry-point interactive sharing of symbolic meaning within a range of flexible to rigid interpretive frameworks which separates personal from interpersonal interpretive meanings in order to establish and maintain an organization-wide standardized interpretive framework at a sufficient level of abstraction so as to include individual and interpersonal concerns in coaligning optimal organizational functioning (see table 2.3).

An organization's *information system* thus permits the rapid coalignment of organizational activities within a menu entry point and rigid indexical system through high-speed information exchange. An organization's *communication system* allows for open to fixed entry points into flexible to rigid interpretive systems of personal, departmental, and organizational levels of meaning which coalign organizational activities. Communication is prior to and necessary for establishing, maintaining, updating, repairing, and changing an organizational information system. Organizational information and communication systems, aided by computers and telecommunications technology, are revolutionizing the way we do work by coaligning people with people, people with machines, machines with machines, and machines with people, all more precisely and rapidly than ever before. This high-speed coalignment process in turn is significantly modifying the speed of organizational response to internal and external economic forces.

Table 2.3   AN ORGANIZATION'S INFORMATION AND COMMUNICATION SYSTEM

Organizational Characteristics	Information Characteristics	Communication Characteristics
Access Points	Menu Entry	Open to Fixed Entry
Interpretive System	Rigid Framework	Flexible to Standardized
Function	Rapid Information Exchange	Framework Meaningful Differentiation
Coalignment Process	Common Level	Diverse Levels
Organizational Goal	Coordination/Control	Integration/Control

Information and Communication Systems' Coalignment to Create a Competitive Advantage

Information and communication systems are creating organizational coalignments which, according to Porter and Miller (1985:152), affect competition in three ways.

1. They change industry structure and, in so doing, alter the rules on how one must compete.
2. They create competitive advantage by giving companies new ways to outperform their rivals.
3. They spawn whole new businesses, often from within a company's existing operations.

Such capabilities create competitive advantage which may be temporary or sustainable. American Airlines and BMW developed information and communications technology systems which *changed the structure* of the airline and auto industry, giving them a sustainable competitive advantage. Several years ago American Airlines introduced a computer-aided reservation system which allowed travel agents to access airline rates, schedules, and seat assignments. This technology provided travel agents with easy access to American flights and provided American Airlines with a monitoring procedure for the size, timing, and cost of flights, allowing for quick adjustment in ticket rates. This forced other large airlines to follow suit and other small airlines to buy time on the American Airlines computer. This in turn allowed American Airlines to give access to their flights first and to monitor their competitors' schedules and load capacity, providing American Airlines with a long-term sustainable competitive advantage. BMW installed a "smart" manufacturing system. BMW can now build customized cars, each with its customer preference in regard to motor size, transmission type, interior features, and exterior features, as well as body color, on a normal assembly line. This places pressure on other manufacturers to follow suit, providing BMW with a short-term competitive advantage.

IBM and General Electric obtained sustainable competitive advantage from the use of information and communication technology. IBM spent $350 million to convert its twenty-five-year-old factory in Lexington, Kentucky, into one of America's most automated plants. Before the plant was automated, labor accounted for almost 33.3 percent of manufacturing cost. Now it has shrunk to 5 percent of manufacturing cost, providing IBM with a long-term sustainable competitive advantage. GE's factory of the future in Louisville, Kentucky, created a dishwasher plant with a 15 percent increase in productivity and a 25 percent decrease in cost, providing a short-term comparative advantage.

Sears and Western Union have spawned entire new businesses from the use of information and communication capabilities. Sears installed a large and extensive credit control system to serve its department store charge cards. This service quickly generated as much profit from interest on credit as Sears earned from store sales. Sears then spawned a new full-service charge card (Discover) aimed at challenging VISA and Mastercard from its niche in retail credit. This new card doubled Sears's income from credit and created a sustainable competitive advantage. Western Union turned its telegraph system into an Easy Link Network Service. This network allows complex high-speed data communication from personal computers, telecommunication facilities, and other electronic devices throughout the world. This service was not needed before the speed of information technology created a demand for such a network.

More efficient and expanded service and control over product design, as in the case of American Airlines and BMW; *increased quality control and decreased labor cost,* as in the case of IBM and GE; and an *expansion of income* from credit and networking, as in the case of Sears and Western Union—all were motivated by a search for competitive advantage from information and communication capabilities. Competitive advantage in these cases (1) changed the structure of an industry, (2) gave companies new ways to outperform their rivals, and (3) spawned whole new businesses.

An Organization's Information and Communication System can be Used to Continuously Improve Organizational Coalignment, Creating a Sustainable Competitive Advantage

Sustainable competitive advantage, according to Coyne (1986), requires that customers perceive (1) a consistent difference in important attributes between the producer's products or services and those of one's competitors, (2) that the difference is the direct consequence of a capability gap, and (3) that both the difference and the capability gap can be expected to endure over time.

At the heart of the use of an organization's information and communication system to create a sustainable competitive advantage is the use of communication to continuously improve current organizational linking or coalignment patterns. Four dynamic communication processes, each with its own theoretic rationale, form the basis for such a continuous improvement of organizational coalignment processes based on world-class benchmarking. These are: (1) negotiation linking, (2) a New England self-managed teamwork meeting, (3) a cross-functional teamwork program, and (4) a best practices benchmarking program (Cushman and King, 1992).

(1) A Negotiated Linking Program. A unit or function is created within an organization whose purpose is to continuously scan the globe in order to locate resources in the form of customers, partners, technologies, and/or consultants which are capable of enhancing an organization's competitiveness. Such resources may include land, labor, capital, market entry, distribution channels, technology, training, and so on. This unit then

- interacts with the unit holding the potential resource in order to locate its interests, concerns, and contributions to coalignment;
- develops the form of coalignment preferred by both units, such as acquisition, joint venture, alliance, partnership coalition, collaboration, licensing technology leasing, transfer, and/ or training.
- determines the world-class benchmarking targets in market shares, productivity, quality, flexibility, and/or rapid response time to be met before coalignment can take place.

The organizational negotiated linking program then formulates the negotiated coalignment agreement aimed at mobilizing external resources for organizational usage.

(2) A New England Self-Managed Teamwork Meeting. A unit or function is created within the organization to implement a worker continuous improvement program within a New England town meeting format. Its goal is to improve an organization's productivity, quality, flexibility, adaptability, and/or response time. It is an attempt to eliminate nonessential, nonproductive, or "bad" work and replace it with "good" work. These New England style town meetings last from one to three days. They begin with the division head calling together twenty to one hundred workers, suppliers, and/or customers.

The meeting then proceeds in the following manner:

- The division head opens the meeting with a presentation of key market issues, the organization's vision in responding to these issues, how the organization and its competitors are responding to this vision, and specific organizational needs for increased productivity, quality, flexibility, adaptability, and rapid response time. The division head leaves at this point in the meeting.

- Teamwork facilitators take over and generate a list of bad work to be eliminated and good work to be undertaken in responding to the various areas of concern.

- The group is then divided into teams of five to ten members to analyze, discuss, and debate potential areas for improvement.

- Each team then provides a cost-benefit analysis and action plan for the solutions recommended.

- The division head then returns and listens to a cost-benefit analysis and action plan from each group.

The division head acts on all high-yield ideas by selecting a team champion, training the team champion in project management, and empowering a team to implement the change by setting performance targets, measurement criteria, time frame, and feedback procedures. The worker improvement team then implements the action plan.

(3) A Cross-Functional Teamwork Program. A unit or function is created to set up cross-functional teams whose goals are to map and then improve cross-functional organizational processes. Many of the most significant improvements in organizational performance have come from mapping important cross-functional organizational processes and then asking those involved in the process to simplify and/or improve the functioning of that process. This approach has been very profitable for organizations since many of these processes have developed and expanded overtime without anyone examining the entire process and exploring its improvement.

Here cross-functional teams are set up and assigned the task of mapping the decision, implementation, and review levels of important organizational processes. The cross-functional team is then asked to evaluate and make improvements in the process mappings. This is accomplished in four steps:

- developing a clear understanding of the process goal;
- identifying the necessary and sufficient critical success factors for achieving that goal;
- mapping and improving the essential subprocesses to meet these critical success factors;
- rank ordering each subprocess and evaluating its productivity, quality, flexibility, adaptability, and how to make improvements.

The unit and/or function then implements the change process and fine-tunes its subprocesses.

(4) A Best Practices Benchmarking Program. A unit or function is created to scan the globe for world-class competitors and to study how various parts of these organizations succeeded in setting world-class benchmarking standards in regard to productivity, quality, flexibility, adaptability, and response time. This unit usually

- located such organizations and makes a site visit;
- develops a case study of the processes involved;
- trains personnel at its own organization in ways to adapt these innovations to its organization.

This unit then sets up monitoring and feedback procedures for and implements the change.

Continuous improvement programs aimed at improving organizational coalignment through negotiated linking, New England town meetings, cross-functional teamwork, and case studies in world-class benchmarking are necessary elements in establishing a *world-class organizational information and communication capability.* Continuous improvement programs are essential information and communication processes in high-speed management. Let us examine the practical bases of continuous improvement programs by observing the four dynamic communication processes functioning first in a small local organization, the Danville, Illinois, Bumper Works.

The Danville, Illinois, Bumper Works.   In 1978 Shahid Khan, a naturalized U.S. citizen from Pakistan, borrowed $50,000 from the Small Business Loan Corporation and took $16,000 of his own savings to establish the one-hundred-person Bumper Works in Danville, Illinois. This company designed and manufactured truck bumpers. Between 1980 and 1985, Khan approached the Toyota Motors Corporation on several occasions, attempting to become a supplier of bumpers for their trucks, but without much luck.

In 1987, Toyota called together a group of one hundred potential suppliers and released their design, quality, quantity, and price range specifications for a new truck bumper. The officials at Toyota also indicated that they expected increased quality and a reduction in price each year from the supplier. By late 1988, only Khan's Bumper Works company could produce a product which met Toyota Motors' exacting requirements. In 1989, Toyota sent a manufacturing team to Danville, Illinois, *to negotiate the contract and coalignment agreement* between the two firms. The negotiations failed because the Bumper Works could not produce twenty different size bumpers and ship them in a single day. If they could not do this, it would slow down the production of all Toyota trucks, increasing their price dramatically (White, 1991:A7).

Khan called a *New England town meeting* of workers from his own and Toyota Motors' Japanese factories to explore how this problem might be solved within Toyota's design, quality, quantity, and price requirements. It was decided that the Bumper Works would have to switch the factory from a mass production to a batch production line and that a massive stamping machine which took ninety minutes to change each cutting die would have to be modified so as to make such changes in twenty minutes (White, 1991:A7).

Next, the workers at both the Bumper Works and Toyota Motors set up *cross-functional teams* to make a process map of current production procedures. They studied, simplified, and restructured the process so as to allow for batch production. The large stamping machine was studied for modifications that would speed up die changes. All this was done with considerable help from Toyota Motors, who had solved these same problems, but in a different way, back in Japan (White, 1991:A7).

Then the Bumper Works remodeled assembly line was ready to begin production. For six months employees with stop watches and cost sheets observed the restructured process and *benchmarked its operations against the world-class standards of the Toyota plant in Japan*—but still could not meet Toyota's quality, quantity, and speed of delivery specifications. They videotaped the process, studied it, modified it, and sent it to Japan for review. In July 1990 Toyota Motors sent a team over to help retrain the workers. They returned again in December of 1990 to fine-tune the process, meeting Toyota Motors' contract requirements.

The new production line increased productivity 60 percent over the previous year, decreased defects 80 percent, cut delivery time by 850 percent, and cut waste materials' cost by 50 percent. A manual and videotape of the manufacturing process were prepared for training, the first of their kind at Bumper Works, and continuous improvement teams were formed in order to meet contract requirements for Toyota Motors of increased quality and decreased costs for each subsequent year.

Now that representatives of each unit involved in the value chain linking the Bumper Works and Toyota Motors had communicated their interests, concerns, and contributions to the coalignment process, each firm's management was able to forge a linking process that was satisfactory to the units involved and optimizing to the value-added activities of each organization in order to create a sustainable competitive advantage. Khan, the owner of Bumper Works, has profited from this experience and is building a new plant which will employ two hundred workers in Indiana and supply truck bumpers for a new Isuzu Motors plant located there (White, 1991:A7).

Having explored in some detail the unique contributions made to organizational coalignment by a firm's information and communication system and the relationship between a properly developed and appropriately maintained organizational coalignment and sustainable competitive advantage, we are now in a position to explore environmental scanning as a theoretic framework for guiding an organization's coalignment with its external environment.

An Overview of the High-Speed Management Principles to be Presented and Applied in the Remainder of the Book

Like competition itself, competitive advantage is a constantly moving target. For any company in any industry, the key is not to get stuck with a single simple notion of its source of advantage.

The best competitors, the most successful ones, know how to keep moving and always stay on the cutting edge.

Today, time is on the cutting edge. The ways leading companies manage time—in production, in new product development and introduction, in sales and distribution—represent the most powerful new sources of competitive advantage.
(Stalk, 1988:41)

Within every organization there are tacit assumptions about how individuals and groups approach and perform tasks. These tacit assumptions create an organization's mind-set and define how members of that organization perceive and interact with customers, investors, and fellow employees. These tacit assumptions which govern and guide perception and interaction create an organization's information and communication climate. Our analysis in this chapter has taught us something about the broad outline of such a set of tacit assumptions in successful organizations.

Our analysis of *environmental scanning taught us that the main profit generator in international business lies increasingly in an efficient and accurate international information system which has the capacity to ascertain instantly and on a twenty-four-hour a day basis where the cheapest capital is to be found, where the most appropriate technology is, where skilled people can be hired, and where opportunities to employ these resources most profitably are to be located and how to do so.*

Our analysis of *value chain theory taught us that the distinctive issue in international, as contrasted to domestic, strategy can be summarized in two key dimensions of how a firm competes.* The *first* is termed the *configuration* of a firm's activities worldwide, or where in the world each activity in the value chain is to be performed, including in how many places. The *second* dimension is what is termed *linking,* which refers to how like activities performed in different countries are coordinated with each other.

Our analysis of *the nature, function, and scope of an organization's information and communication system suggests that the basic function of management appears to be the coalignment, not merely of people in coalitions but of institutional action—of technology and task environment—into a viable system and of the organizational design appropriate to it.* Management, when it works best, keeps the organization at the nexus of several streams of necessary action.

Our analysis of *international competition within an industry has taught us that what separates successful from unsuccessful international competitors is the effective use of a firm's information and communication system to achieve organizational integration, coordination, and control in an innovative, adaptive, flexible, and rapid response or high-speed management manner.* These then are our tacit assumptions regarding the character of a successful organizational climate. We now direct attention to an overview of the specific topics, principles, strategies, and techniques which allow for the theoretic and systematic implementation of high-speed management.

The art of high-speed management has as its goals the development of a steady flow of low-cost, high-quality, easily serviced, high-value, and innovative products which meet the needs of the customers, and of quickly getting these products to market before one's competitors in an effort to achieve market penetration and large profits. Success in achieving these goals will rest in great part on the appropriate use of information and communication technology to integrate, coordinate, and control the organizational activities involved in achieving these goals. The remaining chapters in this book will be divided into three sections dealing with three organizational coalignment processes: *integration, coordination,* and *control.* Each section will contain several chapters dealing with the specific theory, principles, and techniques of high-speed management relevant to that coalignment topic and contain multiple examples of their appropriate use (see table 2.4).

Organizational Integration Processes

Successful organizations are able to *focus* their energies and resources so as to produce an innovative, adaptive, flexible, efficient and rapid response to environmental change. Such a focused response requires the use of information and communication to integrate people, technologies, and resources into a common stream of activities. Part one of this book contains three chapters which deal with the three sets of management coalignment skills central to organizational integration. These are the principles, strategies, and techniques of *organizational leadership, organizational climate,* and *organizational teamwork.*

Organizational leadership (chapter 3) explicates the coalignment principles, strategies, and techniques involved in moving from such traditional theories as power, trait, behavioral, and situational leadership focusing on environments involving incremental and continuous change to transformational, network, and discontinuous leadership theories, which focus on rapid and turbulent change. This latter type of high-speed management leader must anticipate discontinuous

Table 2.4   HIGH-SPEED MANAGEMENT COALIGNMENT PROCESSES AND TOPICS

Section 1 Organizational Integration Processes		
Chapter 3 Organizational Leadership	*Chapter 4* Organizational Climate	*Chapter 5* Organizational Teamwork

Section 2 Organizational Coordination Processes		
Chapter 6 R & D and Marketing Interface	*Chapter 7* R & D, Marketing and Manufacturing Interface	*Chapter 8* R & D, Marketing, Manufacturing, and MIS Interface

Section 3 Organizational Control Processes	
Chapter 9 Information and Communication in Process Mapping	*Chapter 10* Information and Communication in Planning and Linking

change and articulate a compelling vision for rapidly reorienting to that change. Then he or she must coalign a firm's values, structures and empowerment patterns, outsourcing and linking with other firms in order to meet speed-to-market targets, and then create an organizational tension capable of generating quickly the learning and implementation necessary to becoming competitive. The chapter ends with an examination of Jack Welch, General Electric Corporation's CEO, as an exemplar of a high-speed management leader.

Organizational climate (chapter 4) explicates the coalignment principles, strategies, and techniques involved in creating and implementing a corporate value, socialization, and monitoring system for focusing all of a firm's stakeholders on achieving its goals. This chapter discusses the rituals, myths, and social dramas involved in developing a lean, agile, and creative firm which rewards learning and rapid change. The corporate climates of GE and IBM are examined as specific instances of high-speed management climates.

Organizational teamwork (chapter 5) seeks to determine what teamwork is, when it should and should not be employed, and what types of teamwork are best for solving what types of problems. The unique features of self-managed, cross-functional, benchmarking, and outside linking teams are explored in relationship to their appropriate use in a high-speed management environment. Successful teamwork is characterized as a mutually constructed and publicly agreed to goal, which integrates the interests, concerns, and contributions of all the team members in energizing the effort necessary to achieve the firm's goals. Organizational teamwork thus operationalizes a firm's integration processes by exploring the different types of work patterns present in organizations and indicates where, when, and how organizational teamwork can function to energize the creativity, quality, and productivity needed to meet organizational goals. Then we explore examples of the appropriate use of high-speed management teams at Toyota, NUMMI, General Electric, and Ford Motor Corporation.

Organizational Coordination Processes

Successful organizations not only focus their energies and resources through the coalignment of organizational integration processes as described in part one of this book, they also coalign their activities with others in order to exchange information between units in the organizational coordination processes (the topic of part two of this book). Such a coalignment process requires the use of information and communication processes to coordinate the various units' and subunits' necessary lines of activities. Three such coordination processes will be examined in part two of this book. These coalignment processes will focus on the coordination activities involved in (1) the R & D and marketing; (2) R & D, marketing, and manufacturing; and (3) the R & D, marketing, manufacturing, and Management Information System (MIS) interface.

   The R & D and marketing interface (chapter 6) explicates the coalignment tools available, dominant strategies employed, and specific patterns of coaligning activities required to coordinate the R & D and marketing functions of the value chain. Here we explore environmental assessment, product portfolio modeling, and structured innovation as tools useful in the coalignment of various strategies of the R & D and marketing interface. Next, we investigate the specific information and communication patterns of coordination when marketing needs to be involved in the R & D process, when marketing provides information to R & D, and when R & D needs to be involved in the marketing process. We illustrate our analysis by examining the R & D and marketing interface in the Mitsushita Electric Company and the General Electric Company.

   The R & D, marketing and manufacturing interface (chapter 7) explicates the coalignment tools available, dominant strategies employed, and specific patterns of coordination activities required to coalign these organizational functions in the value chain. Here we explore robots, integrated flexible systems, computer-assisted design, computer-aided manufacturing, and computer-integrated manufacturing systems as useful tools in coalignment. We then explore the economics of sourcing, scale, focus, scope, and time as strategies for coalignment. Finally, we investigate the specific patterns of coalignment activities in subunit coordination, interunit coordination and between-unit coordination. We illustrate this analysis by examining the R & D, marketing, and manufacturing interface in the Allen Bradley Corporation and The Limited Company.

The R & D, marketing, manufacturing and MIS interface (chapter 8) explicates the coalignment tools available, dominant strategies employed, and specific patterns of coalignment of activities required to coordinate these necessary functions in the value chain. Here we explore database management, network management, applications programming, design management, systems support management, and executive information systems as useful tools for coalignment. We then explore six strategies for coalignment: business systems planning, critical success factors, an applications portfolio, a stages approach, a value chain approach, and a high-speed management approach. Next we investigate the specific information and communication patterns employed to coalign the activities involved in constructing a data architecture, a transportation architecture, a management process architecture, an investment architecture, and an applications map. We illustrate our analysis by examining the R & D, market, manufacturing, and MIS interface in The Limited Corporation.

Organizational Control Processes

Successful organizations not only focus their energies and resources through coaligned *organization integration* processes and link necessary value chain function through coaligned *organization coordination processes,* but they also plan, benchmark, monitor, and correct coalignment functions through *organization control processes.* Mockler (1972:2) offers a precise conceptualization of organizational control when he states:

> Management control is a systematic effort to set performance standards with planning objectives, to design information feedback systems, to compare actual performance with these predetermined standards to determine whether there are any

deviations and to measure their significance, and to take any action required to assure that all corporate resources are being used in the most efficient way possible in achieving corporate objectives.

Organizational control takes place at two points in a firm's activities: in the process mapping and monitoring of ongoing organizational activities and in the organizational planning and linking stage.

Process mapping (chapter 9) explicates how an organization can monitor its ongoing integration, coordination, and control processes through organizational communication audits used to monitor the critical success factors necessary to locate activities where turnaround time can be reduced in the coalignment processes. Here we explore how to conduct communication audits of customers, competitors, and our own organization's value chain, and how to benchmark world-class performance. Next we explore the structure, function, and implementation of strategies for reducing turnaround time. Finally, we explore the implementation of such strategies in Toyota and the General Electric Corporation.

Information and communication planning and linking (chapter 10) explicates how environmental scanning focused on industrial competitors, the organization's value chain, and the utilization of new information and communication technologies can be employed to develop and implement an organizational information and communication master plan. Next we explore the structure, function, and implementation of such a plan. Finally, we explore the implementation of such a plan in Toyota, Ford, and The Limited.

This concludes our overview of the information and communication processes of integration, coordination, and control, which are integral to the principles, strategies, and techniques of high-speed management. The ensuing chapters provide the detail, explication, and illustration of this innovative, adaptive, flexible, efficient, and rapid response management system. These information and communication principles, strategies, and techniques await your discovery. Search well!

PART I

Organizational Integration Processes

> *To be sure, the fundamental task of management remains the same, to make people capable of joint performance by giving them common goals, common values, the right structure, and the ongoing training and development they need to respond to change. But the meaning of this task has changed, if only because the performance of management has converted the workforce from individuals composed largely of unskilled laborers to one of highly educated knowledge workers.*
> (Drucker, 1988:65)

Organizational integration has as its goal the tying together, energizing, and creating of a focused collective effort by all of a firm's various stakeholders. Three organizational communication processes converge to make such a collective effort possible. *First, organizational leadership* processes employ human communication to provide a firm's stakeholders with a clear, focused, and energizing vision, specific performance targets, and empowered point men for coaligning significant organizational performance. *Second, organizational culture* employs human communication to provide a firm's stakeholders with a common set of values, socialization, monitoring, and reward systems capable of motivating, guiding, and providing satisfaction for the coalignment of significant collective performance and a positive corporate climate. *Third, organizational teamwork* employs human communication to provide its stakeholders with the means to create, operate, continuously improve, and terminate

53

various organizational structures, functions, and processes aimed at coaligning joint performance in achieving organizational goals. Let us explore in turn each of these human communication processes aimed at creating organizational integration, first in their general and then in their high-speed management context.

3

High-Speed Management Leadership:
A Global Perspective

*The 1990s vision of the effective corporate leaders casts
the CEO as global warriors rather than national ones, selling
wares anywhere in the world from manufacturing operations
dotting the globe. They are proponents of the joint venture with
another company to obtain better technology or instant access
to markets. And they have a new respect for quality to win over
consumers who are bombarded with more choice than ever.*
(Prokesch, 1987:8)

The turbulent economic environment confronting most corporations
has caused a radical reassessment of the most appropriate type of
leadership required in order to prosper in such an environment. Out
of this soul-searching has arisen a new breed of corporate leader—
the high-speed management leader, based on a new set of leadership principles. This new conception and the principles it invokes
are redefining the relationships of organizations to workers, investors, customers, competitors, communities, and governments
throughout the globe.

What has prompted this reconceptualization of corporate leadership is the growing perception that organization survival itself is
at stake. This new leadership style is based upon a strong commitment to meeting customer needs, developing, producing, and marketing world-class products, utilizing the most efficient resources
available from around the globe, and acquiring and/or forming joint
ventures with competitors in order to maintain and/or increase market shares and investor confidence. When corporate survival is at
stake, market leadership, profits, and stock prices are the primary
indicators of effective global leadership. In such an environment,
CEOs are cutting their workforce, closing factories, moving offshore

to manufacture as business dictates without regard for the effect of these movements on individuals, communities, or a nation's balance of trade. Change is the only constant—corporate survival, the only concern.

Corporations are embracing a radically new concept of doing business. The organization has a floating structure that involves one business this year, another the next. Such businesses take in raw materials at multiple points throughout the world, transform them into components of a product, and ship them to core markets for assembly where they are sold. Where the raw materials are taken in and transformed into components depends more on where the value of currency is low, the technological capability is high, and the government is willing to give the corporation either financial or tax breaks than on any other set of constraints. The time has come to think of organizations as global monopoly players which assemble a set of modules located in different places, each contributing flexible portions of a constantly changing transportable whole.

In order to understand these changes in organizations and how they impact leadership behaviors, we need to (1) examine from within this new environment the strengths and weaknesses of prior conceptions of effective leadership; (2) explore the nature, function, and scope of effective high-speed management leadership; (3) illustrate the use of high-speed management leadership by a world-class firm; and (4) discuss the critical factors governing effective global leadership.

Prior Conceptions of Leadership: Their Strengths and Their Weaknesses in a Global Environment

Corporate leadership is America's scarcest natural resource. . . . The time has come to talk about how corporations, our wealth-producing institutions, can develop leadership with the courage and imagination to change our corporate life-style.
(Tichy and Devanno, 1986:27)

Leadership is a topic which excites intense interest among the public and researchers alike. To the public, "leadership" evokes images of powerful, dynamic personalities, national and international heroes. To researchers, leadership evokes images of the differences between a manager and a leader and of the causes and consequences of effective leadership. Managers are viewed as directors and monitors of ongoing organizational activities. Leaders, on the other hand, have the ability to create and articulate a vision in which followers want to participate, to set an agenda for obtaining that vision, and then to passionately pursue that vision and agenda in such a manner as to motivate others to do the same (Tichy and Charon, 1989:99). Managers as such are more concerned with how things get done, whereas leaders are more concerned with what things mean to people and how to effectively communicate those meanings (Zelznick, 1977; Dumaine, 1993). Several researchers have demonstrated that such a leader accounts for between 23 and 44 percent of a corporation's sales, profitability, stock value, and productivity (Liberson and O'Connor, 1972). While a careful review of the existing research reveals well over sixty separate approaches to leadership effectiveness, their diversity can conveniently be grouped under five general types of perspectives: power, trait, behavioral, situational, and transformational. Let us explore each in turn and their strengths and weaknesses within a global context (Yukl, 1989).

Power Perspectives

A number of approaches to leadership have emerged which examine the various sources of a leader's power and determine his or her impact on organizational effectiveness. Most of these approaches employ French and Raven's (1959) topology: reward power, coercive power, legitimation power, expert power, and referent power. Power theories attempt to explore the influence of a leader's various types of power on employee satisfaction and organizational performance. Research tracing the effect of different types of leadership power on employer and organizational performance reveals the following results. The use of *reward power* was *not* systematically related to either *employee satisfaction* or *organizational performance*. The use of *coercive power* and *legitimation power* led to *low satisfaction* and *low performance*. The use of *expert power* or *referent power* led to *moderate employee satisfaction and organizational performance* with the interaction effect of using both, yielding *high satisfaction* and *high performance* (Yukl 1981). The interaction of *expert power,* or a leader's special knowledge and technical skill, and *referent power,* or the admiration, respect, and desire for approval from a leader, has been termed *charismatic leadership.*

All power approaches to leadership suffer from two important weaknesses. The sources of expert and referent power are a function of the leader's prior abilities. Such abilities are difficult if not impossible to acquire but once present can be improved. In addition, charismatic leaders, while effective, may have a national or regional rather than global perspective which, as we shall see later, may have certain harmful effects. Having said all this, leaders who lack sufficient power to make necessary changes, reward competent subordinates, and punish or expel troublemakers will find it difficult to develop a high-performance organization.

Trait Perspectives

Underlying a trait conception of leadership is the assumption that some people are more likely to become leaders than others. It therefore becomes necessary to determine what traits a leader must have, to locate those individuals who have those traits, and through training and practice refine those traits in order to develop competent leaders. The most extensive and successful program of this type was undertaken by the Managerial Assessment Center of the American Telephone and Telegraph Company. The correlations found between individual traits and managerial success by this center are reported in table 3.1.

Research conducted by Miner (1978) and his associates found managerial traits to be associated with leadership success in twenty-one different samples of managers in large hierarchical organizations.

With the recent trend toward flatter organizations with the diffusion of power or empowerment, the traits that relate most consistently to leadership effectiveness are high self-esteem, high energy, emotional maturity, tolerance for stress, belief in an internal locus of control, the judicious use of empowerment, the use of focused goals and a clear agenda, and the ability to create and communicate an effective organizational vision (Yukl, 1989:260–265).

To date, all trait approaches to leadership suffer from one important weakness. The traits isolated for effective leadership are culture-specific, unlike the unique traits characteristic of cross-cultural or global leadership.

Behavior Perspectives

This line of inquiry into effective leadership behaviors has been based upon the description of effective leadership behaviors and their impact on organizational performances. According to Yukl (1989:251), leaders need to make decisions "based on information that is both incomplete and overwhelming, and they require coop-

Table 3.1   MOST EFFECTIVE TRAITS OF MANAGERIAL SUCCESS AT AT&T

Trait	Correlations
1. Oral Communication Skills	.33**
2. Human Relations	.32**
3. Need for Advancement	.31**
4. Resistance to Stress	.31**
5. Tolerance to Stress	.31**
6. Organizing and Planning Skills	.28**
7. Energy	.28**
8. Need for Security	−.20**
9. Ability to delay gratification	−.19**
10. Goal Flexibility	−.18*
**p<.01	
* p.<.05	

Source: Bray, Campbell, and Grant, 1974

eration from many people over whom they no authority. The descriptive research shows that [such] . . . work is inherently hectic, varied, fragmented, reactive, and disorderly." Two separate approaches have been pursued, one focusing on leadership roles, and the other on leadership styles and their effects upon organizational performance. Mintzberg (1973) delineated three general leadership *roles* and the leadership behaviors appropriate to each.

1. Interpersonal role
   a. figurehead
   b. leader
   c. liaison
2 Information processor role
   a. information monitor
   b. information disseminator
   c. spokesperson
3. Decision maker role
   a. entrepreneur
   b. disturbance handler
   c. resource allocator
   d. negotiator

Two programs of leadership studies, one at Ohio State University and the other at the University of Michigan, have contributed to an understanding of how leadership styles affect organizational performance. In the Ohio State studies, two major dimensions of effective leadership style emerged—leader consideration and initiation of structure. *Consideration* refers to a leader's regard for the comfort, well-being, status, and contributions of followers. *Initiation of structure* refers to clearly defining one's own and others' roles and setting clear expectations of performance (Stogdill, 1974). These two dimensions of a leader's functioning toward subordinates were found to be highly correlated with employee turnover and grievance rates, two measures of employee satisfaction and organizational effectiveness. The most preferred leadership style generating low employee turnover and low grievance rates involves employing *high consideration* and *high initiating structure*. The second most preferred is low consideration and high initiating structure (Yukl, 1981).

At the University of Michigan, Blake and Mouton (1978) located two dimensions of effective leadership style—*leader's concern for people* and *leader's concern for task*. This led to the construction of the widely used managerial grid, which plots each leader's scores on both of those dimensions and then classifies leadership style into four groups:

1. *Impoverished* (low concern for people, low concern for task)
2. *Country club* (high concern for people, low concern for task)
3. *Team or domestic* (high concern for people, high concern for production)
4. *Authoritarian* (low concern for individual, high concern for production)
5. *Middle-of-the-road* (an intermediate concern for people and an intermediate concern for task).

Rensis Likert (1961) employed these same two underlying dimensions to develop his System 4 analysis of leadership style and employee rewards. *System 1* leaders make all work-related decisions and order workers to carry them out. Rigid performance standards are used to reward. *System 2* leaders issue orders, but workers have some freedom to comment on orders and some flexibility in carrying them out. Workers who meet and exceed goals are rewarded. *System 3* leaders set goals and issue general orders after discussion with workers, and workers are free to carry them out in the manner they prefer. Rewards are given for goal attainment. *System 4* leaders (ideal type) set goals and apportion work as a team member coequal with workers, after coming to a consensus on what to do and how to do it. Both economic and social pressures are used as rewards.

The strength of behavior approaches to effective leadership is their focus on specific communication behaviors which lead workers to perform well. Behavioral approaches suffer from at least one weakness. To date, all behavioral approaches tend to be leader/worker specific. Global leadership appears to involve behaviors intersecting the leader/customer, leader/investor, leader/government, and leader/competitor relationships as well.

Situational Perspectives

Situational approaches to leadership all argue that which leadership approach is best depends on the types of workers, tasks, and organizations one has. Hersey and Blanchard's (1977) situational perspective argues that two components of workers' maturity—job maturity and psychological maturity—determine which leadership style is most effective and when a given leader needs to change leadership styles. *Job maturity* refers to a subordinate's task-relevant skills and technical knowledge. *Psychological maturity* refers to a subordinate's motivation, feelings of self-confidence, and commitments. Hersey and Blanchard believe the relationship between a leader and subordinates moves through four leadership stages, each of which requires the leader to employ different styles. In the *initial stage*—when subordinates first enter the organization—a telling style is necessary for the leader. Subordinates have to be instructed in their task and familiarized with the organizational culture. In the *second stage,* employees begin to become familiar with their job and the organization and a selling style is necessary for the leader. In the *third stage,* workers become very good at their job and strong members of the organizational culture. Here the leader needs to employ a participative style. In the *fourth stage,* employees are seasoned workers and thinking about retirement from the culture. Here a leader needs to employ a delegating style (see figure 3.1).

Kerr and Jarmier's (1978) situational perspective argues that under certain conditions each of the leadership functions outlined in table 3.2 is capable of being neutralized or substituted for by other elements in an organization. When the organization has a strong culture and repetitive tasks or a mature workforce and repetitive tasks, then the functions performed by a supportive or instrumental leader are achieved irrespective of the leader.

Figure 3.1

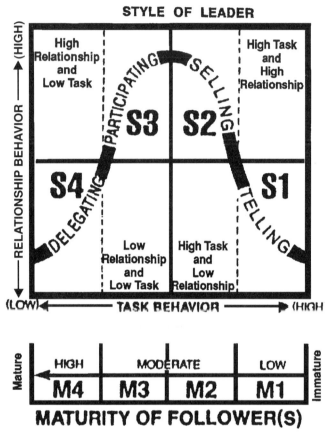

Source: Kerr, S. and Jarmier, J. M. (1978). "Substitutes for leadership: Their meaning and Measurement," *Organizational Behavior and Human Performance*, 22:375–403.

The strength of situational approaches to leadership is in the recognition that leadership involves a management team and is not an individual effort. Variations in skills among members of a management team, worker skills and maturity, and environmental constraints determine what leadership roles, skills, and styles must be brought to bear in a given context. The chief weakness of a situational leadership is the diffusion of responsibility for action within the management team, rather than focusing responsibility on the leader of the team, thus allowing for the deflection of responsibility to others.

Table 3.2 STYLE OF LEADER

	Substitute or Neutralizer	Supportive Leadership	Instrumental Leadership
A. Subordinate Characteristics:			
1. Experience, ability, training			Substitute
2. "Professional" orientation		Substitute	Substitute
3. Indifference toward rewards offered by organization		Neutralizer	Neutralizer
B. Task Characteristics:			
1. Structured, routine, unambiguous task			Substitute
2. Feedback provided by task			Substitute
3. Intrinsically satisfying task		Substitute	
C. 1. Cohesive work group		Substitute	Substitute
2. Low position power (leader lacks control over organizational rewards)		Neutralizer	Neutralizer
3. Formalization (explicit plans, goals, areas of responsibility)			Substitute
4. Inflexibility (rigid, unyielding rules and procedures)			Neutralizer
5. Leader located apart from subordinates with only limited communication possible		Neutralizer	

(Based on Kerr and Jarmier, 1978)

What has four decades of leadership research revealed regarding effective organizational leadership? *First,* an effective leader must have expert and referent or charismatic power. *Second,* an effective leader should have such positive traits as good oral communication and human relations skills, a strong need for advancement, resistance to stress, tolerance for uncertainty, organizing and planning skills, and high energy. In addition, the leader should not have a need for security and an ability to delay gratification and be unwilling to pursue goal flexibility. *Third,* an effective leader must perform several roles. There are the interpersonal, information processor, and decision-making roles, initiating and carrying out an organization's tasks while manifesting an appropriate concern for subordinates. *Finally,* effective leadership is a team effort in which a leader adjusts his or her leadership style to worker maturity, environmental change, and shifting organizational goals by employing telling, selling, participative, and delegating strategies.

The central weakness of these leadership theories is their dependence upon an environment which is relatively stable and in which a leader and/or a leadership team has the time to incrementally fine-tune its policies.

The Nature, Function, and Scope of High-Speed Management Leadership

Today is an age of global competition, rapid technological change, and too much productive capacity. Chief executives are beginning to march to a set of standards they never dreamed of embracing in the past.

The new order eschews loyalty to workers, products, corporate structure, businesses, factories, communities and nations. All such allegiances are viewed as expendable under the new rules. With survival at stake, only market leadership, strong profits, and high stock prices can be allowed to matter.
(Prokesch, 1987:3:1)

A tight fit among market opportunities, corporate strategy, and the internal integrative system of an organization is the hallmark of a successful corporation. The test of strong organizational leadership is maintaining such a tight fit in a turbulent environment. The task of managing incremental change in a stable environment is relatively simple and straightforward. The leadership merely fine-tunes existing policies within the organization's integration processes. But turbulent change requires a leadership to undertake frame-breaking change. Frame-breaking change requires the creation of a new vision, and the significant realignment of existing organizational integration processes in order to implement that vision.

In a turbulent global economic environment, organizations must develop the capacity to respond rapidly to changes in their environment by dramatically revamping a firm's vision, mission, product mix, value structure, knowledge, alliance, and technological base, i.e. its core capabilities. A new kind of leadership is required to guide these activities. Three trends have converged in the past several years which allow a rather clear characterization of this new high-speed management leadership pattern. This characterization emerges from the convergence of the research on (1) transformational leadership, (2) network leadership, and (3) leading an organization through discontinuous change. Let us explore each of these trends in turn and characterize the emergent outcome.

Transformational Leadership

The most effective leaders in a volatile economic climate recognize the need for frame-breaking change through scanning the environment for opportunities for and threats to organizational success. They then construct and implement a new vision aimed at changing the direction of and repositioning their firms for short-term success. However, as Tushman, Newman, and Romanelli (1986) indicate, such visionary leadership is rare. In their study of forty instances of frame-breaking change, over 80 percent were precipitated by a financial crisis in which the CEO was replaced, while only 20 percent involved existing CEOs who recognized the need for discontinuous change. In a turbulent global environment, change is the only constant, and leaders must be capable of responding transformationally to environmental change. "What is required of this kind of leadership is an ability to help the organization develop a vision of what it can be, to mobilize the organization to accept and work towards achieving the new visions, and to institutionalize the change that must last over time" (Tichy and Ulrich, 1987:59). Transformational leaders thus have a core set of responsibilities to provide an organization with a new vision, mobilize commitment to that vision, and institutionalize the changes needed to implement the vision. In meeting these core responsibilities, such a leader must (a) exercise a unique set of skills, (b) focus a firm's goals and means for achieving these goals, and (c) restructure the firm so as to facilitate rapid change.

Transformational Leadership Skills. Byrd (1987) argues that transformational leadership requires five unique skills: (1) anticipating skills, (2) visioning skills, (3) value-congruence skills, (4) empowerment skills, and (5) self-understanding skills.

Anticipatory skills, according to Byrd (1987:36), entail "projecting consequences, risks and trade-offs (having foresight), actively seeking to be informed and to inform (scanning and communicating), and proactively establishing relationships (building trust and influence)." Anticipatory skills include the ability to see and understand patterns of environmental forces, to know when to reassess or challenge assumptions, to see the value and limitations of alternatives, to recognize "hybrid" behaviors and to balance human and technical interest (Hunsicker, 1985).

Visioning skills involve those processes of communication which lead people to want to be a part of an exciting and involving vision. When effectively internalized, such a vision provides inspiration and a direction to behavior. However, commitment to a vision occurs only when people feel they are actively involved in creating it. The skills associated with vision entail creating mental and verbal pictures of desirable future states in which others can participate and feel they have a necessary part to play.

Value-congruence skills involve those processes involved in articulating values which can give appropriate direction to organizational activities. Values are often internalized so deeply that they define personality and behavior. Transformational leaders must be in touch with workers, investors, and consumer values, and be able to articulate and appreciate congruence among them. Value-congruence skills entail knowing, understanding, articulating, and integrating these values into a workable system.

Empowering skills involve allowing the stakeholders of an organization to share the achievement and responsibilities of the organization. It involves decentralization of power and status in order to achieve commitment and flexibility. The skills associated with empowerment entail being willing to share power, rewards, control, and visioning with others in an organization. It means the creating of a team, not just a leader and a group of followers.

Self-understanding skills involve a recognition of one's own strengths and weaknesses and the location of others who can synergize with the strengths and compensate for the weaknesses. Self-understanding skills entail the use of a variety of tools to recognize one's strengths and weaknesses, realizing that ego strength is a requirement of leadership but must be moderated by help from others.

Refocusing a Firm's Goals and Means for Achieving These Goals. Such transformational changes require the revamping of an organization's mission and values, power and status relationships, and the leadership team. *Frame-breaking change always involves a new definition of corporate mission and a reformulation of an organization's values to support the change in mission.* AT&T changed its corporate mission and had to modify its corporate value system to become more competitive, aggressive, and responsive to consumer demands. Similarly, shifts took place in the corporate mission and values of GE, Apple Computer, and others.

Frame-breaking change involves altered power, status, and interaction patterns. Some individuals and groups lose and some gain in this process. What is important is that the organization's integration, coordination, and control processes be adjusted to reflect these changes. Decentralization at AT&T and GE required a new conception of who has what power, status, and needs for communicating with whom.

Frame-breaking change may involve the use of a new leadership team. Change is always a high-energy activity. In order to proceed rapidly, minimize disruptions, and maximize benefits, the CEO must install trusted leaders at key points in the change process to lead the change. This requires a leadership team with synergy to overcome pockets of resistance, risk, and uncertainty. The leadership team must direct frame-breaking change and provide the energy, vision, resources, and role models for a new corporate order.

Restructuring the Firm's Goals As a Means for Achieving These Goals. Ostroff and Smith (1992), two consultants with McKinsey and Company, found that those organizations which responded rapidly to successive transformational visions by effectively altering and elevating organizational performance had ten common operational directives across firms, industries, and economic environments.

1. *Organize primarily around process, not task.* Base performance objectives on customer needs, such as low cost or fast service. Identify the processes that meet (or don't meet) those needs—order generation and fulfillment, say, or new-product development. . . .
2. *Flatten the hierarchy by minimizing subdivision of processes.* It's better to arrange teams in parallel, with each doing lots of steps in a process, than to have a series of teams, each doing fewer steps.
3. *Give senior leaders change of processes and process performance.*
4. *Link performance objectives and evaluation of all activities to customer satisfaction.*
5. *Make teams, not individuals, the focus of organization performance and design.* Individuals acting alone don't have the capacity to continuously improve work flows.
6. *Combine managerial and nonmanagerial activities as often as possible.* Let workers' teams take on hiring, evaluating, and scheduling.
7. *Emphasize that each employee should develop several competencies.* You need only a few specialists.
8. *Inform and train people on a just-in-time, need-to-perform basis.* Raw numbers go straight to those who need them

in their jobs, with no managerial spin, because you have trained front line workers—salespeople, machinists—how to use them.

9. *Maximize supplier and customer contact.* ... That means field trips and slots on joint problem-solving teams for all employees all the time.

10. *Reward individual skill development . . . instead of individual performance alone.*

The research on transformational leadership provides a clear outline of the initial skills, uniqueness, and operational features of a high-speed management leader who must respond rapidly to successive transformational change. Research on managing the network organization adds to this outline.

Network Leadership

As Snow, Miles, and Coleman (1993:6) argue, firms that are to be competitive in the 1990s need a leader who can

- search globally for opportunities and resources;

- maximize returns on all the assets dedicated to business, whether owned by the manager's firm or by other firms;

- perform only those functions for which the company has or can develop expert skills;

- outsource those activities which can be performed quicker, more effectively, or at lower cost, by others.

In order to meet these leadership imperatives, a network leader must (1) expand and strengthen a firm's core competencies, and (2) assume the role of coalignment broker.

Expanding and Strengthening a Firm's Core Competencies. In the dynamic and competitive global environment facing most leaders today, the only real source of sustainable competitive advantage, as we have seen, is the ability to respond rapidly and transformationally to the changes in market forces. A leader can achieve this ongoing renewal only by identifying, developing, and expanding a firm's core competencies. The term *core capabilities* refers to those portions of a firm's value chain "which allow it to consistently distinguish itself along dimensions that are important to its customers" (Bartness and Carney, 1993:81). Leaders interested in success in today's globally competitive environment must focus on locating and then continuously improving such capabilities. However, core capabilities create no competitive advantage if they are easy to imitate by one's competitors. Core competencies that are difficult to imitate and continuously improve are what effective leaders seek to create. We believe that there are at least three separate and always combinable means for converting value-added organizational functions and/or business processes into strategic capabilities which are difficult to imitate and thus a source of products with a sustainable competitive advantage. These are (1) knowledge-based competencies, (2) alliance-based competencies, and (3) technology-based competencies (Obloj, Cushman, and Kozminski, 1994).

Knowledge-based competencies arise when, in comparing a firm's value chain with the value chain of all of the firm's competitors, one locates some single or combination of value-added organizational function(s) and/or business process(es) in which one excels in comparison to one's competitors. The question will then arise as to how the firm should strategically link and configure those value-added activities with its customers in order to produce a product which has a sustainable competitive advantage. In such cases, it is one's own firm's unique knowledge in the form of value-added activities which, when grouped into capabilities in linking with the customers, yields a competitive advantage (Barton, 1992).

Alliance-based competencies reside in comparing a firm's value chain with a firm's competitors and finding that while some aspects of a firm's value chain can produce value-added activities, some portions of the firm's value chain of most concern to the customer are not present or not functioning at an appropriate level. Under such conditions, an organization may choose to form one or more linking arrangements with other firms which are performing well in these customer sensitive areas in order to obtain sustainable competitive advantage. Such linkages may take the form of mergers, acquisitions, equity partnerships, consortia, joint ventures, development agreements, supply agreements, and/or marketing agreements (Nohria and Garcia-Pont, 1991:105; Prahalad and Hamal, 1990).

Technology-based competencies reside in comparing a firm's value chain with a firm's competitors and finding that while some aspects of a firm's value chain can produce value-added activities, some portions of a firm's value chain of most concern to the customer cannot function without the addition of some new state-of-the-art technology. Under such conditions, the firm's entire value chain may be in need of modification in order to reap the benefits of the addition of this new technology. The knowledge necessary to obtain this value-added advantage resides in the innovative and appropriate use of these new technologies (Stalk, Evans, and Schulman, 1992).

The Role of Coalignment Broker.   Successful leaders in network organizations must proceed through several operational steps in developing a firm's core competencies in a nonimitable manner. Such a leader must

1. understand pent-up customer demand,
2. be aware of competitors' core competencies,
3. identify one's own core competencies,
4. decide how one's own core competencies can be strengthened through outside linkages,
5. develop a vision, set of priorities, and operations for forging a strong set of inimitable process-oriented linkages, and
6. then continuously improve these linkages and core capabilities through teamwork, benchmarking, and further linkages (Bartlett and Goshal, 1993).

The organizational network management literature thus gave rise to a new leadership role, namely, that of a *coalignment broker,* which functions both within and between firms and which must be added to our transformational leadership role and skills in order to make clear the characteristics of high-speed management leadership. In a network organization a leader does not plan, organize, and control resources that are held in-house; rather, such a leader serves as a coalignment broker across firms, many of which are not under a single firm's control. Such a coalignment broker must have three skills: that of architect, lead operator, and caretaker of interorganizational coalignment (Snow, Miles, and Coleman, 1993).

Leaders who act as *architects* facilitate the emergence of specific operating networks which can function at given levels of quality and productivity within a specific high-speed management time frame. Leaders who act as *lead operators* must establish the correct coalignment between functional units and firms, giving them a clear vision, specific missions, and performance targets for assisting in fulfilling both firms' goals. Then a monitoring, reward, and adjudication system for conflicts must be put in place to guarantee high performance. Finally, network leadership requires constant *caretaking,* namely coaching, resource enhancement, and fine-tuning in order to maintain a high performance. Here the tools of continuous improvement teams, benchmarking, and new external linkages come into play. In addition to the top management team, each firm, according to Bartlett and Goshal (1993:124–129), must develop three additional levels of leadership: the business manager who is a strategist, architect, and coordinator; the country manager who is an environmental scanner, builder, and contractor; and the functional or process manager who is a monitor, cross-pollinator, and champion.

Whereas the research on transformational leadership yields a focus on anticipating chance, visioning, empowerment, and value-congruence skills for directing and motivating worker involvement, the research on network leadership adds to this the role of *coalignment broker* who has the skills to create outside linkages with firms, who can enhance one's own firm's core competencies and function as an architect, lead operator, and caretaker of these linkages. We are now in a position to explore the contributions of the literature on managing organizational discontinuities to our characterization of a high-speed management broker.

Leading Discontinuous Organizational Change

The research literature on managing organizational discontinuities focuses on the roles and skills involved in transforming a firm from one vision and/or set of core competencies to another. This literature yields two rather specific sets of insights for the high-speed management leader. *First,* organizations will go through periods of rapid and dramatic change during which the vision and core competencies to be acquired are *known,* and on other occasions the vision and core competencies to be acquired are *unknown. Second,* the leaders who will successfully guide change must employ some roles and skills which are *unique* to and some *common* to each of these types of change (Burdett, 1993:10).

Unique Change Skills. Differential roles and skills are involved in leading a change and setting performance targets where the vision and/or core competencies are known (stable change) and those where they are unknown (unstable change). Table 3.3 contains a list of these differences.

Common Change Skills. Common to both types of change is the need to create a positive learning environment in which a firm's

Table 3.3   TYPES OF CHANGE SKILLS

Known	Unknown
Communicated single vision	Communicated multiple visions
Set clear performance targets	Set flexible performance targets
Manage organizational change	Manage organizational constraints
Improve core competencies	Outservice multiple core competencies
Empower decision-making	Centralize decision-making
Follow fixed time frame	Follow multiple time frames
Flex time performance ahead of competition	Flex performance against competition
Create tension and release it	Minimize tension
Bring core skills inhouse	Leave core skills out-of-house
Limit outside linkages	Increase outside linkages
Benchmark	Make suppliers benchmark
Employ teams	Make suppliers employ teams
Set boundaryed organizational system	Set boundaryless organizational system

employees are guided on a journey of organizational renewal in which they redefine the assumptions underpinning the meaning and measures of (a) performance, (b) work, and (c) the organizations itself. The *first* of these transformations, namely *performance,* requires a redefinition of a firm's critical success factors. The *second, work,* requires a redefinition of *empowerment.* The *third,* a redefinition of the *firm,* requires a knowledge of outside linking or networking possibilities (Burdett, 1993).

In order to understand the pattern of possibilities for success in such a transformation, a high-speed management leader must have an estimate of the time available to get a product to market ahead of its competitors and some knowledge and skill in expanding and/or contracting a firm's span of attention for meeting these time deadlines. The major leadership skills involved in meeting these time deadlines are:

a. creating an organizational tension sufficient for motivating a firm's leadership and workers to leave their old core competencies and move to a new set;

b. creating a learning framework to guide the change in core competencies; and

c. targeting objective critical success factors, empowerment goals, and networking links to be established within the prescribed time frame (Burdett, 1993:13–14).

A leader must be careful in attempting to create the tension necessary for change to create also a positive learning environment. If one creates too much tension without guiding the productive channeling of that tension into positive learning situations, emotion renders the employees motionless and work halts. If one creates too little tension then employees hold onto old habits and resist change. There are methods available to leaders for creating a positive tension which can lead to the appropriate level of learning and implementation of new core competencies. Among these are benchmarking with both the best in the industry and the best, period; moving from seniority to meritocracy; improving the quality and openness of performance feedback by including peer and subordinates in the process; removing those, especially those at senior levels, who represent poor role models; encouraging risk; taking non-decision-making levels out of hierarchy; rewarding success; discouraging concepts of turf; striving for synergies; and focusing on outputs (Burdett, 1993:16).

Two examples will serve to illustrate the use of all the above skills and tools for creating a known and unknown transformational change. In the mid-1980s the Chrysler Automotive firm was having trouble designing and producing cars in a short enough time span to compete with Ford and Toyota, the leading U.S. and Japanese firms. The CEO Lee Iaccoca decided to discontinue the firm's old core competencies in design, engineering, and producing, and transform the firm's core competencies to Ford's and Toyota's lean production models. The firm made a commitment of $1 billion over five years to construct and implement a new R & D and production center. To create a strong and positive tension for the acquisition and implementation of these new knowledge, technology, and parts alliance competencies, all the old competency units were closed and Chrysler outsourced the design, engineering, and production of its new car models from Japanese firms (Levin, 1992).

During the first three years of new competency acquisitions, all the tools for extending a firm's span of attention were employed and during the final two years of new competency implementation, all the tools for shortening a firm's span of attention were employed in order to produce new models within a two-year time frame. In addition, the implementation process benchmarked Chrysler's performance against the best Ford and Toyota facilities in the world. The workforce was downsized by cutting both managers and workers who could not learn and implement the new skills, and all the types of change tools for known competencies were exploited to create a world-class R & D and production center. By 1991 the Chrysler auto division had been completely restructured, new core competencies were in place, and a steady flow of new products was on the way to market, expanding Chrysler's market shares and types of cars offered from a single platform. Chrysler's stock went up and the firm was in an excellent competitive position to turn the firm over to a new management team upon Iacocca's retirement (Schonfeld, 1992:56–57; Taylor, 1992:82).

In the early 1990s the American Telephone and Telegraph Company faced a crisis and an opportunity of unknown proportions on two fronts (Andrews, 1993a:1). *First,* new developments in cellular technology were beginning to reveal the broad outline of a revolution in long distance phone, computer, and visual transmission services. Motorola had begun a program to launch sixty-eight low-level satellites that could create a global wireless telephone revolution. *Second,* new developments in electronic games, radio, and multimedia technology were indicating the broad outline of a revolution in centralizing TV, telephones, radio, and computer communication in a single unit. AT&T was heavily involved in computer and long distance communication through wire cable and high-level satellites. To protect itself from becoming outdated in terms of knowledge and technology, AT&T CEO Robert Allen embarked on a broad acquisition and alliance program in both of these areas. AT&T paid $12.6 billion to acquire McCaw Cellular, giving them control of a vast wireless network and bringing the core knowledge and technology involved in-house. Next, it invested heavily in ten firms involved in multimedia research and development and set up alliances with these firms while keeping them outside AT&T primary core competencies. *Finally,* AT&T embarked on setting up a strong set of alliances with local cable television and telephone companies to supply either cable or wireless service (Andrews, 1993b:3–1). The results have been an increase in sales, profits, and stock prices and AT&T is now poised to transform its firm in any or all of these directions (Kirkpatrick, 1993:35–66).

A high-speed management leader has time as a controlling interest—speed-to-market—in order to outperform one's competitors. A high-speed management leader also must fulfill at least three new leadership roles: that of transformational leader, network leader, and a leader of discontinuous change.

An Example of High-Speed Management Leadership in a World-Class Firm

The search for internal synergies, the development of strategic alliances, and the push for new ventures, all emphasize the political side of a leader's work. Executives must be able to juggle a set of constituencies rather than control a set of subordinates. They have to bargain, negotiate, and sell instead of making unilateral decisions and issuing commands. The leader's task, as Chester Barnard recognized long ago, is to develop a network of cooperative relationships among all the people, groups, and organizations that have something to contribute to an economic enterprise.
(Kantor, 1989:90)

As an example of a high-speed management leader to analyze, we turn to Jack Welch, the CEO of the General Electric Company (GE). He was selected for three reasons.

First, his thirteen-year reign as CEO of General Electric has produced rather dramatic results. GE's sales rose from $27.9 billion to $62.2 billion; profits rose from $2.9 billion to $4.7 billion; stock appreciation went from $31 per share to $93 per share with stockholder equity reaching $73.9 billion. GE thus became the *fifth* largest industrial corporation in America, the *third* largest in profits, and the *second* largest in stockholder equity (*Fortune,* 1993:185).

Second, GE is one of only eight U.S. multinational firms to make a profit in each of the last twenty years. In addition, each of GE's fourteen businesses are number one or two in market shares in the world with a thirteen-year increase in productivity of over 110 percent and average increases in quality and response time of over 300 percent.

Third, Jack Welch has won *Foreign World Magazine*'s award for outstanding leader in the world, *Fortune* magazine's Leadership Hall of Fame Award, and numerous other leadership awards. In addition, over twenty of GE's former top executives have become successful CEOs of such global firms as GTE, Allied Signal, Goodyear Tire, Owens-Corning, Ryland Group, General Dynamics, Wang Laboratories, Sundstrand, Rubbermaid, M/A Communications, USF&G, Zorn Industries, Clean Harbor, and Systems Computer Technology.

Let us examine briefly Jack Welch as a high-speed management leader (i.e., transformational, network, and discontinuities leader) across three of his anticipated needs for a transformation in the General Electric Corporation.

Transformation #1: To the Most Competitive and Valuable Firm in the World

In 1981, Jack Welch became CEO of the General Electric Corporation and anticipated his first need for a transformational change. Welch (1988:12) recalls his thoughts:

> At the beginning of the decade . . . we faced a world economy that would be characterized by slower growth with stronger global competitors going after a smaller pie. In the context of that environment we had one clear-cut major competitor: Japan, Inc. . . . powerful . . . innovative . . . and moving aggressively into many of our markets.

In an attempt to create and operationalize a transformational vision, Welch set two clear and simple goals for his firm and outlined the operational targets for reaching these goals.

1. *To become the most competitive corporation in the world.* This principle is currently operationalized to mean that each of GE's thirteen businesses should

a. invest only in businesses with high growth potential where GE can become the number one or two in market shares in the world;
b. increase productivity and grow 5 percent per year;
c. decentralize power and responsibility downward in order to make each business unit as fast and flexible as possible in responding to global competition;
d. develop low-cost, high-quality, easily serviced products which are customer oriented so as to yield increased market shares in order to fund the R & D and acquisitions necessary to remain number one or two;
e. monitor carefully the ability of each business to meet productivity and financial targets; and
f. intervene when necessary to make each business become a "win-aholic" (Cushman and King, 1994a:1994b).

2. *To become the nation's most valuable corporation.* This principle is currently operationalized to mean the "most valuable" in terms of market capitalization. This principle manifests itself in a number of specific ways at GE:

a. keep earnings rising at 5 to 10 percent per year;
b. keep stock appreciation and yield at about 15 to 20 percent per year;

  c. shift earning mix so 50 percent can come from a high growth
     area;
  d. keep supplier productivity rising at about 5 to10 percent
     per year;
  e. maintain exports as percent of sales at about 50 percent;
     and
  f. maintain management's reputation as an entrepreneurial,
     agile, knowledgeable, aggressive, and effective competitor
     (Cushman and King, 1994a and 1994b).

Welch created an organizational tension in 1981 by redefining
his firm's goals and targets. He then released the tension in a series
of dramatic and now famous moves. *First,* he cut GE's 150 independent
business units down to 14, each positioned in a high-growth
industry in which GE ranked number one or two in market shares in
the world. These businesses were aircraft engines, broadcasting,
defense electronics, electric motors, engineering, plastics, factory
automation, industrial power systems, lighting, locomotives, major
appliances, medical diagnostics, financial service, and communications
(Sherman, 1989:40). *Second,* between 1981 and 1993, Welch
sold over 200 of GE's business units worth $12 billion while acquiring
and combining over 300 businesses worth $26 billion into 14. He
closed 78 production facilities, and invested $25 billion in automating
the remaining 200 U.S. units and the 130 abroad in twenty-four
countries, making them world-class manufacturing facilities. *Third,*
Welch shed over 150,000 workers, one out of every four workers. He
reduced nine layers of management to five, releasing one out of
every four managers. *Fourth,* he decentralized power, expanded his
managers' span of control, built an all new executive team, and
restructured every business, replacing thirteen of fourteen business
leaders (Cushman and King, 1994).

Welch realized that GE would have to undertake frame-breaking
changes if they were to meet this challenge and become a world-class
competitive organization. Welch (1988:2) sketched his vision
and described its roots.

> Our experience during the late '70s in grappling with world competition
> etched very clearly on our minds the belief that companies
> that held on to marginal businesses—or less than
> world-competitive operations of *any* sort—wouldn't be around
> for very long. That analysis led us to a strategy that said we had
> to be number one or number two in each one of our businesses
> . . . or we had to see a way to get there . . . or exit if we

couldn't. The product businesses had to achieve global leadership positions in cost, quality and technology. Our services businesses had to define and attain leading niche positions in the broad spectrum of markets they served. That was—that is—our strategy: simple, even stark.

In 1988, Welch stood back and reflected on this effort:

Now, how we went at this can be described from two totally different perspectives. One perspective would use words like "downsizing," "reducing," "cutting." We think that view misses the point. We see our task as a totally different one aimed at liberating, facilitating, unleashing the human energy and initiative of our people.

At the heart of this change and institutionalization process was Welch's (1988:3) use of empowerment.

Sure we saved. Simply by eliminating the company's top operating level, the geographic sectors, we saved $40 million. But that was just a bonus that pales in importance to the sudden release of talent and energy that poured out after all the dampers, valves and baffles of the sectors had been removed. We can say without hesitation that almost every single good thing that has happened within this company over the past few years can be traced to the liberation of some individual, some team, some business.

So we reduced the number of management layers in the company to get closer to the individual—the source of that creative energy we needed.

In reducing these layers, we are trying to get the people in the organization to understand that they can't do everything they used to do. They have to set priorities. The less important tasks have to be left undone. Trying to do the same number of tasks with fewer people would be the antithesis of what we set out to achieve: a faster, more focused, more purposeful company.

As we became leaner, we found ourselves communicating better, with fewer interpreters and fewer filters.

We found that with fewer layers we had wider spans of management. We weren't managing better. We were managing less, and *that* was better.

Finally, Welch and his new GE management team demonstrated self-understanding in what the institutionalization of change had done for the organization. Welch (1988:3) continues:

We found that the leaders—people with a vision and a passion—soon began to stand out. And when they did, we found our own self-confidence growing to the point that we began to delegate authority further and further down into the company. Businesses were allowed to develop their own pay plans and incentives that made sense for *their* marketplaces. They were given the freedom to spend significant sums on plant and equipment on their own, based on *their* needs, *their* judgement, *their* view of their marketplace. Freeing people to move rapidly and without hestitation makes all the difference in the world . . . we have found what we believe is the distilled essence of competitiveness—the reservoir of talent and creativity and energy that can be found in each of our people. That essence is liberated when we make people believe that what they think and do is important . . . and then get out of their way while they do it.

Transformation #2: To Speed Simplicity and Self-Confidence

In April of 1988 this first massive reengineering was all but complete and Welch began to anticipate the need for a second transformation in GE. Welch (1988:4) reflects:

> . . . today the world is even tougher and more crowded. Korea and Taiwan have become world-class competitors, as hungry and aggressive as Japan was in 1981. Europe is on fire with a new entrepreneurial spirit and leadership that is among the world's best. Many of its most aggressive companies, like Electrolux and ASEA of Sweden, Philips of Holland, and Siemens and Bayer of Germany, are after our markets through acquisitions and joint ventures—just as we are going after theirs.
>
> At the same time, the Japanese are more sophisticated and aggressive than ever—building servicing plants outside Japan, including dozens just over the Mexican border.

By 1988, GE's challenges were internal and even larger than in 1981. Welch (1988:1–2) reflects: "We had to find a way to combine the power, resources, and reach of a *big* company with the hunger, the agility, the spirit, and fire of a small company." The rationale for this change was simple: that only the most productive, high-quality, and rapid response firms were going to win in the 1990s. If you can't produce a top quality product at the world's lowest price and get it to market in less time than your competitors, you're going to be out of the game. In such an environment, 5 percent annual increase in productivity and quality will not be enough; more will be needed. Welch argued that now a firm must (1) define its vision in broad, simple, and strategic terms; (2) maximize its productivity, quality, and speed-to-market; and (3) be organizationally and culturally innovative and flexible and rapid in responding to shifting customer demand for low-price, high-value products. He then called for GE to reorient its internal vision to "speed, simplicity and self-confidence." In order to meet this internal vision, two new goals and sets of targets were put in place.

   3. *To develop a skilled, self-actualizing, productive, and aggressive workforce capable of generating and employing practical and technical knowledge.* This principle is operationalized currently to mean GE wants to create an environment in which GE will be viewed as a challenging place to work and that will significantly enhance worker skills so that they can find another job if the company no longer needs them—a place where employees are ready to go but eager to stay. In order to actualize this goal, GE must

   a. develop employee awareness that the only road to job security is increasing market shares;
   b. develop employees who are more action oriented, more risk oriented, and more people oriented;
   c. develop employees who relentlessly pursue individual and group goals;
   d. develop employee skills and performance through timely and quality education programs;
   e. hold employees responsible for meeting productivity and financial targets; and
   f. reward high performance and deal effectively with low performance (Cushman and King, 1994b).

   4. *To develop open communication based on candor and trust.* This principle is operationalized to mean sharing with all employees the corporation's vision, goals, and values, opening each employee up to discussion regarding his or her strengths, weaknesses, and the possibility for change. This is accompanied by

   a. speaking openly and listening carefully to discussions aimed at preparing, articulating, refining, and gaining acceptance for unit visions;
   b. showing candor and trust in sharing and evaluating personal and business plans; and

c. motivating employees to become more open, more self-confident, more energized individuals in generating and employing practical and technical knowledge (Cushman and King, 1994b).

Two new mechanisms were put forward to create a tension capable of meeting these new goals—a reengineered corporate culture and a continuous improvement program. A new corporate culture was devised and put in place by GE stakeholders to aid in the development of speed, simplicity, and self-confidence. This new culture focused on improving organizational productivity, quality, and response time, and contained the following leadership values for management.

These management values were prefaced with a statement that "G.E. leaders, always with unyielding integrity,"

1. "create a clear, simple, reality-based, customer-focused vision and are able to communicate it straightforwardly to all constituencies";

2. "set aggressive targets, understanding accountability and commitment, and are decisive";

3. "have a passion for excellence, hating bureaucracy and all the nonsense that comes with it";

4. "have the self-confidence to empower others and behave in a boundaryless fashion";

5. "believe in and are committed to Work=Out as a means of empowerment and are open to ideas from anywhere";

6. "have, or have the capacity to develop, global brains and global sensitivity and are comfortable building diverse global teams";

7. "stimulate and relish change and are not frightened or paralyzed by it, seeing change as opportunity, not threat";

8. "have enormous energy and the ability to energize and invigorate others";

9. "understand speed as a competitive advantage and see the total organizational benefits that can be derived from a focus on speed." (Tichy and Charon, 1989:18–19)

Next GE put in place a continuous improvement program aimed at rengineering GE's organizational processes by increasing the firm's productivity and quality while decreasing its response time. The program included a self-managed team program called "workout," a cross-functional team program called "process mapping," a bench-marking "best practices" program, and an aggressive outside linking program (Cushman and King, 1994b).

The practical objective of "workout" was to

> get rid of thousands of bad habits accumulated since the cre-
> ation of GE 112 years ago. The intellectual goal was to put the
> leaders of each business in front of 100 or so employees, eight
> to ten times a year to let them know what their people think
> about how the company can be improved and then make the
> leaders respond to those changes. Ultimately we are restructur-
> ing the leader-subordinate relationship to challenge both to make
> GE a better place to work. It will force leaders and workers to
> combine in creating a vision, articulating the vision, passion-
> ately owning the vision, and relentlessly driving it to comple-
> tion. (Tichy and Charon, 1989:113)

By the end of 1993, over seventy thousand employees will have
participated in three-day workout town meetings with remarkable
results. In GE's plastics division alone, over thirty workout teams
have been empowered to make changes. One team saved GE plastics $2 million by modifying one production process, another en-
hanced productivity fourfold, while a third reduced product delivery
time 400 percent (Workout, 1991: 1–2). Another business, NBC, used
workout to halt the use of report forms that totaled more than two
million pieces of paper a year (Stewart, 1991:44). GE Credit Services
used workout to tie its cash registers directly to the mainframe,
cutting the time for opening a new account from thirty minutes to
ninety seconds. Similar results have been reported from workout
projects in GE's other businesses, demonstrating a remarkable
companywide reorientation of coalignment processes between worker
capabilities and organizational needs.

While this internal transformation of GE's value chain was taking place, CEO Welch also realized that some other global organizations were achieving greater productivity, quality control, flexibility,
adaptability, and rapid response time than GE, even with the workout program in place. In the summer of 1988, GE began its "Best
Practices Program," aimed at locating those organizations which had
outperformed GE in a given area, developing a case study of how
they did it, and then employing these case studies as world-class
benchmarks for improving GE's performance.

GE scanned the globe and located twenty-four corporations
which had outperformed GE in some area. They then screened out
direct competitors and companies which would not be credible to
GE employees. Welch then invited each corporation to come to GE
to learn about its best practices and in return to allow GE to come

to their companies and study their best practices. About one-half of the companies agreed. They included AMP, Chapparral Steel, Ford, Hewlett Packard, Xerox, and three Japanese companies. GE sent out observers to develop case studies and ask questions. These best practices case studies have been turned into a course at Crotonville, GE's leadership training center, and is offered to a new class of managers from each of GE's fourteen businesses each month (Stewart, 1991:44–45).

Finally, as GE's top management team reviewed the projects which had been successful from both their workout and best practices programs, they noticed a difference in the types of product which saved up to $1 million and those which saved $100 million. The latter always involved changes in organizational processes which spanned the entire value chain. They cut across departments and involved linking with suppliers and customers. All emphasized managing processes, not functions. This led GE to establish its cross-functional teamwork program aimed at mapping and then improving key organizational processes. Such process maps frequently allowed employees for the first time to see and understand organizational processes from beginning to end. They demonstrated also the need for a new type of manager, a process manager who could coalign an organization's total assets. They allowed employees to spot bottlenecks, time binds and inventory shortages, and overflows.

Since implementing such a cross-functional teamwork program, GE appliances has cut its sixteen-week manufacturing cycle in half, while increasing product availability 6 percent and decreasing inventory costs 20 percent. The program has cost less than $3 million to implement and has already returned profits one hundred times that (Stewart, 1991:48). Product mapping programs have provided also an empirical basis for changing how GE measures its management and workers' performance. GE now employs world-class cross-functional process benchmarking standards to evaluate its various business performances and to award its bonuses and merit awards for process improvement (Cushman and King, 1993).

The 1990s, according to Welch (1988:4), will be a "white-knuckle decade for global business . . . fast . . . exhilarating," with many winners and losers. But GE, according to Welch, is ready. His transformational vision, mobilization, and institutionalization in the 1980s have put GE in position to meet these new threats head-on with minimal stress, and with the communication, speed, flexibility, and efficiency of a creative firm. Welch foresaw this development in 1988 (1988:4).

We approach the '90s with a business system, a method of operating, that allows us to routinely position each business for the short- and long-term so that while one or more are weathering difficult markets, the totality is always growing faster than the world economy.

No one in the world has a set of powerful businesses like ours. They've never been stronger. And big, bold moves are enhancing their global competitiveness: . . . Plastics by expansion in the U.S., Europe and the Far East . . . GE's numerous domestic acquisitions . . . Aircraft Engine with its European partnership . . . Factory Automation's worldwide venture with Fanuc of Japan . . . Medical Systems' French and Japanese acquisitions . . . NBC's new station and programming initiatives . . . joint ventures by Lighting in the Far East and most recently, Roper's acquisition by Major Appliance. The list of moves goes on and on and will continue at an even faster pace. Our business strategy, grounded in reality, has become real. Our businesses are number one or two in their marketplaces.

To go with our business strategy, we've got a management system now in place and functioning that supports that strategy—one that is lean, liberating, fast-moving—an organization that facilitates and frees and, above all, understands that the fountainhead of success is the individual, not the system.

Transformation #3: The Push to Become a Major Player in the Pacific Rim Markets

In 1992 Jack Welch began to reflect on the need for a third transformation in GE. He believed that the slow 3 percent projected growth rate for European, U.S., and Japanese core markets over the next several years would limit GE's growth. He believed that if GE were to remain a global leader, it must take steps to position itself in the major emerging markets of the Pacific Rim, China, India, Mexico, and Southeast Asia. These markets are growing and will continue to grow at 8 to 12 percent per year for the next ten to twenty years. In addition, GE's growth in revenue from these areas had gone from $10 to $20 billion in the last three years (Smart, Engardio, and Smith, 1993:64–70). Welch believed that to remain a global leader, GE had to shift its center of gravity from the U.S./Europe relationship to the U.S./Pacific Rim markets. This was to be accomplished through a two-pronged strategy with specific performance targets for each.

    5. *To become a multipolar, multicultural firm.* This principle is operationalized currently to mean that while GE's fourteen businesses are currently number one or two in Europe and the United States and should defend this status, they must now become number one or two in the major markets of the Pacific Rim—China, India, Mexico, and Southeast Asia. In order to actualize this goal, GE must (a) develop profit centers in each of these markets; (b) develop a multicultural pool of business leaders and employees; (c) integrate Pacific Rim nations into their R & D, manufacturing, sales, and service systems; (d) extend GE's management system into these major markets; and (e) increase investment in GE from the region (Smart, Engardio, and Smith, 1993).

      6. *To employ GE's strong infrastructure in technology transfer, management training, and financial services to broadly and deeply penetrate these markets.* In order to do this GE is (a) developing joint ventures in technology transfer with firms in the region; (b) training foreign nationals in the United States and then sending them back to Asia to head GE units; (c) exporting GE's training programs to the region; (d) using GE financial services to fund projects in the region which use GE products; and (e) making small $10 million investments throughout the region to hedge against foreign currency fluctuations and other forms of economic instability (Smart, Engardio, and Smith, 1993).

      Thus far, the results of these strategies have been promising. GE's reality-based action training programs have taken managers from Asian cultures and trained them in management skills in the United States. Next, these managers were shipped off to the Pacific Rim's major markets to interview old, new, and potential GE customers, competitors, and business managers. Finally, GE asked these managers to develop market penetration plans and a value chain, reengineering plans to better position the firm's business in the region. Similarly, GE's middle management training programs are rotating promising multicultural leaders through different businesses and markets in Asia in order to create a truly global multipolar, multicultural leader (Smart, Engardio, and Smith, 1993).

      GE has invested over $100 million in factories to produce medical imaging equipment, plastics, appliances, and lamps in India. GE sales in India will go from $400 million to $1 billion by the year 2000. GE has moved boldly into China where the government plans to add $100 billion in power generators, one hundred jet engines, one thousand medical imagers, and over two hundred locomotives in the next four years. GE Capital has been creative in helping the Chinese government set up a new development bank to fund these activities.

In Indonesia GE is part of a $2 billion power plant project and offered an array of technology transfer projects to help upgrade Indonesia's industrial capacities (Smart, Engardio, and Smith, 1993).

In Malaysia, GE now owns a 49 percent interest in UMW Corporation. In Mexico, GE has over twenty factories with twenty-one thousand employees who have upheld GE appliances as a household name. GE will have over $1.5 billion in sales this year, up from $900 million last year. GE Broadcasting has joined with Rupert Murdoch's Star TV system to launch a new business and news channel throughout the Asian region. Finally, GE Capital, a $155 billion per year financial arm, has made $200 million in funds available for loans to small business in Asia. In short, GE is on the move again, transforming its firm, people, and resources to fit the needs of customers in the Pacific Rim (Stewart, 1993:64–70). In so doing, it brings GE's unique brand of management to Asia. GE's blend of entrepreneurial spirit with a hard-driving and intensely competitive focus transfer into an obsession with performance, an ability to shift strategy rapidly to take advantage of change, an appetite for risk taking and deal making, and an engineer's yen to run productive, high-quality, and rapid response operations. In addition, GE's CEO Jack Welch may be one of the world's best transformational, network, and discontinuities leaders. He is looking to position GE as a dominant player in the Pacific Rim region while maintaining a dominant position in Europe and the Americas (Smart, Engardio, and Smith, 1993).

Critical Success Factors of a High-Speed Management Leader

The basic function of [leadership] appears to be the coalignment not merely of people in coalitions but of institutional action—of technology and task environment into a viable domain, and of organizational design and structure appropriate to it. Leadership functions well when it keeps the organization at the nexus of several necessary streams of action.
(Thompson, 1967:21)

We began our investigation of corporate leadership with a review of the literature covering four decades of research. Beginning with power perspectives and proceeding through trait, behavioral, and contingency perspectives, we traced the role of leadership in corporations from charismatic leadership through situational leadership. We then noted that these perspectives all presupposed a relatively stable business environment based on incremental change. However, with the advent of a turbulent global economic environment and the need to deal with discontinuous change, a new high-speed management leader has emerged. This type of leader focuses on transformations, network management, and managing organizational discontinuities. There are five critical success factors for this final type of leader; he or she must

1. have accurate information on customer pent-up demand, competitor core capabilities, product life cycle timelines, and one's own core capabilities;
2. effectively anticipate and communicate a vision of the next transformation, goals, targets, and a time frame for implementing the known or unknown change;
3. select the nonimitable core competencies to be acquired and adjust the firm's span of attention and tension levels so as to motivate this enhancement within the time frame required;
4. act as a broker of these new coalignment patterns both inside and outside the firm;
5. institutionalize a monitoring and reward program for the transformed performance target in following known and unknown patterns of change.

4

High-Speed Management Corporate Climate

> *Organizational culture is the pattern of basic assump-*
> *tions that a given group has invested, discovered, or devel-*
> *oped in learning to cope with its problems of external*
> *adaptation and internal integration, and that have worked*
> *well enough to be considered valid, and, therefore, to be*
> *taught to new members as the correct way to perceive,*
> *think, and feel in relation to those problems.*
> (Schein, 1984:3)

At the core of an organization's integration processes are its pre-
scriptive values, rules, reward and punishment systems—its corporate culture. A culture is a complex of values which contains a vision
of that culture's ideal of excellence (Weaver, 1964). A culture in this
sense is an orientation system from which its most powerful and
humble members can borrow to give dignity, direction, and a sense
of belonging to their lives. From within a culture's vision, this ideal
of its own excellence, comes the culture's power to inspire and to
motivate significant effort. A *culture* is by nature restrictive. It provides a preferred viewpoint on the world and asks its members to
seek out and establish their personal identity within that vision or
experience the threat of their primary reference group's denying the
validity of their existence.

A corporate culture services at least three functions: legitimation, motivation, and integration. *First,* a culture provides its members with socially legitimate patterns of interpretation and behavior
for dealing with culturally relevant problems. *Second,* a culture

---

Portions of this chapter are based on material in D. P. Cushman, S. S. King, and
T. Smith, "The Rules Perspective on Organizational Communication Research."
In G. H. Goldhaber and G. H. Barnett (eds.), *Handbook of Organizational
Communication.* Norwood, N.J.: Ablex, 1988: 55–94.

provides its members with a hierarchy of values, a motivational structure which links individual identities to culturally relevant roles and values. *Third,* a culture provides its members with a symbolically integrated framework that regulates social interaction and goal attainment through the creation of cultural meanings (Gutknecht, 1982).

Corporate climate is the degree of fit between an organization's culture and the values and interests of the individuals and groups upon whom the organization depends for its effective functioning (Cushman, King, and Smith, 1988). However, as several researchers point out, individuals and groups who interact within an organization's domain have values and interests of their own, which may or may not intersect with an organization's culture in a productive way (Philipsen, 1981). Understanding these intersections and the resultant information and communication climate they create is important in grasping a corporate culture's ability to legitimate, motivate, and integrate its activities. *Four groups appear particularly significant in respect to organizational goal attainment: the government, investors, workers, and consumers.* The fit between these four audience's values and interests and the corporation's culture is termed *corporate climate* (Quick, 1988:45–56).

It will be the purpose of this chapter to analyze in some detail the relationship of corporate culture to organizational performance in a volatile economic environment by exploring (1) the corporate climate created by IBM, (2) the corporate climate created by General Electric, and (3) to draw out of these analyses the critical success factors involved in these core integrative processes. Prior to entering into the main body of our analysis, we will develop the analytic tools to be employed in such an analysis and to justify the selection of IBM and GE as corporations worthy of our analysis.

The term *corporate culture* denotes two very different but interrelated things. On the one hand, culture refers to a *conceptual reality,* to core values for orienting a person to the perceptual world, to specific ways of thinking. On the other hand, culture refers to a *phenomenal reality,* to culturally specific patterns of behavior. Socialization into this phenomenal reality provides one's everyday activities with a sense of direction, a sense of what is appropriate and inappropriate behavior. A corporate culture is made operational by socializing its members into the value system involved and by learning the rituals, myths, and social dramas that demonstrate how the organization's core values are to be linked conceptually and phenomenally to reality. A *myth* is a symbolic narrative—a story that manifests a culture's core values. It specifies ways of linking the corporation's values to thought and action in a manner which holds a grip on the communal imagination by overcoming difficulty. A *ritual* is a pattern of thought and behavior, the correct performance of which constitutes participation in the culture by paying homage to the culture's sacred values. A *social drama* is a dramatic presentation of a breach in cultural values, the cases it causes for the community, the redress of the offender, and how the offender is dismissed or reintegrated into the community (Philipsen, 1981).

Our examination of corporate culture will focus on *locating the organization's core values, exploring the method for socializing members into those values, and analyzing the rituals, myths, and social dramas which link corporate values to actual cognitive and behavioral processes.* Corporate climate involves the degree of fit between an organization's operationalized value system and the values and interests of those individuals and groups with whom interaction must occur, namely investors, workers, and consumers. The degree of positive or negative fit will significantly affect a culture's ability to legitimate, motivate, and integrate an organization's activities in pursuit of its goals. Our exploration of corporate climate will attempt to examine each of these intersects, to evaluate the goodness of fit, and to assess the effect of corporate climate on organizational performance (Calori and Sarnin, 1991:48–74).

IBM and General Electric were selected as the bases for our inquiry because IBM was believed in 1994 to have a corporate culture which was injurious to a firm and prevented adaptation to environmental change (Lohr, 1994:3–1), while GE was believed to have the best corporate culture in America for adapting to environmental change (Welsh, 1994:58). In addition, IBM and General Electric offer theoretically interesting contrasts in their corporate cultures. IBM is an industry-based competitor; General Electric is multi-industrial in its base. IBM has a strong nurturing corporate culture, while General Electric has a strong self-reliant culture. IBM has a strong sense of community responsibility; General Electric has little. These qualities make the two corporations interesting case studies and an excellent base for the examination of critical success factors.

The Corporate Climate Created by IBM

The late Thomas Watson Jr. of IBM liked to tell Kierkegaard's tale about a man who relished watching the annual flight of wild ducks.

Each year he sowed a nearby lake with feed so the ducks would stop to eat. Some of the ducks gave up flying south and wintered at the lake instead. In time they grew fat and lazy. Why bother to fly when you have everything laid on for you right here?

In spite of this caution, IBM became a tame duck company in a wild duck industry. It is paying the price. So are its employees. Worldwide, since 1986, 180,000 of them have been let go or soon will be.
(McMenamin, 1994:126)

Now, Mr. Gerstner, IBM CEO, is increasingly addressing what may be his greatest challenge: fundamentally changing IBM's culture. Without a basic shift in attitude and behavior, IBM, he warns, will continue to squander its technology and talent.
(Lohr, 1994:3–1)

International Business Machines, or IBM, in 1993 was the third largest corporation in America with $62.7 billion in sales, the fifty-sixth in profits when it lost $8.1 billion, and twelfth in stockholder value (Teitelbaum, 1994:220). IBM sells mainframes, micro-, mini-, and personal computers as well as softwar, peripherals, and service for com puters. IBM's performance over the last ten years has gone from riches to rags. Four times in the last twelve years, 1982–1993, its management team has topped the list of the most admired in America and three times topped the last 90 to 93 of least admired by *Fortune* magazine (Welsh, 1994). Ten times in the last ten years IBM has led the computer industry in sales. However, over the past three years IBM lost $15 billion. This prompted the IBM board of directors in April of 1993 to replace its CEO, John Akers, and replace him with Louis Gerstner (Hays, 1994:A1). Let us examine in some detail IBM's (a) corporate values, (b) socialization process, (c) monitoring, (d) central rituals, myths, and social dramas, and (e) corporate climate and the effect of its climate on corporate performance.

IBM's Corporate Values

In 1957 IBM joined the exclusive fraternity of American corporations grossing $1 billion or more per year. In 1987 IBM passed the $1 billion mark the first week in January and ended the year grossing $54 billion. What accounts for this phenomenal growth rate? Tom Watson Jr., one of the firm's CEOs during this period, firmly believed it was IBM's corporate culture.

> I firmly believe that any organization, in order to survive and achieve success, must have a sound set of beliefs on which it premises all its policies and actions.
>
> Next, I believe that the most important single factor in corporate success is faithful adherence to those beliefs.
>
> And finally, I believe that if an organization is to meet the challenges of a changing world, it must be prepared to change everything about itself except those beliefs as it moves through corporate life. (Watson, 1963:1)

The basic values that guide IBM's corporate culture are expressed as seven principles which guide action.

1. *Respect for the individual.* This principle manifests itself in a number of ways based on the rights and dignity of the individual and specifies that IBM should:

> Help each employee to develop his/her potential and make the best use of his/her abilities.
>
> Pay and promote on merit.
>
> Maintain two-way communication between manager and employee, with opportunity for a fair hearing and equitable settlement of disagreements (IBM, 1985a).

As a management principle, this results in an emphasis on job security which has been part of the company policy since 1914, an "open door" communications policy, maintenance of good human relations, continual opportunity for advancement, and a respect for individual achievement (Watson, 1963; IBM, 1985).

2. *Service to the customer.* By 1985 IBM had earned the rank of America's most admired corporation for the fourth year in a row in *Fortune*'s annual survey of corporate reputations (Hutton, 1986), and with good cause. Their dedication to the best possible service is based on principles such as:

> Know customer needs and help them anticipate future needs.
>
> Help customers use products and services in the best possible way.
>
> Provide superior equipment maintenance and supporting services. (IBM, 1985)

This service to the customer depends on the team of employees who are committed to the IBM principles. IBM begins with the highest standards for the selection of all personnel (Watson, 1963; IBM, 1985).

3. *Superior accomplishment of all tasks.* IBM's expectations for a superior performance from all of its employees in whatever they do sets a tone for dealing with all its constituencies—managers, employees, stockholders, suppliers, customers. Nothing is left to chance. Managers are admonished to:

Lead in new developments.

Be aware of advances made by others, better them where possible, or be willing to adopt them to fit the needs of the corporation.

Produce quality products of the most advanced design and at the lowest possible cost. (IBM, 1985)

4. *Managers must lead effectively.* Sensitivity, intelligence, and aggressive management are demanded to make every individual in the corporation an enthusiastic partner in IBM. In order to achieve this, managers have to follow certain procedures:

Provide the kind of leadership that will motivate employees to do their jobs in a superior way.

Meet frequently with all their people.

Have the courage to question decisions and policies.

Have the vision to see the needs of the Company as well as the division or department.

Plan for the future by keeping an open mind to new ideas, whatever the source. (IBM, 1985)

5. *Obligations to stockholders.* Stockholders are considered the persons having the capital which created the jobs in IBM, and because of this IBM has obligations to them. These require IBM employees to:

Take care of the property the stockholders have entrusted to the company.

Provide an attractive return on invested capital.

Exploit opportunities for continuing profitable growth. (IBM, 1985)

6. *Fair deal for the supplier.* Even the often overlooked supplier of goods and services should be treated fairly and impartially by:

Selecting suppliers according to the quality of their products or services, their general reliability, and competitiveness of price.

Recognizing the legitimate interests of both supplier and IBM when negotiating a contract.

Avoiding suppliers' becoming unduly dependent on IBM. (IBM, 1985)

7. *IBM should be a good corporate citizen.* Competition is essential for protecting the immediate and long-term public interest, but the competition should be vigorous and in a spirit of fair play, with respect for competitors and respect for the law, improving the quality of society, creating an environment in which people want to work and live, and making the world a better place (IBM, 1985).

In addition to these general values, IBM's corporate culture consists of several well-articulated goals for the corporation, department, and unit roles. For example, in 1983 IBM set the following general goals for the 1980s: to grow with the industry; to exhibit product leadership across the entire product line—to excel in technology, values, and quality; to be the most efficient in everything—to be a low-cost producer, seller, and administrator; and to sustain profitability which funds growth. Specific division, department, and individual performance plans are set up and monitored on a yearly basis for meeting these goals (IBM, 1983). In addition to these organizational goals, IBM's corporate culture consists of several well-articulated role-specific duties. For example, the five basic duties of a manager are to employ, to teach, to supervise, to promote people who deserve it, and to discharge when necessary. Specific rituals are then set up for the performance of each duty, such as interviews, personnel reports, and employee counseling (IBM, 1985).

Socialization

Socialization is the systematic means by which firms bring new members into the culture. It encompasses the processes involved in making one a member of the group, learning the ropes, and learning how one can think, act, and communicate in order to get things done. IBM's socialization process involves several steps.

Step one: Careful selection of entry-level candidates. IBM in a given year interviews over 200,000 prospective employees, selecting fewer than 1 percent. IBM recruits from approximately 350 colleges across the country, focusing on the top 32 institutions (Harvard, MIT, CIT, Illinois, Penn State, Purdue, Stanford, University of Texas, UCLA, etc.) where selected IBM executives act as liaisons to the school. About 50 percent of all candidates have technical degrees in the natural sciences (engineering, math, physics); another 40 percent have business degrees, with the remaining 10 percent from the arts and social sciences. Candidates go through a three-level interview process. *First,* trained recruiters use standardized procedures in employee selection. Trainers never attempt to oversell the company and use an extensive filtering process of deselection. Recruiters conduct multiple interviews aimed at locating individuals whose personal values already conform to IBM's corporate beliefs. They are particularly careful to select employees who are motivated to learn, can handle change, are group achievement oriented, are in the top of their class (average G.P.A. is 3.68), have demonstrated social leadership, and present themselves well. *Second,* they are brought into corporate headquarters and administered an IBM aptitude test in their respective areas of expertise on which they must score high. *Third,* they are interviewed and hired by line managers who have all this data before them. This careful screening process increases receptivity for the second stage of socialization (Pascale, 1985).

Step two: Humility-inducing experience. In the first month of on-the-job training, new employees are placed in difficult situations and frequently work long hours on problems that cannot be solved without help. Early training sessions at IBM often cause employees to work from 8:00 A.M. to 2:00 A.M. for several days in a row. Lunches are confined to the workroom. Humility tends to flourish under certain conditions, particularly long hours and intense work that pushes one to the limit. One learns to be humble, to seek the help of others, to become a member of the group, and to defer to experience.

Step three: In-the-trenches training. This leads to a mastery of one's core discipline under the rules and values established by the organization. For example, let's take a close look at the training program for an IBM marketing representative whose initial training program lasts one year with about 75 percent of the training taking place at a branch office and 25 percent at one of IBM's education centers (IBM, 1985d).

IBM marketing representatives do sell IBM products, but they are hardly salesmen or saleswomen in the conventional sense of those words. Many of the products they sell have to do with computer systems: central processing units, terminals, input/output devices, printers, storage units, controllers, and other elements that make up an information processing configuration. The marketing representatives can work with almost any kind of equipment or system needed to solve almost any kind of business problem. Their orientation is the customer, not a particular set of products or systems. To sell a full range of systems and products, many calling for substantial capital investment, marketing representatives must know two things. First, they must know IBM's business; that is, they must know in depth the capabilities of the products and systems they recommend. Second, they must know their customers' businesses and know the kinds of problems their customers face in daily operations (IBM, 1985c).

The training program called "The Core Curriculum" for marketing representatives is twenty-two weeks of this first year. The entire program focuses on what a marketing representative actually does in performing his or her job at IBM. People in these positions are assigned to an IBM branch office where they spend three to five weeks becoming knowledgeable about IBM's policies, practices, and its full line of products. In addition, they study the needs of IBM customers and in particular the ways in which IBM's processing products and systems can help solve problems encountered in the marketplace. After this session, they are sent to Dallas, Texas, for three weeks to be trained in what is called computer concept and marketing. The next move is to be returned to the branch office for five to nine weeks to test how well this information can be applied in a real work situation. Application design and marketing is the next move, with a segment of training taking place again in Dallas on design applications, problem identification, and problem solving, followed by a stint back at the branch applying what has been learned. This last segment of training lasts for five to seven years (IBM, 1985d).

An intensive period of training follows again in Texas for three weeks of systems and account marketing training in various operating systems, including processing applications. Here, according to Buck (1986:78),

> IBM conducts one of the most ambitious and sophisticated case studies ever developed for sales training—the Armstrong Case Study, focusing on a fictitious international conglomerate with hotel chains, marinas, retail outlets, and manufacturing and sporting goods divisions. There are detailed profiles of engineers, financial executives, marketing people, the chief operating officer and the chief executive officer. The profiles incorporate personality characteristics, attitudes and even past decisions.

Back to the branch office go the marketing representatives, again for six to eight weeks, before returning to Dallas for one week of training during which the concentration is on learning one particular industry. After learning one area well, the employee returns to the branch office to search out clients and become familiar with the territory.

Once the marketing representatives have completed all of this training and begun to settle into their areas, they are sent to marketing school for two weeks, either in Dallas or in Poughkeepsie, New York, to polish their marketing skills. This training program has been utilized for approximately five years. The program is carefully monitored by IBM and subject to change when there is reason to believe that any part of it does not achieve what it was set up to do (IBM, 1985a).

Step four: Training and retraining program. Each year all IBM employees are required to undergo at least four weeks of training focusing on implementing IBM's corporate culture in their respective jobs. In addition, each promotion is followed by at least two weeks' worth of additional training on the application of IBM's culture to the new job. Finally, remedial training sessions are held for those employees having difficulty in applying IBM's values to the job at hand. There is also a middle-management school on how to manage managers. There are schools for experienced middle-level managers and senior managers. IBM's Executive Resource Program seeks out and plans the careers of all those who are considered to have high potential. In another program, promising young managers are brought in as assistants to high-ranking IBM executives. Finally, to broaden their perspective, future managers attend programs at Harvard's Advanced Management Program, the London School of Economics, MIT's and Stanford's Sloan Program, and the Aspen Institute of Humanistic Studies. IBM schedules over 1.5 million hours of training for its employees each year at an estimated cost of $700 million (Sellers, 1985:92). Pascale (1985:30–31) summarizes the culmination of this socialization process.

> The first phase of socialization aims to attract the right trainees predisposed toward the firm's culture. The second instills enough humility to evoke self-examination; this facilitates "buying in" to the firm's values. Increasingly, the organizational culture becomes the relevant universe of experience. Having thus opened one's mind to the company's way of doing business, the task is now to cement this new orientation. The most effective method for doing so is via extensive and carefully reinforced field experience. It takes six years to grow an IBM marketing representative, twelve years for a controller. . . . The gains

from such an approach are cumulative. When all trainees understand there is one step-by-step career path, it reduces politics. There is no quick way to jump ranks and reach the top. Because the evaluation process has a long time horizon, short-term behavior is counterproductive. Cutting corners catches up with the trainee. Relationships, staying power and a consistent proven track record are the inescapable requirements of advancement. Those advancing, having been grown from within, understand the business not as financial abstraction but as a hands-on reality. Senior managers can communicate with those at the lowest ranks in the "shorthand" of shared experience.

Monitoring

Meticulous attention is given at IBM to tracking division, department, and individual performance in order to reward those who excel and correct the behavior of those who err. The evaluation systems employed are comprehensive, consistent, and interlocking, focused on determining adherence to corporate values and effectiveness in meeting corporate goals. Pascale (1985:31) illustrates:

> One example of comprehensive, consistent, and interlocking systems are those used at IBM to track adherence to its value of "respecting the decency of the individual." This is monitored via climate surveys; "Speak up!" (a confidential suggestion box); open door procedures; skip level interviews; and numerous informal contacts between senior-level managers and employees. The Personnel Department moves quickly when any downward changes are noted in the above indices. In addition, managers are monitored for percent of performance appraisals completed on time and percent of employees missing the required one week a year of training.

In addition, every year each worker fills out an opinion survey. Are you being challenged by your job? What work pressures do you find? Do you think IBM is following its core values? How do you evaluate your pay in light of your duties? How do you evaluate your pay relative to other companies? How do you evaluate IBM's top management? How do you evaluate your manager? Are you satisfied with your career development? and so on. This information is reviewed by each level of management, and where problems arise, action is taken. Jobs are redesigned, management improved, pay levels modified, and more.

IBM's compensation strategy is threefold. *First,* provide a base salary and set of fringe benefits which create job security. IBM's guaranteed salaries are competitive industrywide and its fringe benefits lead the industry. *Second,* the pay package must include strong incentives and motivation to improve. IBM has a complex bonus system built on productivity relative to individual and unit goals, with 75 percent of all workers meeting their annual productivity quotas and 25 percent of this group exceeding their quotas by a margin sufficient to quality for bonuses. *Third,* awards and rewards are given for exceptional performance in the form of cash, gifts, trips, and publicity for accomplishments. IBM's suggestion box awards return 25 percent of the money saved by a suggestion from the employee. Many such awards have exceeded $100,000 per year.

Two of IBM's most important award programs are the corporate technical awards and IBM fellowships. IBM makes technical awards for achievement to about 250 people per year for initiating product innovations or new products. These go to individuals or teams of workers. One award for $1.78 million went to two design teams of forty-eight members each who developed the IBM PC. IBM Fellows are individuals who propose important projects. Ten such projects have been funded for up to five years each to develop new innovations (Buck, 1986:185–186).

At IBM, deviations from cultural expectations are dealt with face-to-face in counseling and corrective action sessions, discussions of performance appraisal reports, and by a device known as the "penalty box." Pascale (1985:31–32) explains:

> Included in IBM's mechanisms for respecting the individual is a device known as the "Penalty Box." Often a person sent to the "penalty box" has committed a crime against the culture—for example, harsh handling of a subordinate, overzealousness against the competition, gaming the reporting system. Most penalty box assignments involve a lateral move to a less desirable location—a branch manager in Chicago might be moved to a nebulous staff position at headquarters. For an outsider, penalty box assignments look like normal assignments, but insiders know they are off the track. Penalty boxes provide a place for people while the mistakes they've made or the hard feelings they've created are gradually forgotten—and while the company looks for a new useful position. The mechanism is one among numerous things IBM does that lend credence to employees' beliefs that the firm won't act capriciously and end a career. In the

career of strong, effective managers, there are times when one steps on toes. The penalty box is IBM's "half-way house" enabling miscreants to contemplate their errors and play another day. (Don Estridge, maverick pioneer of IBM's success in personal computers and currently head of that division, came from the penalty box.)

When counseling and corrective action sessions, discussions of performance appraisal reports, and the penalty box fail to bring corrective action, separation from the organization ensues. However, it is noteworthy that IBM had one of the lowest turnover rates for employees of any major company in the United States (IBM, 1984).

Rituals, Myths, and Social Dramas of IBM

The rituals, myths, and social dramas employed by a corporation in operationalizing its core values, in the last analysis, determine how effective an organization is in translating those values into attitudes and behaviors. While it is impossible in the short space provided by this chapter to sample all of IBM's values, we shall explore the operationalization of three: respect for the individual, service to the customer, and being a good corporate citizen.

1. *Respect for the individual* is IBM's top value. The most important ritual in regard to this value was the company's policy of no layoffs. The most significant test of such a policy comes in times of industry recessions. Between 1969 and 1972, more than 12,000 employees were moved from areas with light work loads to locations where they could be used more productively. More than 5,000 employees were retrained for new jobs. Again in 1975, during a severe recession, nearly 3,800 employees were placed in new positions to balance workloads. It cost the company a great deal of money in the short run, but won respect in the long run. During 1985 and 1986, when Exxon, General Motors, AT&T, and almost all other computer firms cut substantially their workforce to help reduce costs, CEO Akins produced what Harvard Business School professor D. Quinn Mills described as "probably the most massive redeployment by a company in decades, all without firing a single employee" (Lewis, 1985). IBM offered 15,000 workers early retirement. It had a normal attrition rate of 24,600 workers, made 23,400 new hires, and redeployed 21,500 employees into new jobs as programmers and sales agents after extensive retraining. What was most remarkable was

what a survey taken in June 1988 of these redeployed workers revealed: that 90 percent considered the change of job voluntary and 70 percent saw the move as a promotion even though most moves were lateral (Sellers, 1988:73). A similar shift of some 21,000 workers took place in 1988. Full employment has been a ritual at IBM through good times and bad, demonstrating management's respect for the individual in his or her right to work.

2. *Customer service* is another of IBM's core values. Several rituals have been put in place to make sure that customer service is operationalized into behavior. IBM employs annual account-planning sessions where both line and customer support people spend from three days to a week reviewing the entire status of an account. At these meetings, the customer's business conditions are examined; there is a review of all computer applications and installations, their backlog, maintenance records, and so on. An action plan is set up and reviewed with the customer to upgrade, downsize, or substitute equipment where needed. In IBM, top corporate accounts systems analysts, programs, and applications personnel are permanently stationed on site. For smaller customers' demonstrations, training sessions and on-line maintenance personnel are provided to answer questions and assign systems applications personnel. Over 85 percent of all problems are solved during the first contact. In addition, IBM conducts joint study agreements with customers where new products are installed, monitored, and assessed at no cost to the customer. On other occasions, IBM invites a dozen or so customers to an industrial council such as banking to discuss their needs and evaluate IBM equipment relative to the competition. Similarly, marketing reps make out reports on customer satisfaction. These include statements of opportunity for new products which are investigated and responded to within ninety days (IBM, 1985b). Finally, each sales representative is given a bonus for each product sold. If within five years that account is lost to another company, the bonus is charged back to the office and rep making the sale. This provides an incentive to monitor each account regularly and to be sure that each customer is happy with the product, that the product is serviced regularly, and that the product meets the customer's needs (Buck, 1986).

3. *IBM is a good corporate citizen.* Perhaps the most significant ritual here is illustrated by IBM's plant closing in Shreveport, Illinois. Here IBM donated the plant facility to the local community and in conjunction with the community remodeled the plant for use by other businesses, helped bring in other firms, and left town having created

more jobs in that facility than were eliminated by the plant's closure. All IBM employees were assigned to other locations. Thus no jobs were lost, no income was lost in the community, and several new firms were brought to the area creating new opportunities for employment.

IBM's Corporate Climate

Between 1957 and 1987, IBM's uniquely nurturing corporate culture fostered on unprecedented growth in sales, profits, and stockholder value, topping the Fortune 500 in each category (Farnham, 1994:50). IBM's corporate culture was structured to foster organizational excellence at a time of slow, gradual, and consistent growth. It was a time of incremental change.

Between 1987 and 1994, this all changed. The computer industry, like so many other industries, experienced the emergence of a global economy and along with it the onset of volatile economic change in the form of quick market saturation, unexpected competition, and rapid technological change. In short, incremental change gave way to *discontinuous change*. The same corporate culture which had served so well to foster excellence from 1957 to 1987 was now IBM's chief hindrance. It was too slow and began to retard and lead to costly organizational adaptations. By 1992, life-long employment was halted; by 1993, IBM's new CEO began hiring managers from outside the firm in order to break the culture's hold on management; and in May of 1994, Gerstner introduced an entirely new corporate culture into the firm aimed at reordering all the organization's priorities and performance criteria (Hays, 1994b:A1). This new culture has eight core values:

1. The marketplace is the driving force behind everything we do.
2. At our core, we are a technology company with an overriding commitment to quality.
3. Our primary measures of success are customer satisfaction and shareholder value.
4. We operate as an entrepreneurial organization with a minimum of bureaucracy and a never-ending focus on productivity.
5. We never lose sight of our strategic vision.
6. We think and act with a sense of urgency.
7. Outstanding dedicated people make it all happen, particularly when they work together as a team.
8. We are sensitive to the needs of all employees and to the communities in which we operate. (Hays, 1994b:A8)

Next, Gerstner began the struggle involved in reengineering IBM's rituals, myths, and social dramas, as well as its socialization and monitoring systems. Gerstner announced that anyone who could not support these values should leave. "Most galling to employees," according to Hays (1994:), "was Mr. Gerstner's decision to relegate the respect for the individual to number 8." By June of 1994, Gerstner saw the departure of six of eleven members of his board of directors and three of the members of his top management team who had been brought in from the outside (Lohr, 1994:3–5; Dobrzynski, 1993:23). On more than one occasion in the ensuing month, Gerstner delivered public speeches admonishing management and employees alike for failing to adapt to the change. Lohr (1994:3–5) reports:

> Mr. Gerstner is trying to eradicate many IBM traditions. At the top of his hit list is a practice known as "push back" which was originally intended to allow employees to constantly challenge policies to insure better decision-making. In fact, he said, it comes to mean "if I don't like your decision, I'm not going to follow it. . . . We have people here fighting decisions that were made three years ago."

Only time will tell how successful this new culture will be. It frequently takes five to ten years to successfully put in place a new system with the rituals, myths, social dramas, socialization, and monitoring capability of the old culture which can coordinate investors, management, workers, and customers into an efficient system (Arnst and Verity, 1993:24–25).

Two critiques are leveled against Gerstner's new culture from both inside and outside IBM. First, management has limits in a high-tech firm where technological vision and bold risk taking are crucial to success, and this culture fosters neither. Second, this culture puts its chips on customer satisfaction, but the customer is the rearview mirror, not a guide to the future in the computer industry (Lohr, 1994:c).

Effect of IBM's New Corporate Climate on Corporate Performance

Currently IBM's workforce has been cut from 400,000 to 350,000 with more cuts scheduled for next year. This along with the new culture and CEO Gerstner's lack of openness has created a pensive workforce. IBM's stock has changed from a high of $150 per share to $42 per share, causing stockholder shock. Customers still strongly support

IBM products, with IBM leading in market shares in the mainframe and PC markets and among the top three firms in supercomputers, mid-range, and work stations (*The Economist*, 1993:23–25).

The Corporate Climate Created by General Electric

As foundations of a strong culture, the shared values play a double role. They serve as powerful, built-in motivational power for members, and they provide guides for corporate goals, policies, strategies and actions.
(Reimann and Weiner, 1988:37)

The General Electric Corporation, GE, is the fifth largest corporation in America, with annual sales of $60.8 billion; second in profits, with $4.3 billion; and first in stockholder equity (Teitelbaum, 1994:220). GE has three divisions: *technology,* consisting of aerospace, aircraft engines, medical equipment, plastics, and semiconductors; *core manufacturing,* consisting of consumer products, appliances, and power systems; and *financial services,* known as GE Capital, NBC, and Employers Reinsurance. GE operates 200 manufacturing facilities in the United States and 130 abroad in twenty-four countries. GE has ranked third in the nation as an industrial exporter, first in electronic sales, and first in appliance sales for five straight years, and its management teams have ranked first in these same areas over the same period of time.

Whereas IBM's history of the past ten years yields a progression from riches to rags, GE's history over that same time frame is a progression from moderately rich to very rich (Porter and Parker, 1993:452). Let us examine in detail GE's (a) corporate values, (b) socialization process, (c) monitoring, (d) control rituals, myths, and social dramas, and (e) the effect of its organizational climate on corporate performance.

GE's Corporate Values

As already mentioned, Jack F. Welch Jr. took over as CEO for GE in 1981. Since then, the company has undergone a radical change. He began with 150 independent business units, cutting down to 14 businesses in high-growth areas where GE ranks number one or two in their respective markets. During that period Welch sold $12.9 billion of GE's holdings while acquiring $17.1 billion in new holdings, moving out of such low profit areas as housewares and TVs and into such high-profit areas as broadcasting, high-tech manufacturing, investment banking, and medical systems. He boosted sales from $27.9 billion in 1982 to $60.8 billion in 1988 and profits from $3.1 billion to $4.3 billion, while productivity rose 110 percent and stock appreciation 273 percent (Teitelbaum, 1994:200).

GE's Management Values
GE leaders, always with unyielding integrity:

•

Create a clear, simple, reality-based, customer-focused
vision and are able to communicate it straightforwardly
to all constituencies.

•

Set aggressive targets, understanding accountability and commitment, and
are decisive.

•

Have a passion for excellence, hating bureaucracy and
all the nonsense that comes with it.

•

Have the self-confidence to empower others and behave in a boundaryless
fashion. They believe in and are
committed to Work-Out as a means of empowerment and
are open to ideas from anywhere.

•

Have, or have the capacity to develop, global brains and
global sensitivity and are comfortable building diverse global teams.

•

Stimulate and relish change and are not frightened or
paralyzed by it, seeing change as opportunity, not threat.

•

Have enormous energy and ability to energize and invigorate others. They
understand speed as a competitive advantage
and see the total organizational benefits that can be
derived from a focus on speed.

GE VALUE STATEMENT
Business Characteristics

Lean
    What — Reduce tasks and the people required to do them.
    Why — Critical to developing world cost leadership.

Agile

>   What — Delayering.
>
>   Why   — Create fast decision making in rapidly changing world through improved communication and increased individual response.

Creative

>   What — Development of new ideas—innovation.
>
>   Why   — Increase customer satisfaction and operating margins through higher value products and services.

Ownership

>   What — Self-confidence to trust others. Self-confidence to delegate to others the freedom to act while, at the same time, self-confidence to involve higher levels in issues critical to business and the corporation.
>
>   Why   — Supports concept of more individual responsibility, capability to act quickly and independently. Should increase job satisfaction and improve understanding of risks and rewards. While delegation is critical, there is a small percentage of high-impact issues that need or require involvement of higher levels within the business and within the corporation.

Reward

>   What — Recognition and compensation commensurate with risk and performance—highly differentiated by individual, with recognition of total team achievement.
>
>   Why   — Necessary to attract and motivate the type of individuals required to accomplish GE's objectives. A #1 business should provide #1 people with #1 opportunity. (Tichy and Charon, 1989:119)

Individual Characteristics

Reality

>   What — Describe the environment as it is—not as we hope it to be.
>
>   Why   — Critical to developing a vision and a winning strategy, and to gaining universal acceptance for their implementation.

Leadership

>   What — Sustained passion for and commitment to a proactive, shared vision and its implementation.
>
>   Why   — To rally teams toward achieving a common objective.

Candor/Openness
> What — Complete and frequent sharing of information with individuals (appraisals, etc.) and organization (everything).
>
> Why — Critical to employees knowing where they, their efforts, and their business stand.

Simplicity
> What — Strive for brevity, the "elegant, simple solution"—less is better.
>
> Why — Less complexity improves everything, from reduced bureaucracy to better product designs to lower costs.

Integrity
> What — Never bend or wink at the truth, and live within both the spirit and the letter of the laws of every global business arena.
>
> Why — Critical to gaining the global arena's acceptance of our right to grow and prosper. Every constituency; shareowners who invest; customers who purchase; community that supports; and employees who depend, expect, and deserve our unequivocal commitment to integrity in every facet of our behavior.

Individual Dignity
> What — Respect and leverage the talent and contribution of every individual in both good and bad times.
>
> Why — Teamwork depends on trust, mutual understanding, and the shared belief that the individual will be treated fairly in any environment. (Tichy and Charon, 1989:119)

GE's Core Values

To reiterate from Chapter 3, the core values which guide GE's new corporate culture are means to achieve the following organizational goals.

1. *To become the most competitive corporation in the world.* This principle is currently operationalized to mean that each of GE's sixteen businesses should:

   a. Invest only in businesses with high growth potential where GE can become the number one or two producer.
   b. Divest themselves of business with low growth potential.

c. Decentralize power and responsibility downward in order to make each business unit as flexible as possible in responding to global competition.

d. Develop low-cost, high-quality, easily serviced products that yield high profits in order to fund the R & D and acquisitions necessary to remain number one or two.

e. Monitor carefully each business's ability to meet productivity and financial targets.

f. Intervene when necessary to make each business become a "win-aholic."

Alliances, joint ventures, acquisitions, marriages of convenience, and strange bedfellows are materializing all over the world to challenge GE's efforts to become number one or two in market shares. For example

a. Philips of Holland purchased Westinghouse's lighting business. GE, formerly first in the world in lighting share, is now number two.

b. Electrolux of Sweden purchased White Consolidated of the US, threatening GE's number one position in major appliances.

c. Brown Boveri of Switzerland and ASEA of Sweden merged, making GE's power systems division, which had been number one for the better part of a century, number two.

In all these instances GE's operating businesses must respond or be placed in corporate jeopardy.

2. *To become the nation's most valuable corporation.* This principle is currently operationalized to mean the "most valuable" in terms of market capitalization. This principle manifests itself in a number of specific ways by GE:

a. Keep earnings rising at 10 to 15 percent per year

b. Keep stock appreciation and yield at about 15 to 20 percent per year

c. Shift earning mix so 100 percent can come from a high-growth area

d. Keep productivity rising at about 15 to 20 percent per year

e. Maintain exports as percent of sales at about 50 percent

f. Maintain management's reputation as an entrepreneurial, agile, knowledgeable, aggressive, and effective competitor

3. *To develop a skilled, self-actualizing, productive, and aggressive work force.* This principle is currently operationalized to mean GE wants to create an environment which will be a challenging place to work and which will significantly enhance workers' skills so that they can find another job if the company no longer needs them—a place where employees are ready to go but eager to stay. The directives here are:

a. To develop employees' awareness that the only road to job security is increasing market shares.
b. To develop employees who are more action-oriented, more risk oriented, and more people oriented
c. To develop employees who relentlessly pursue individual and group goals
d. To develop employees' skills and performance through timely and quality education programs
e. To hold employees responsible for meeting productivity and financial targets.
f. To reward high performance and deal effectively with low performance

4. *To develop open communication based on candor and trust.* This principle is operationalized to mean sharing with all employees corporation objectives, facts, and vision, opening each employee up to discussion regarding his or her strengths, weaknesses, and the possibility for change. Management is encouraged

a. To speak openly and listen carefully to discussions aimed at preparing, articulating, refining, and gaining acceptance for unit visions.
b. To show candor and trust in sharing and evaluating personal and business plans.
c. To motivate employees to become happier, more self confident, more energized individuals.

In addition to these core values, GE's corporate culture includes several well-articulated business units and individual targets that, when met or exceeded, receive the appropriate internal support. For example, in 1986 three businesses substantially exceeded their financial targets: plastics with an 18.2 percent profit margin, medical equipment with a 37.2 percent profit margin, and financial services with a 44.4 percent profit margin. Because they significantly exceeded their financial targets, each in turn received significant internal investment aimed at making them even more competitive. In the case of plastics, the investment exceeded $1 billion over three years (Mitchell and Dobrzynski, 1987).

Socialization at GE

GE's socialization process involves several steps.

Step one: The selection of a stable work force. GE interviews on college campuses for specific job needs, but since the organization purchases, sells, and closes many units these provide a ready pool of well-trained, seasoned personnel with clear track records from which to draw to fill available job openings. For example, if a person has worked for a unit for several years and the company acquires, sells, or closes another unit which has personnel who can perform this person's job better, he or she will be replaced. In all cases managers seek aggressive, entrepreneurial, and self-sufficient employees with excellent performance records. This principle holds equally for managers and workers alike. Welch has replaced thirteen of fourteen chief operating officers for independent business units in the past eight years.

Step two: In-the-trenches training. All new and old managers taking new positions are placed in these positions for six months prior to receiving extensive training. During this period they are encouraged to assume risk, delegate authority, work in teams, and develop a vision of what their jobs could be. Available to them during this six-month period are position papers on unit plans, quality productivity, and financial reports. Also available is *First Addition,* a video magazine dealing with corporate policy, issues and concerns; videotapes of instructions on how to deal with specific problems; and video interviews and conferences conducted by top executives with employees, managers, investors, and customers. By the end of six months, each manager also has several evaluations of his or her own performance by supervisors, coworkers, and employees, and a basket full of errors one has made and problems one must deal with. It is at teachable moments like this that GE prefers to provide its managers with formal training.

Step three: Training and Retraining. GE provides its managers with four separate formal education opportunities. What is a good manager? Jack Welch argues quite forcefully that it is

> "Somebody who can develop a vision of what he or she wants their business, their unit, their activity to do and be. Someone who is able to articulate to the entire unit what the business is,

and gain through sharing of the discussion—listening and talk-ing—an acceptance of the vision. And someone who then can relentlessly drive implementation of that vision to a successful conclusion." (Mitchell and Dobrzynski, 1987:96)

GE Management Development Center at Crotonville. Crotonville's mission, according to Welch, "is to make its GE managers more ac-tion oriented, more risk oriented and more people oriented." It is supposed to develop leaders, not just managers. Each year five thou-sand managers attend two- to four-week courses at Crotonville. These are extensive courses in survival training, "a business Outward Bound experience" (Mitchell and Dobrzynski, 1987:98). According to Noel M. Tichy, training director at Crotonville:

> "First, participants do preparatory case studies, bone up on the business problems, and learn to work in teams. That's where rafting comes in. The teams build rafts, then race each other on the Hudson River. Or they spend a few days performing other physical tasks to build trust among team members. Later they visit the business and meet with customers—or anyone else they wish. Then, they make recommendations and present them to the appropriate vice-president. Besides team work and ana-lytic skills, the course teaches people that they can handle big problems." (Mitchell and Dobrzynski, 1987:97)

Crotonville focuses on problems of change, in particular, problems involved in global change and corporate adaptation.

National Technology University. GE helped found the National Technology University, which offers courses via telecommunication to most GE facilities. Installation of satellite dishes, terminals, and various other types of equipment allows students to participate in-teractively in courses or tape them for use at home. One recent course presented an integration of various aspects of GE's business. This course stressed a team approach to design, manufacturing, and marketing. Examples of success stories from within GE illustrated the analysis.

Advanced Education Course. A variety of graduate education programs where the company pays tuition and offers the opportu-nity for work-related study on company time is available in most areas where GE workers are assigned. The advanced courses in en-gineering, manufacturing, computing, finance, and management information systems are a combination of classes taught in-house, regular graduate classes at local universities, and work-related theses.

Bel Air Conference. The top managers of GE each year gather at the Bel Air Conference to recognize corporate accomplishment, reflect on corporate challenges, and celebrate being a member of the cultural elite. This conference is held for line, middle-, and upper-level managers and is known as the "company picnic."

There are numerous subcultures for managers within GE, each of which serves as a network for assisting the talented in a turbulent environment. The groups of managers who work together at Crotonville, in National Technology University courses, and at Bel Air become friends, access each other's talent, and in times of change provide a network for job opportunities within GE's union units. If a plant closes, a unit is sold, or downsizing occurs, old friends are called on in the hopes of locating new opportunities. Like war buddies, the veterans of these programs form a fraternity.

Monitoring

Like most large companies, GE employs performance evaluations which provide skip up, down, and across levels at 360-degree reviews, productivity and financial target monitoring procedures, examinations in technical areas, as well as frequent employee interviews with supervisors. What sets GE apart from many other organizations is the openness, candor, and trust they expect at each of these evaluations. After acquiring NBC at the height of its popularity with the public, Welch accused one hundred of their top officials of being tied to the past and told them that they would have to change or they would go. Welch warned, "I'll guarantee you there is somebody out there who will want to do it" (Mitchell and Dobrzynski, 1987:95). Later, he replaced the chief operating officer with the former head of GE's financial services business and cut seven hundred employees.

Once formal, stable, and paternalistic, the new GE is open, change oriented, aggressive, argumentative, and confrontational. Unions have been told to cut wages 50 percent and take layoffs, or GE will move to Korea; managers have been told they can't handle their units and were demoted or let go; new acquisitions have been stripped of their top management and downsized. "It's a brawl," says Frank Doyle, senior vice president for corporate relations. He continues, describing the GE style, "It's argumentative, confrontational. Working at GE can be a shock to newcomers. There is a much higher decibel level here. I told Jack [Welch] that what passes for conversation in here would be seen as a mugging by RCA people" (Mitchell and Dobrzynski, 1987:94). Monitoring at GE is frequent and systematic and in the words of Welch performed with "openness, candor and trust" (Mitchell and Dobrynski, 1987:93). Managers either adjust to this style and become productive or they are gone.

Compensation at GE is excellent. Base salaries are at the top of the industry and these are supplemented by an extensive bonus, reward, and recognition system. Fringe benefits are high, educational opportunities are high, with deselection being based on performance and one's ability to cope with GE's corporate style. In 1988, 25 percent of all managers received a bonus averaging $1,400 cash. In 1991, several managers each received a bonus exceeding $4 million (Hansell, 1994:D8).

Rituals, Myths, and Social Dramas of GE

At GE each of the corporate values interacts with the others to create a unique corporate climate. Two examples will illustrate our point.

Shortly after becoming CEO, Welch cut his headquarters staff about in half and pushed decision-making power down to the chief operating officer of each business unit. Outside of monitoring its business plans and financial targets on a quarterly basis, each unit is allowed to make its own decisions. This freedom to act, according to several business heads, reaped significant results. Brian Rowe, head of GE Aircraft Engines, says it made it possible to quickly redesign GE's midsize jet engine, allowing GE to increase its market share by 40 percent of the expense of Pratt and Whitney, yielding 240 solid orders in one year worth $1 billion. Glen Hiner, head of plastics, boasts getting approval for the building of a new $3.5 million plant within two months. Prior to the Welch era, this would have taken years. Roger W. Schipke, head of GE major appliances, turned his unit around in a year after several years of decline by spending $1 billion on automation and redesigning products. Market shares grew 11 points, profits 16 percent, the quality of products increased, and the price decreased. Schipke's motto was "automate, emigrate or evaporate" (Mitchell and Dobrzynski, 1987:95).

To promote openness, candor, and trust, Welch in 1986 created the Corporate Executive Council, which brings together each quarter the heads of all fourteen businesses, the corporate headquarters staff, and the CEO team for a frank discussion of business plans.

"It's open-kimono time," says Schipke. Business plans are held up to scrutiny, and participants say that no one is shy about criticizing. Yet everyone is expected to help out, offering suggestions that might work in another part of the company. At one recent meeting, business heads picked up pointers from Hiner about a drug-testing program that is working out well in the plastics unit. Schipke recalls a meeting where he and Hiner had a discussion about product design. "And now we've got 16 pounds of GE plastic in each of our top-line refrigerators." (Mitchell and Dobrzynski, 1987:97)

These rituals are each illustrative of how GE operationalizes its corporate culture—in an attempt to become the most competitive corporation in the world, to become the nation's most valuable corporation; to develop a skilled, self-actualizing, productive, and aggressive workforce; and to develop open communication based on candor and trust as applied to corporate processes. Attention is now directed to the fit between these values and operationalization and those of GE's various constituencies.

GE's Corporate Climate

There are several groups upon whom GE depends for corporate success and with whom its culture must interact successfully for these relationships to be mutually rewarding. We will now explore the interests and values of each group and their positive or negative interactions with GE's corporate culture.

Investor confidence. Investor confidence in an organization rests on eight variables: (1) innovativeness; (2) ability to attract, develop and keep talented people; (3) quality of management; (4) long-term investment value; (5) community and environmental responsibility; (6) quality of products and services; (7) financial soundness; and (8) corporate assets. It is significant that in 1987, *Fortune* magazine polled eight thousand top executives, outside directors, and financial analysts regarding the most admired corporation in the United States employing the above-mentioned criteria. GE, a conglomerate, ranked number one in electronics and appliances with a score of 7.77. The top ten companies in America irrespective of corporate focus scored between 9.00 and 7.90 averaging across all categories. GE's score put them in the top twenty most admired corporations in America. GE's corporate performance was rated lowest in community and environmental responsibility, and in ability to attract, develop and keep talented people. GE ranked highest in innovativeness, quality of management, and long-term investment value. As previously indicated, GE's sales and profits, its productivity, and its reward to investors are all up. It is currently number three in the United States in market value and number one in stockholder equity with an annual return to investors of 20 percent over the past twenty years (*Fortune*, 1992:16).

GE is thus a high-growth corporation that investors feel must strengthen its community and environmental responsibility, its ability to attract and retain people, and its stockholder equity. It is also equally clear that GE's corporate values do strongly intersect those of their investors.

Worker commitment. GE is going through one of the most wrenching corporate culture changes in its history. It is moving from a formal, stable, and paternalistic culture to an open, change-oriented, and self-actualizing culture. Many employees remain from the old culture and they are for the most part dismayed, confused, and disillusioned (David, 1988:92–106). Some employees are also present who have been attracted by the new culture as new employees who have adjusted to the change and find it liberating. The result is twofold. *First,* workers with strong union ties, hourly employees, unchanged former employees, and some newly acquired units are upset. *Second,* trying to do more work with fewer personnel, uncertainty about unit viability in low-growth areas, and individuals who do not function well in an open, aggressive, argumentative, and confrontational environment create high stress and workers who are "paralyzed by fear" (David, Dec. 7, 1988).

GE's corporate culture has thus diffused through the top two-thirds of the corporation and needs to continue to the other third. However, given GE's propensity to acquire high-growth corporations with different values then their own, this diffusion will always be incomplete. Given that all high-growth areas eventually saturate, it remains to be seen how well this corporate culture can intersect employee values and interests.

Consumer interest. GE has no higher value than increasing market shares, no greater crime than decreasing market shares. The result is a clean, lean, and agile corporation adjusting to consumer needs in high-growth areas. Customer interest in high-quality, low-cost, serviceable products is thus GE's primary concern. Consumer interests and values, and corporate interests and values, converge.

GE will become a blessing to consumers by providing the kind of products wanted, in the form needed, to the dissatisfaction of GE's competitors.

Effect of Corporate Climate on Corporate Performance

In summary, our analysis of GE's corporate culture and the organizational climate it creates suggests two claims. *First,* GE's corporate values do intersect the values of their investors and consumers and a major portion of their employees. This corporate culture and the climate it creates are very conducive to high organizational performance. In 1993, GE ranked sixth in the nation in sales, third in the nation in profits, and first in the nation in market value. *Second,* GE has several areas in which its cultural socialization and monitoring processes could be improved: (a) in regard to community and environmental responsibility; (b) in its ability to attract, develop, and keep talented people; and (c) in the tendency among some employees and managers to employ illegal or immoral business practices such as bribes and fraud to achieve or exceed performance targets and achieve upward mobility (Larsen, 1994:1).

This final area deserves some discussion. In the last several years, GE's management team has been accused of trying to corner the industrial diamonds market and set prices with the DeBeers Corporation; spending millions from U.S. government contracts to bribe Israeli military officers to buy jet engines; overcharging the U.S. government on military contracts; and developing an investment scheme aimed at misleading stockholders on GE Finance's profit margins. The question arises, does an entrepreneurial culture employing extensive empowerment and setting high performance targets by nature generate such problems, or are these merely the product of bad managers? Welch has promised to take actions to halt such behaviors. Whether these can be corrected with either a corporate value or style change is questionable, and these issues may place limits on the improvement of GE's performance under its current value system.

The Critical Information and Communication Factors in This Core Integrative Process

While a strategic culture is more likely to respond effectively to environmental changes, it is no guarantee of successful strategy creation. To be truly effective over the long term, the company

must keep the focus on key values that promote critical success factors.
(Reimann and Weiner, 1988:40)

IBM and GE have each developed their own unique corporate culture and corporate climate. One was for a time nurturing, paternalistic, secure, and adaptive while the other was entrepreneurial, empowering, self-reliant, self-actualizing, change oriented, and adaptive. Each has operationalized its organizational rituals, myths, and social dramas to create the attitudes and behaviors necessary to implement their core values and have constructed socialization and monitoring processes to inculcate, reward adherence to, and punish deviations from these values. *Both* corporations were successful in responding to *incremental change* while only GE has succeeded in responding effectively to *discontinuous change.*

Our analysis does, however, yield the suggestion that a high-speed management corporate culture, one capable of dealing with both incremental and discontinuous change, must emphasize (a) entrepreneurial skills and empowerment as values; (b) a lean, agile, and creative set of business values; (c) clear, precise, and diverse targets for monitoring corporate goals; (d) a simple, reality-based set of individual values based on integrity and candor; and (e) a leadership value system which is simple, reality based, aggressive, self-confident, change oriented, and rooted in high energy, with a focus on excellence.

Communication theorists, researchers and practitioners can employ such a corporate culture and climate analysis as a valuable tool in explaining, predicting, and controlling the effectiveness of a corporate culture and the organizational climate it creates on organization performance. *It allows one to understand, evaluate, and change the manner in which corporate culture and climate serve as core information and communication processes of organizational integration.*

5

High-Speed Management Teamwork

Bosses are not necessarily good leaders, subordinates
are not necessarily effective followers. Many bosses couldn't
lead a horse to water. Many subordinates couldn't follow a
parade. Some people avoid either role. Others accept the
role thrust upon them and perform badly. At different points
in their careers, even at different times of the work day,
most managers play both roles, though seldom equally
well. . . . But the reality is that most of us are more often
followers than leaders. Even when we have subordinates,
we still always have bosses. For every committee we chair,
we sit as a member on several others.
(Kelly, 1988:143)

Teamwork is the third essential component in the use of communication to achieve integration within a high-speed management process. A strong high-speed management leader is necessary for
integration in order to provide an organization with a vision, a set of
priorities for transforming the organization to that vision, and the
motivation and the reengineering plan for moving vigorously to
achieve that vision. A strong corporate culture which can generate a
positive corporate climate is necessary in that an organization's vision, priorities, motivation, and reengineering are operationalized
within its corporate culture. The way in which a corporate culture's
value system, socialization, and monitoring system are able to yield
organizational behaviors which intersect the values and interests of
employees, consumers, and investors in a favorable manner will
determine if the reengineering effort will be successful. A strong
sense of corporate teamwork is necessary in that in the final analysis it is through team effort that work gets done, that products are
designed, manufactured, marketed, and serviced, and that profits

are made. It is through corporate teamwork that corporate visions and values are brought to the bottom line, transformed into increasing productivity, product quality, and product value. *An organization's potential for change and limits on that potential are determined by a corporation's teamwork.*

For a strong sense of corporate teamwork to become operational requires the presence of several specific attitudes and behaviors. *First,* a team must have a common focus, direction, or goal. What makes the focus, direction, or goal of a team unique is the presence in the mind of each team member of a mutually constructed and publicly agreed to or shared goal. It is this collaborative effort in establishing and publicly committing to a shared goal in front of one's coworkers which separates a mere collection of individuals or group from a collaborative team (Obloj, Cushman, and Kozminski, 1995).

Second, a team's performance is constrained, channeled, and focused by a concern for the appropriate integration of all the team's components in goal attainment. Corporate team components normally include R&D, manufacturing, marketing, sales, and service functions. When the unique interests of each team component are clearly articulated, collectively understood, and appropriately integrated, the "team's creativity, energy and focus ignites, fueling the engines of the individual and the firm making a new level of competitiveness, quality and performance possible" (Barrett, 1987:24).

Third, the members of a team must have a permanent dissatisfaction with the status quo and a desire to improve every aspect of a firm's activities. In short, teams must be change oriented, they must want to fix things before they are broke. They must want to continuously improve the firm through collective efforts (Ju and Cushman, 1994).

Fourth, when coworkers collaborate to form a mutually constructed and publicly committed to goal whose attainment is channeled and constrained by an appropriate concern for the integration of all team members, then they manifest a specific set of values such as mutual respect, trust, and confidence, which are unique to effective teamwork and create a team synergy. Such collaboration guided by respect, trust, and confidence generates a level of creativity, energy, and integration which produces a focused force more powerful than the sum of the individual contributions. A team's creativity, energy, and integration is multiplicative, not merely additive.

Given the unique and important role which corporate teamwork plays in the organizational integration process, it becomes necessary for managers to acquire a basic knowledge of the skills with which to develop, manage, and participate in corporate team-work processes. It will be the purpose of this chapter to provide that knowledge and skill by (1) determining how and where team-work should be employed to improve organizational performance; (2) exploring what research tells us about the effective use of team-work; (3) examining how self-managed teams work; (4) examining how cross-functional teams work; and (5) outlining critical success factors for these two types of teamwork.

How and Where to Employ Teamwork

Survivors in this turbulent epoch are finding that teamwork and cooperation ignite and fuel the engines of the individual and the enterprise, and they make a new level of competence possible.
(Barrett, 1987:24)

Teamwork within the organizational context may take many forms. There are executive teams, management teams, and worker teams. Teams are set up to develop products; integrate manufacturing, marketing, and services; and increase quality, productivity, and coordination. There are four very important types of teams in most high-speed management organizations, and they constitute a firm's continuous improvement program. They are self-managed, cross-functional, benchmarking, and outside linking teams.

The main body of the theory of continuous improvement should be constituted by a practical knowledge that enables managers to analyze their firm's environments and value chains. As we have already discussed in chapter 2, an analysis of a firm's environment should focus on a unique dynamic created by the behavior of customers and strategies of competitors. A value chain analysis should enable a firm to pinpoint its special strengths, competencies residing either in specific unit functions, business processes, or linkages. Therefore, the theoretical framework reduces to the following core questions:

1. What products and product's attributes do customers want?
2. What strategies do competitors pursue, and do they develop products that intersect desirable attributes?
3. What core competencies enable an organization to provide the desirable product's attributes better than its competitors?
4. What areas must a firm improve to develop or sustain competitive advantage in providing products and cope with competitors?

5. What tools and strategies should be used during the continuous improvement process in order to ensure success?

The main goal and a bottom line of the continuous improvement process is successful adaptation to the customer.

The most common uses for teamwork involve continuous improvement programs, collective efforts aimed at improving an organization's productivity, product quality, and response time. Within this context, five types of teamwork activities can be observed: problem solving, coordination, learning, linking, and decision making.

When a unit or organization is confronted with a common problem which requires a joint solution, one everyone can employ with equal agility, then *self-managed teams* are normally employed to incrementally *resolve the problem.*

When several units in an organization require improved coordination in order to integrate diverse interests, concerns, and contributions to a common goal, then *cross-functional teams* are normally employed to achieve this incremental *increased coordination and integration.*

When a unit or several units in an organization need to master an unusually productive business process employed by another world-class organization, then *benchmarking teams* are normally formed to discontinue current processes and to *acquire or master this learning process.*

When a unit or organization finds it necessary to control its outsourcing with suppliers, form a joint venture with another firm, or form an alliance with several other firms in order to meet organizational goals, then *outside linking teams* are formed to *negotiate, operationalize, and monitor these linking processes.*

Self-managed, cross-functional, benchmarking, and linking teamwork in the past have been and in the future will be employed in an attempt to enhance organizational functioning, as demonstrated in table 5.1 (Obloj, Cushman, and Kozminski, 1995).

Research Findings on Effective Teamwork

When there is collaboration, when there is coordination, when there is communication, then there is integration, then there is unity, then there is direction and the concentration of energy and talent on the objective. There is enormous force focused upon the task whenever and wherever the magic of integrated effort is manifest.
(Barrett, 1987:2)

Table 5.1   TYPES OF CONTINUOUS IMPROVEMENT AND CHANGE

Types of Change		
	Incremental Change	**Discontinuous Change**
Types of Teamwork	*Self Managed Teams* within functional units	*Benchmarking Teams* between firms
Types of Teamwork	*Cross Functional Teams* within business processes	*Outside Linking Teams* between firms

Several studies conducted by consulting firms who provide training in the various forms of teamwork involved in organizations have found to their dismay that more often than not such forms of teamwork fail to accomplish their goals. Arthur D. Little in 1991 surveyed five hundred firms involved in teamwork and continuous improvement training programs and found that only one-third of the firms surveyed felt that their programs were having a significant impact on their competitiveness (*The Economist,* 1992:68). A. T. Kearney surveyed over one hundred British firms in 1991 and found that only 20 percent believed their teamwork and continuous improvement programs had achieved "tangible results" (*The Economist,* 1992:68). McKinsey's surveyed sixty firms that had undertaken at least two years of serious efforts at employing teamwork programs and found that most had ground to a halt with the firms reporting that continuation was not worth the cost and effort involved (Port, Cary, Kelly, and Forest, 1992:68). Finally, Rath and Strong asked ninety-five firms to analyze whether "TQM efforts had met such goals as raising market shares or increasing customer satisfaction. Rath and Strong obtained positive evaluations from only 26 percent of the firms surveyed" (Port, Cary, Kelly, and Forest, 1992:68).

If so many firms which provide training in teamwork and continuous improvement programs are finding the majority of their clients dissatisfied, what can we learn from the research of these programs regarding the appropriate and inappropriate uses of teamwork in their organizational context?

Three separate findings shed considerable light on the appropriateness and inappropriateness of teamwork: team embeddedness, leader-team interface, and overall organizational competency. Let us explore each in turn.

The concept of *embeddedness* emerges as the most distinctive feature of teams within large collectivities. Work team development within an organizational context is significantly influenced by the types of team embeddedness in the organization. Three types of connectedness appear particularly important. *First,* there is *task embeddedness* (Cohen 1991). This involves the types of task the team has been given—a learning task, problem-solving task, integration task, performance task, and so on—and what is to be done with the results of the team effort. *Second,* there is *social embeddedness,* the relation between the team and its connectedness with the organization's structural and cultural system. The question here is what corporate unit, values, and corporate climate variables impact the team's developmental process. *Third,* there is *psychological embeddedness,* which focuses on how the individual personalities of team members interface (Cohen et al., 1969). Teams are made up of individuals with unique interests and interaction styles. These interests and interaction styles significantly influence the development of team processes.

Where team embeddedness intersects the teamwork processes in such a manner as to prevent the team from (1) developing mutually constructed and publicly agreed to or shared goals and/or (2) appropriately integrating the team's members by addressing their unique interests, concerns, and contributions to that shared goal, then the task embeddedness, social embeddedness, and psychological embeddedness will lead to inappropriate teamwork activities.

The *interface* between an organization's or team's leadership and team members is equally important. Fiorelli (1988:1) in a study of nineteen teams within an organizational context found that the personality of the team leaders was the chief determinant of team members' behaviors. Lefton and Buzzotta (1987) support and extend Fiorelli's analysis in their study of twenty-six top-level management teams operating in large corporations. They found that teamwork was most significantly influenced by the team's interface with the organizational leader's interaction style. The diverse patterns of work groups were found to be a straightforward function of the types of interface found in the group leader. They isolated four distinct patterns and established the frequency with which each occurred in large organizations.

First, there was a *hierarchical pattern* in which groups have strict procedures for the downward transmission of instructions and downward control of outcomes. The leader prefers after an initial meeting to interact with team members singly. The group tasks are divided up and assignments made to each member who then reports directly to the leader. Group members are encouraged to be positive, not critical, and to ratify the leader's conclusions. "Group members work together not to generate new and better ideas but to implement the leader's ideas" (Lefton and Buzzotta, 1987:8). This pattern of group work occurred in 33 percent of the teams studied.

Second, there was a *formalistic pattern* in which the group leader utilizes a bureaucratic style of interaction. Here the leader discourages collaboration to limit unforeseeable consequences. After an initial meeting, members are assigned individual tasks, told to do them the way the organization always does them, and told to take care not to rock the boat. Here the leader believes that "genuine collaboration can be disruptive. Intellectual sparks once ignited, can kindle anything from a small fire to devastation. A formalist leader avoids this risk by dousing the spark" (Lefton and Buzzotta, 1987:9). This pattern of group work occurred in about 19 percent of the cases under study.

Third, there was a *circular pattern* in which group leaders insist on collaboration, camaraderie, and collegiality in dealing with group members but not in dealing with the team task. This pattern dominates whenever harmony and equality are the key group values. Compromise and appeasement take the place of the open and critical evaluation of the problem. "The circular pattern is almost always present whenever the leader of a group says things like: 'around here, we're all one big happy family' and 'we are people who get along with one another" (Lefton and Buzzotta, 1987:9). This form of group work occurred in 9 percent of the cases under study.

Fourth, there was the genuine *teamwork pattern* in which leaders encouraged the development and attainment of a mutually constructed, publicly agreed to shared goal whose attainment was channeled and constrained by an appropriate concern for the integration of all the team's components, thus manifesting mutual respect, trust, and confidence in the teamwork process. Leaders, while remaining in charge, encouraged the teams to set goals, do planning, and implement actions that would serve the entire team's needs. What distinguishes this teamwork pattern from others is the prevalence of candid and committed interplay. The candor is evident in the ease and frankness that marks discussions; team members argue and disagree without embarrassment or discomfort. In place of the zestful malice so often seen among adversaries, there is constructive openness of partners. The commitment is evident in the degree of involvement; each member believes that the work of the team is important and that he or she can affect the outcome. As a result, the team goes about its work with spirited seriousness. A high degree of synergism usually results (Lefton and Buzzotta, 1987:9). This pattern occurred in about 40 percent of the instances under investigation. The patterns of communication behaviors characteristic of each sequence as reported by participants on a 5-point scale are listed in table 5.2.

Each of the above patterns of group work occurs within all organizations. Each has its own outcomes and organizational leadership style. The important thing for organizational leaders to understand is how to match a team's leadership style to the preferred team outcomes. The important thing for team members to realize is which type of leader a team has and thus what are considered productive communication activities for team members under that style.

Finally, an organization's overall performance as an indicator of its general knowledge and competence level is important as team embeddedness and the leadership-team interface. Recently, Ernst and Young (Port, et al., 1992), examined 584 firms employing teamwork in their continuous improvement programs and found a strong correlation between the successful use of different types of teamwork and the overall competency levels of an organization as reflected in general profitability and productivity levels.

More specifically, the Ernst and Young study found that if a firm had a return on assets (ROA) of less than 2 percent and a value added per employee (VAE) of under $47,000, they should follow the position of the model found in table 5.3 for *novices*. If a firm had a ROA of 2 to 6.9 percent and a VAE of $47,000 to $73,999, then they should follow the pattern for *journeyman*. If a firm had an ROA of 7 percent or higher and a VAE of $74,000 and up, they should follow the pattern for *master* firms.

Thus bodies of research literature provide us with three specific recommendations on when and where teamwork will and will not work.

1. When a firm's task, social, and psychological embeddedness allows teamwork to develop mutually constructed and publicly agreed to goals and/or appropriately integrate each team member's unique interests, concerns, and contributions, then teamwork should be employed.
2. When the leadership of a firm provides an appropriate team

Table 5.2 SELF-ASSESSMENT OF THE TOP-LEVEL TEAMS IN TEN ACTIVITIES

	Coordination within Team (1)	Profitability/ Cost Awareness (2)	Communications (3)	Conflict/ Disagreement (4)	Meetings (5)	Organization/ Control (6)	Decision Making/ Problem Solving (7)	Goal Setting/ Planning (8)	Coordination with Other Units (9)	Critique and Feedback (10)	Total
Hierarchical	4.3	3.9	3.7	3.3	4.0	3.3	2.9	2.9	2.3	2.4	3.3
Formalistic	1.9	1.6	2.2	2.3	1.4	1.4	2.4	1.4	2.0	2.7	1.9
Circular	0.4	1.0	1.2	1.3	0.7	0.7	0.7	0.7	1.1	1.0	0.9
Teamwork	3.4	3.5	2.9	3.1	3.9	4.6	4.0	5.0	4.6	3.9	3.9
Totals	10.0	10.0	10.0	10.0	10.0	10.0	10.0	10.0	10.0	10.0	10.0

Source: Lefton, R. E. and Buzzotta, V. R. "Teams and Teamwork: A Study of Executive Level Teams," *National Productivity Review* (Winter 1987–88), 11.

Table 5.3   CORRELATIONS BETWEEN TEAMWORK AND COMPETENCY LEVELS IN AN ORGANIZATION

Levels	Return on Assets	Value Added/Employee	Skills
Novice	Less than 2 percent	Under $47,000	Train and Facilitate self-managed teams
Journeyman	2–6 percent	$47,000–$73,999	Train and facilitate cross-functional teams
Master	7 percent	More than $74,000	Train and facilitate benchmarking teams

Adapted from Port, Cary, Kelly, and Forest, 1992:66–67

leader interface with a team, then teamwork should be employed.

3. When the overall performance of a firm has been appropriately assessed, then only that form of teamwork appropriate to its general level of competence should be employed.

Having explained in some detail how teamwork is employed in continuous improvement programs and what research tells us about the effective use of teamwork, we are now in a position to explore in this chapter how self-managed and cross-functional teams function. In the final two chapters of the book we will discuss the function of benchmarking and outside linking teams as important in organizational control processes.

Self-Managed Teams

There are a number of different ways to describe and apply self-managing teams. Usually they involve an increased amount of behavioral control and decision making autonomy at the work group level.... Self-managing work teams are typically introduced with the objective of simultaneously improving productivity for the organization as well as the quality of working life for employees.... Self-managing teams have been described as possessing a relatively whole task; members who each possess a variety of skills relevant to the group task; workers' discretion over such decisions as methods of work, task scheduling, and assignment of members to different tasks; and compensation and feed-

back about performance for the group as a whole.
(Manz, 1992:13–15)

Self-managed teams are normally employed to map and solve problems within a firm's functional units, and as such seek continuous improvement through an incremental change in existing unit policy. Traditionally there are two types of self-managed teams— problem-mapping teams or New England town meeting teams, and problem-solution teams or solution-implementation teams.

Problem-Mapping and Solution-Implementation Self-Managed Teams

Self-managed teams are the first element of the continuous improvement practice vital as a tool for effective problem mapping. *Problem mapping* is a team activity oriented toward locating, defining, and solving problems occurring in the workplace. The use of self-managed teams as a tool of problem locating, defining, and solving in work settings, while standard in Japan, is only recently gaining momentum in Europe and the United States.

The self-managed teams appear in many forms and under various names; they are called quality circles in Japan, self-managed or self-directed teams in the United States, and autonomous work groups in Europe, but everywhere they show similar features.

First, self-managed teams are a grouping of several participants from the same work units. As a result, self-managed teams are relatively homogeneous in terms of work environment and tasks of the members (e.g., maintenance unit, assembly line workers, purchasing department). The common tasks and work environment facilitate bestowing on the team well-defined power and responsibility to solve problems connected with the execution of common tasks.

Second, self-managed teams share their members' knowledge base, experience, and skills through cross-training and common problem solving. They expand employees' knowledge base and motivation. All members become capable of playing diverse roles, understanding the unit's purpose, function, and relations with other units, formulating and solving problems (Flynn, McComb and Elroy, 1987:30).

Third, teamwork must be a structured, problem-solving and improvement oriented process. A necessary condition of effectiveness of such process is an empowerment of teams. Empowerment does not mean a think-spread but pinpointing, and therefore it must be clearly related to the problem-mapping and solving process. Only then decisions and resources are moved closely to where action can be taken. As Bohman and Deal (1993:34) succinctly put it:

> In most such cases, the employees who work within the pro-
> cesses every day understand the problems more intimately than
> anyone else. They are the ones, after all, who jump through
> often ridiculous hoops to get their jobs done. And usually, they're
> the ones who remember why the hoops were invented in the
> first place.

While employees who work within an organization's functional units are most knowledgeable about the status quo functioning of the unit, frequently they have a bias in favor of the status quo and lack the problem-solving tools to go beyond that bias. Thus training in the use of problem-solving tools for improving existing performances is necessary. Flynn and Care (1994) outline one set of such tools utilized by a high-performance organization (see figures 5.1–5.11).

In addition to training in problem-solving procedures, each team proceeds through certain steps in obtaining its outcome. In a self-managed team, whether using a problem-analysis or a town meeting approach, a unit or function is created within the organization to implement a worker continuous improvement program within a large group discussion format, like a town meeting. Its goal is to improve an organization's productivity, quality, flexibility, adaptability, and/ or response time. As detailed in chapter 2, the town meeting approach is an attempt to eliminate nonessential, nonproductive, or "bad work" and replace it with "good" work (see figure 5.12).

Let us summarize. The self-managed teams are operating at the workplace environment. They are effective if tasks are well defined, members are cross-trained, and the team is empowered with decision-making competencies that enable it not only to remove evident deficiencies but localize areas for possible improvements. Self-managed teams are a natural and necessary extension of process-oriented, cross-functional teams. While self-managed teams are looking for improvements in their limited natural workspace, cross-functional teams link different workspaces and prevent local improvements from becoming suboptimal from the point of view of processes across the organization (Katzenback and Smith, 1993:120).

Figure 5.1 PROBLEM SOLVING PROCESS

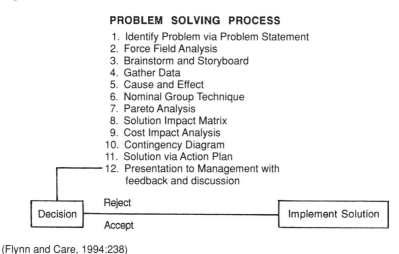

PROBLEM SOLVING PROCESS
1. Identify Problem via Problem Statement
2. Force Field Analysis
3. Brainstorm and Storyboard
4. Gather Data
5. Cause and Effect
6. Nominal Group Technique
7. Pareto Analysis
8. Solution Impact Matrix
9. Cost Impact Analysis
10. Contingency Diagram
11. Solution via Action Plan
12. Presentation to Management with feedback and discussion

Decision — Reject — Implement Solution
Accept

(Flynn and Care, 1994:238)

Figure 5.2 PROBLEM STATEMENT

THERE HAS BEEN AN INCREASE IN SATELLITE BOOKING CANCELLATIONS IN THE PUBLICITY DEPARTMENT OVER THE PAST SIX MONTHS.

(Flynn and Care, 1994:238)

Figure 5.3 FORCE FIELD ANALYSIS

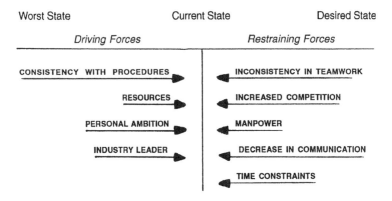

(Flynn and Care, 1994:249)

Figure 5.4 BRAINSTORMING

"What is causing the increase in satellite booking cancellations."

Decrease in manpower
Time constraints
Poor communication between publicity and production
Poor communication between production and shipping
Insufficient confirmed bookings
Tentative bookings
Service of West Coast bookings
Decreased booking supervision
Lack of timely press material to bookers
Stations receiving press material late
Shipping shortages
Insufficient tracking system
Lack of coordination between publicity, production, and shipping
Decreased teamwork in publicity
Station technical problems
Inside technical problems
Vendor technical problems
Outside production personnel not 100 % competent of communications
    equipment
Limited training

(Flynn and Care, 1994:240)

Figure 5.5 STORYBOARD

MANPOWER

Decrease in manpower
Poor communication
Decreased booking supervision
Decreased teamwork
Outside production personnel not 100% competent

PROCEDURES

Limited Training
Insufficient confirming
Tentative bookings
Service of West Coast bookings
Insufficient tracking system
Lack of coordination
Late press material

EQUIPMENT

Station technical problems
Inside technical problems
Vendor technical problems

RESOURCES

Shipping shortages
Time constraints

(Flynn and Care, 1994:241)

Figure 5.6 CAUSE AND EFFECT DIAGRAM

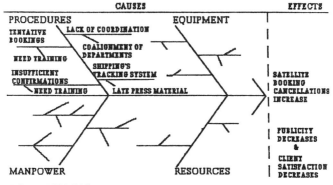

(Flynn and Care, 1994:242)

Figure 5.7 NOMINAL GROUP TECHNIQUE

PROCEDURES

NEED TRAINING	TENTATIVE BOOKINGS	3
	INSUFFICENT CONFIRMATIONS	
LACK OF COORDINATIION	COALIGNMENT OF DEPARTMENTS	2
SHIPPING'S TRACKING SYSTEM	LATE PRESS MATERIAL	7

(Flynn and Care, 1994:243)

Figure 5.8 PARETO ANALYSIS

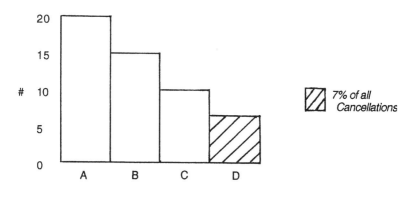

SATELLITE BOOKING CANCELLATIONS

LEGEND: A= MANPOWER
B= TRAINING
C=TECHNICAL
D= SHIPPING
#= NUMBER OF CANCELLATIONS

(Flynn and Care, 1994:244)

Figure 5.9 SOLUTION IMPACT MATRIX

Legend:			A	B	C	D	E	F	G
A-G: Possible Solutions	1	.30	M	L	H	---	M	H	---
	2	.26	---	---	M	---	L	L	M
	3	.15	L	---	M	H	---	---	---
H = 10	4	.09	---	M	---	L	H	M	---
M = 5	5	.06	---	M	L	---	L	---	M
L = 1			1.7	1.1	5.1	1.6	2.7	3.7	1.6

SOLUTION   IMPACT   RATINGS

(Flynn and Care, 1994:244)

Figure 5.10 COST IMPACT ANALYSIS

PART A

Cost considerations: rated (1-5)
    1= Lowest cost
       to
    2= Highest cost

SOLUTIONS

	D vs. D	E vs. E	F F
Manpower	3	5	4
Resources	---	5	2
Training	1	5	3
Time	2	2	3
COST RATINGS	**6**	**17**	**12**

Figure 5.10 COST IMPACT ANALYSIS (Continued)

PART B

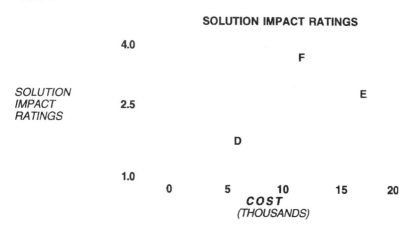

(Flynn and Care, 1994:243)

Figure 5.11 CONTINGENCY DIAGRAM

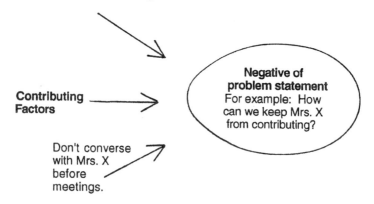

(Flynn and Care, 1994:246)

An Example of a Self-Managed Team: NUMMI

In 1985, General Motors and Toyota Motors Corporation formed a joint venture, New United Motors Manufacturing Inc. or NUMMI, to produce Chevy Nova and the Toyota Corolla at a plant in Fremont, California. The plant was managed and designed by the Japanese but the facility and employees were supplied by General Motors, who had closed the plant and laid off its workforce a year earlier.

Workers at the NUMMI plant earn $15.00 per hour. They do not have the normal United Auto Workers Union coverage (95 percent of their normal pay) if laid off. However, when auto production dropped from 910 cars per day to 650 due to a weakening market demand, no employees were laid off. Instead they were sent, one hundred at a time, from the slowed assembly line to training sessions in new equipment, interpersonal communication, and teamwork skills.

At NUMMI, team absence policies are strict and labor disputes are resolved rapidly. A worker who is absent for any reason on three occasions in a ninety-day period is charged with an offense. Anyone committing four offenses in a year is fired. One worker reported, "If it is the cold and flu season, you had better think twice about taking a day off to get your hair done" (Holusha, 1989:B10). If a worker has a labor complaint, a member of the management team is dispatched along with the union representative in an effort to correct the problem on the spot.

Following Japanese management practices, managers dress in the same uniforms as workers, are placed on the production floor, and eat their meals with workers. At NUMMI, managers are called "group leaders" and supervise four to six work teams. Each work team consists of four to eight members with one member serving as a team leader who is paid fifty cents an hour more than other team members to keep records and assist teammates if they are having trouble finishing their work on time.

Each team is given a set of responsibilities in assembling a car and allowed to design its own jobs in collaboration with teammates and the group leader. Each team rotates its members through each job to prevent boredom and to assure equality of workload. "One of the highest compliments that workers pay to NUMMI is that it is now a fair place to work, where the workload is evenly distributed—unlike the GM days when some worked hard while those in good jobs coasted" (Holusha, 1989:B10).

Team members meet regularly and each member is assigned a work task to refine. In refining a task, team members seek to find more efficient methods to perform the tasks, methods all team

Figure 5.12 PROBLEM SOLUTION CHART

Problem: Eliminater mechanics' wasted line time waiting for work orders

Recommendation: Organize the mechanical maintenance workload of non-critical work orders to ensure the mechanic is busy at all times

Payoffs:
- Reduce backload
- Improve morale
- Reduce idle time
- Free lead hand from paperwork

Action Plan:
- Meet with co-ordinator and mechanics to discuss work distribution
- Highlight workable backlog (work that can be accomplished now)
- Define way to distribute more non-critical work orders to mechanics
- Install an established location board (where to find mechanic)

---

members can utilize. At any point in time, each team member can tell you the work task he or she is refining in order to improve productivity and quality control.

Management also contributes to the increased efficiency and productivity process. Holusha (1989:B10) reports:

> NUMMI managers also have gone to considerable effort to make jobs easier to perform. A visitor touring the plant sees one little touch after another that eliminates bending, stretching, or heavy lifting. Heavy welders are suspended over head and the line rises and fails so that operations are performed at a comfortable height.

One very big issue at NUMMI is the speed and quality of the work. Each work team has a set of tasks which are timed, and the line is set to move at the appropriate time sequence for optimal production. Work teams must move fast to complete their tasks in the time allotted. At each work station on the assembly line, cords hang within easy reach. They are linked to an Andon Board, which shows the status of each operation. The worker who is having trouble completing his or her job in the time allotted is taught that he or she has the "right" and "obligation" to pull the cord to prevent a defective car from continuing down the line.

When the cord is pulled, a bell rings and lights flash. The team and group leaders converge on the problem area to assist the worker. If the cord is pulled again within two minutes, the line is shut down. If a given team consistently has problems, tasks are reassigned, team members are transferred to other teams, or more workers are added to the team.

While the work is hard and the social pressure to increase productivity and quality is great, morale appears to be high. Robert Mandoza, the leader of a work team which installs fenders said, "We have to compete with countries where they pay less wages." A poll of workers indicates that over 90 percent of the workforce preferred working for NUMMI over their old employer, GM (Holusha, 1989:B10). After four years of operation, the plant boasted an extraordinary record of high productivity, low level of defects, and low absenteeism (see table 5.4).

While many aspects of a firm's primary and support activities contribute to worker productivity, quality, and low absenteeism, both management and workers at NUMMI point to their self-managed work teams as the major factor involved. *Self-managed teamwork made a motivational, quality, and productivity difference at NUMMI.*

Table 5.4 HOW NUMMI OUTPERFORMED GM

		NUMMI	General Motors
Productivity	hours of labor per	20 hours	28 hours
Absenteeism	unexcused (% of workforce)	2%	9%
Quality	survey of new car owners in U.S. market after 90 days	(Chevy Nova ranked no. 2)	(no GM car in top 10)

Adapted: 1986 Survey by MIT, published in *New York Times*, January 29, 1989.

Cross-Functional Teamwork

Communication as a process is pervasive to all activities of managers. In fact, the managerial skills of interaction, allocating, monitoring and organization which are so crucial to new program implementation become operationalized only through communicative activity. For example, in the new product development process members of the project team interact with an array of individuals inside and outside the organization, including personnel from other functional areas, advertising representatives, customers, distributors and so on. When making decisions, these managers must both acquire and disseminate information in order to serve a number of distinct purposes, all related to improving the interactions among members of the project team and to the ultimate successful implementation of the project.
(Pinto and Pinto, 1990:202)

Cross-functional teams are normally employed to map and improve a firm's business processes and as such seek continuous improvement through an incremental change in organizational functioning. Traditionally there are two types of cross-functional teams— problem-mapping teams and solution-implementation teams.

Problem-Mapping and Solution-Implementation Cross-Functional Teams

The strategic perspective of an organization as a system presented in chapter 1 stresses two features. *First,* it stresses that an organization should be considered a value chain of systemically intertwined functions and processes containing product/service development, manufacturing, customer service, and management. A map of these processes is the key to a real understanding of how tasks are interrelated and how complex manufacturing, financial, and other operations are accomplished. *Second,* it indicates a necessity to extend organizational analysis into the environment and to build maps of potential linkages of an organization with competitors, consumers, and suppliers. The fundamental way to build reliable maps is by applying cross-functional teams.

Cross-functional teams have a long history in organizational practice. They were used in order to solve particularly complex problems and were called "task forces." In the seventies and eighties they became a more permanent structural element with the development of matrix structures. Today they gain recognition as tools of process mapping. *Process mapping is an elaborate and systemic effort of cross-functional teams directed toward the development of models usually in the form of flowcharts of organizational processes in order to reengineer and simplify them.*

There are three common features of organizational business processes which makes cross-functional teams the best way to map processes. They are repetitive, organically cross-functional, and demand extensive coordination of knowledge and activities. Let us review these characteristics.

First, most of a firm's business processes are repetitive because they constitute a core of standardized cycles of action with the same inputs and outputs, for example, billing customers, maintaining machinery and equipment, and planning and executing production. The repetitive nature of the processes makes them relatively easy to monitor, record, analyze, and subsequently improve.

Second, organizational business processes encompass and cross different functions and therefore require different knowledge bases in order to understand them. In practice they often become much more complex than necessary. Each functional top or middle manager sees only part of the process and naturally enough modifies it over time according to the interests and/or needs of his or her subsystem. The additive effects of such changes and "improvements" lead to growing complexity and major problems at the cross-functional points. These problems often are overlooked for the simple reason that they are not within anyone's functional responsibilities. Walter (1992:16) discussed the experience of Xerox:

> When we then overlaid this process view of our business with our functional organization we made some very interesting observations. First, *just about every process was cross-functional,* in that more than one function participated in delivering parts of the process. . . . The second observation was the most telling. When we then analyzed the process for efficiency and effectiveness, we found 80-90 percent of errors, queuing, duplication of activity were at the functional cross-over points.

Third, most of the organizational business processes have the structure of a double helix, i.e. consisting a flow of material components (parts, people) and a flow of coded information. Such a pattern of organizational processes demands very good coordination of materials and information flow. However, the design of material flow is basically production based, i.e. dominated by primary functions, while the design of information flow results primarily from the needs of management, i.e. dominated by support functions. The different functional bases of design result often in the lack of coordination between the tangible (productive) and intangible (informational) aspects of the process. Cross-functional teams help both to simplify and integrate these processes.

Cross-functional teamwork involves an intense one- or two-day teamwork session which proceeds through a three-step problem-solving process:

1. Develop a clear understanding of the team's mission.
2. Identify the necessary and sufficient critical success factors for fulfilling the mission.
3. Identify and evaluate the business processes essential to meeting the critical success factors (Henke, Krackenberg, and Lyons, 1993:299).

Step one: Mission. The first step in this teamwork process is for the participants to develop a clear understanding of the team's *mission,* that is, what its members collectively are attempting to do. Each team member, because of the unit he or she represents, will have a slightly different perspective regarding the team's mission. It is the purpose of this first step to develop a common understanding of the mission statement, the central focus, the boundaries, what has to be done, and how one can measure when it has been done.

Vagueness and lack of precision in the mission statement will lead to team failure. The team must begin its work by identifying clearly and understanding the team's mission statement and expressing it precisely in three or four short sentences.

Step two: Success factors. The second step, after developing a clear understanding of the team's mission, is to identify the necessary and sufficient *critical success factors* for fulfilling that mission. Hardaker and Ward (1987) note that few teams are in a correct frame of mind to attack this problem. Most members will be attempting to discern what the implications for the mission statement are for the work in their units. They will focus on individual interests in present operations, not on future interests and tomorrow's possibilities.

To break out of this mind-set, a ten-minute brainstorming session is useful in which participants list one- or two-word descriptions of things they believe could have an impact on achieving the mission. Normal brainstorming rules apply, that is: each participant must contribute; all ideas are accepted for the list, no matter how unusual; no one is allowed to challenge or criticize an idea during listing; and the team list is displayed so all can see it.

In brainstorming, the team should think of factors impacting the organization's chief constitutencies. These include workers, customers, investors, and governments. These constituencies are operating within broad frames of influence such as cultures, regions, political climate, economic climate, educational climate, and so on. The typical list contains thirty to fifty items.

Critical success factors (CSFs) are not the "how to" of the mission; they are the subgoals of the mission statement. Each statement should contain a single factor. Consensus, not majority rule, should govern the selection of no more than eight CSFs on the final list. This process normally takes three to six hours.

Step three: Process identification and evaluation. The third step is to identify and evaluate the *organizational processes* essential to meeting the critical success factors. Again a necessary and sufficient rule and consensus is required for including an organizational process on the list. In addition, Hardaker and Ward (1987:14) suggest that each business process description should follow a verb-plus-object sequence; every business process should have an "owner," the person responsible for carrying out the process; and no owner should have more than three or four organizational processes to manage. While the mission statement and CSFs are the product of, and responsibility of, the entire team, the *organizational process statements* are the products of team consensus. The ownership or responsibility for an organizational process, however, is normally assigned to only one of the team members.

Now place the critical success factors and the business processes in random order on a matrix, such as the one in figure 5.14. Then focus on each critical factor in turn and ask which processes must be performed particularly well for the organization to be confident of meeting that critical success factor. Here the attempt is to locate the organizational processes which have the most important impact on the CSF. The facilitator fills in the box for each essential organizational process at the point of intersect with the critical success factor. Again, the intersects must pass the necessary and sufficient test.

If organizations had unlimited time and resources, a team could devote equal attention to all organizational processes. Since most organizations do not have these resources, we must now rank order these activities to obtain a list of priorities for allocating time and money. The most important processes are those which intersect the largest number of CSFs. However, to get a meaningful ranking, we must assess how well each process is *now* being performed.

Now the team must decide on the best way to obtain follow-through on improvements needed and relevant measures for demonstrating that things are improving. This is normally achieved by reconvening the team at agreed upon times to review the Process Quality Management process and examine the implementation results. Particularly important in such a review is to realize that while the mission statement and critical success factors remain constant, the quality ratings of the organizational processes change, creating a change in the priorities graph—that is, a change in what organizational processes are in zones 1, 2, and 3 (see figure 5.13).

An Example of a Cross-Functional Team: IBM

In the mid-1980s, IBM's European manufacturing arm attempted to implement continuous-flow manufacturing in its fifteen European

Figure 5.13 CHARTING CRITICAL SUCCESS FACTORS

Critical Success Factors

Business Processes	1	2	3	4	5	6	Total
1							
2							
3							
4							
5							
6							
7							
8							
etc.							

manufacturing plants. To assist in this process, IBM hired two senior consultants, Maurice Hardaker and Bryan Ward, to set up a series of one- and two-day training sessions in cross-functional teamwork. As already discussed, cross-functional teamwork is an organizational process aimed at getting the whole team committed to some task, to ensure that everyone knows the goal of the task, the critical factors involved in obtaining the goal, and the business processes which must be upgraded or brought on-line to meet the critical success factors. Let us explore how this form of the teamwork process works.

Cross-functional teamwork at IBM Europe began with the vice president for manufacturing and his team exploring carefully the task of creating a continuous-flow manufacturing system in order to understand precisely how such a change would intersect IBM's existing manufacturing operations. Next they focused in on the changes which had to be implemented in the firm's materials management processes. They then invited all the key managers and only those managers involved in this process to a teamwork session. The group was limited to no more than twelve people so that the team would not become unwieldy. The teamwork sessions were held at two sites away from the firm's offices to avoid interruptions. The team leader, the vice president for manufacturing who had called the meeting, was then asked to participate as an observer. The teamwork sessions were led by a neutral outsider consultant.

The first step in the teamwork process is for the participants to develop a clear understanding of the team's mission, what its members collectively are attempting to do. For example, Hardaker and Ward (1987) cite the following mission statement of one of IBM Europe's units as clear and precise.

> "Prepare IBM World Trade Europe Middle East Africa Corporation employees to establish their businesses. Organize high-level seminars for IBM customers and make a significant contribution to IBM's image in Europe. Demonstrate the added value of the International Education Centre through excellence in advanced education internationalism, innovation, and cross functional exchanges." (Hardaker and Ward, 1987:113)

This mission statement has a clear central focus: to organize high-level seminars for IBM customers in order to make a significant contribution to IBM's image in Europe. The mission statement sets clear boundaries for the business: Europe, Middle East, Africa Corporation employees. The mission statement sets measurable criteria of success (to demonstrate the added value of the center through excellence in advanced education, etc.).

The second step, after developing a clear understanding of the team's mission, is to identify the necessary and sufficient critical success factors for fulfilling that mission. Now the team must begin to formulate the critical success factors into statements such as "we must" and "we need." Each statement should be tested against the mission statement to make sure *it is a necessary condition* for achieving the mission and that all the statements taken collectively are *sufficient to achieve the mission.*

Hardaker and Ward (1987:14) provide a hypothetical example of CSFs to illustrate this process. The mission statement for this example might read: For IBM Europe to increase market shares from 23 to 30 percent profitability growth. Seven critical success factors for this mission might read:

1. We need the best-of-breed product quality.
2. We need new products that satisfy market need.
3. We need excellent suppliers.
4. We need to motivate skilled workers.
5. We need excellent customer satisfaction.
6. We need new business opportunities.
7. We need lowest delivery cost.

The third step is to identify and evaluate the business processes essential to meeting these critical success factors. Again a necessary and sufficient rule and consensus is required for including a business process on the list.

In IBM's cross-functional teamwork studies, they used a subjective ranking based on a team consensus which is entered in the quality column of the matrix (figure 5.15): A=excellent performance, B=good, C=fair, D=bad, and E=embryonic or not performed at all. Hardaker and Ward (1987:118) conclude:

> Graphing makes priorities clear; the second part of the *Exhibit,* shows the best way we've found to help the team translate its rankings into an action plan. The quality of each process is plotted horizontally and the number of CSFs the process impacts is plotted vertically. Then the team divides the graph into zones to create groups of processes. We can see immediately that Zone 1 contains the most critical processes. All the processes are important, by definition. But the higher risk (or higher opportunity) processes are found in Zone 1. These activities need the team's closest attention if the company is to improve market shares and profitability within two years.

Please examine carefully figure 5.14 in order to understand how to graph these issues.

Now the team must decide on the best way to obtain follow-through on improvements needed and relevant measures for demonstrating that things are improving. This is normally achieved by reconvening the team at agreed upon times to review the cross-functional process and examine the implementation results. Particularly important in such a review is to realize that while the mission statement and critical success factors remain constant, one can hope that the quality ratings of the business processes change, creating a change in the priorities graph—a change in what business processes are in zone 1, zone 2, or zone 3.

Figure 5.14 TURNING A MISSION INTO AN AGENDA

Graphing makes priorities clear

Number of critical success factor impacts

7				P10
6		P7		
5		P5 P14 P8		
4			P1 P18 P13 P15	P3 P16
3	P4 P12 P2 P11			
2				P9
1				
0				
	E	D	C	B A
	P6 P17			

Embryonic stage

Quality scale
E Embryonic stage
D Bad
C Fair
B Good
A Excellent

Zone 1
Zone 2
Zone 3

P = business process number

Charting a project

Critical success factors

- Quality
- Lowest delivered cost
- New business opportunities
- Excellent customer satisfaction
- Motivated, skilled workers
- Excellent supplies
- New products that satisfy market needs
- Best-of-breed product quality

Business Processes

Business Process	Quality	Count
P1 Research the marketplace	C	3
P2 Measure customer satisfaction	D	4
P3 Advertise products	B	3
P4 Monitor competition	D	6
P5 Measure product quality	C	5
P6 Educate vendors	E	4
P7 Train employees	C	6
P8 Define new product requirements	B	4
P9 Process customer orders	B	2
P10 Develop new products	D	6
P11 Monitor customer complaints	D	3
P12 Negotiate manufacturing designs	C	5
P13 Define future skill needs	C	3
P14 Select and certify vendors	C	5
P15 Promote the company	B	3
P16 Support installed products	E	3
P17 Monitor customer or prospect's business	C	3
P18 Announce new products		

Source: Hardaker, Maurice and Bryan E. Ward. "Getting Things Done." Harvard Business Review, November–December 1987, p. 115

Cross-functional teamwork is but one strategy for stimulating effective teamwork. Hardaker and Ward (1987:122) report that as a result of the cross-functional teamwork sessions and the organizational changes these sessions stimulated, continuous-flow manufacturing was brought on-line at all fifteen facilities with the following effects: "manufacturing cycle times and inventory levels improved, costs dropped, quality rose, and the company became more flexible in meeting customer demand. That may not be the end of the rainbow, but it's not bad from a two-day... session." At IBM Europe, it works successfully to create a common focus, a mutually constructed, publicly agreed to shared goal, whose attainment is channeled and constrained by an appropriate concern for the integration of all team components, thus manifesting the values of mutual respect, trust, and confidence in the organization's teamwork. In so doing, cross-functional teamwork ignited the creativity, energy, and force of the team, fueling the engines of the individual and firm, making a new level of competitiveness, quality, and performance possible (Barrett, 1987:24).

Critical Success Factors for Self-Managed and Cross-Functional Teamwork

What distinguishes the teamwork pattern is the prevalence of candid and committed interplay. The candor is evident in the easy frankness that marks discussion; team members argue and disagree without embarrassment or discomfiture. In place of the zestful malice so often seen among adversaries, there's the constructive openness of partners. The commitment is evident in the degree of involvement; each member believes that the work of the team is important and that he or she can affect the outcome. As a result, the team goes about its work with spiritual seriousness. A high degree of synergism usually results.
(Lefton and Buzzotta, 1987:9)

What then does our analysis of the teamwork research, processing, and instances suggest as the critical success factors involved in developing, managing, and participating in effective corporate teamwork?

General Teamwork: Critical Success Factors

1. All team members must understand and publicly commit to the team mission.

2. Team leaders must clearly and precisely communicate their expectations in regard to the appropriate manner for team members to participate in the teamwork processes.
3. Each participant in the teamwork process must clearly articulate the interests of the units, process, or function he or she represents so that these interests can be appropriately integrated into the team's overall mission and activities.
4. All team members must employ a constructive communication pattern of candid and committed interplay aimed at mission fulfillment.
5. The teamwork process must be guided by a concern for improving teamwork processes with clear criteria and measures of progress in resolving problems.

Self-Managed Teams: Critical Success Factors

1. Training of facilitator.
2. Training of team members in problem solving.
3. Unit head presenting clear goals, targets, and constraints.
4. Team analysis and/or implementation demonstrated for most goals, targets, and constraints.
5. Unit head acting to implement appropriate solutions.
6. Monitoring unit head's decision.
7. Monitoring team performance.

Cross-Functional Teams: Critical Success Factors

1. Training of facilitator.
2. Training of team members in problem solving.
3. Unit heads involved in business processes.
4. Development of clear mission statement.
5. Development of clear critical success factors.
6. Development of clear evaluation of unit functions.
7. Good team interaction.

Organizational Integration Processes: A Summary

The appropriate use of leadership, corporate climate, and teamwork to achieve corporate integration creates a sense of cultural and individual place for all employees within the organization. It creates an environment where workers admire the organization's values and performance and are proud of the role they play in that process because of the appropriateness of the fit—a heavenly fit. But when the organizational integration process goes awry, when the vision is inappropriate, the corporate culture and climate arbitrary and negative, the teamwork process a sham, then the sense of group and individual place is lost—the appropriateness of the fit suffocating—creating a hell of work.

Organizational integration in a turbulent, economic environment begins *first* with *high-speed management leadership,* the anticipation of a need for change, the creation of an appropriate vision for reorientation to change, the use of value congruence and empowerment skills to set priorities, and the use of self-understanding skills to reengineer the change. Then, while an organization renews itself based on the tight fit between the organization and its environment, the leader begins the process for high-speed management leadership anew by anticipating the next change and formulating the next vision.

Second, if change is the only constant in a turbulent economic environment, then the corporate culture and corporate climate which flow from repeated visions must involve repeated adaptations of an organization's values, socialization, and monitoring system to the ever-shifting values and interests of investors, consumers, and workers. A positive corporate climate requires a flexible, adaptive, and focused organizational value, socialization, and monitoring system which intersects the values and interests of investors, consumers, and workers in a positive way.

Finally, organizational teamwork must also reflect this flexibility, adaptation, and focus. Effective teamwork rests on a mutually constructed, publicly agreed upon, shared goal. This goal must be channelled and constrained by a concern for the appropriate integration of all the team's components, producing respect, trust, and confidence which ignites creativity and fuels individual and collective motivation, making a new level of performance possible (Barrett, 1987:24).

PART II

Organizational Coordination Processes

The faster information, decisions, and materials can flow through an organization, the faster a firm can respond to customer orders, adjust to market demand and competitive conditions. . . . The basic idea is to eliminate the organizational slack and bottlenecks, delays, errors, and over-bloated inventories firms accumulate. Then costs drop, customer service improves, quality is higher, and the firm becomes more innovative.
(Turner, 1989:6)

To make such an improvement in speed-to-market, a firm needs a tight coordination system to link its units and subunits into an effective whole. Such a linking system must include the best available tools and technologies for speeding the flow of accurate information between units, a set of effective coordination strategies which meets each unit's needs, and the exact coordination topics for maintaining the appropriate unit interfaces. It is the purpose of this section to provide a discussion of these tools, strategies, and topics by major organizational unit interfaces.

Chapter 6 will explore the R & D and marketing interface. Environmental assessment, product portfolio modeling, and structured innovation as tools for rapidly coordinating the R & D and marketing interface are examined. Such coordination strategies as technology-driven, market-driven, balanced low-budget, and high diverse strategies are discussed. Then the effective coalignment topics are outlined

151

for each unit in a benchmarked organization. Finally, two examples of the effective use of these tools, strategies, and topics are explored, involving the General Electric and Matsushita corporations.

Chapter 7 explores the R & D, marketing, and manufacturing units' interface. Robots, integrated flexible systems, computer-assisted design and computer-aided manufacturing (CAD/CAM), as well as computer-integrated systems (CIS) are explored as tools for effectively coordinating information and communication within and between units. Strategies aimed at guiding coordination including economies of scale, focus, sourcing, scope, and time are discussed. The appropriate topics for discussion between units are then outlined and illustrated by their use in coordinating these units at the Allan-Bradley and the Limited corporations.

Chapter 8 explores the R & D, marketing, manufacturing, and management Information System (MIS) interfaces. Such tools as database management, telecommunication management, applications programming, and design management are discussed for coordinating these units. Such MIS strategies as critical success factors, applications portfolio, the stages approach, the value chain approach, and high-speed management approach are discussed. Then the coordination topics to be employed by each unit are outlined and illustrated as employed by The Limited and VISA corporations.

The rapid flow of accurate and relevant information and communication is central to successful high-speed management firms.

6

The R & D and Marketing Interface

Managers divide work into specialized functions or departments to increase the productivity and efficiency of their organizations. At the same time, though, they create the need for coordinating these divided work activities. Coordination is the process of integrating the objectives and activities of the separate units of an organization in order to achieve organizational goals efficiently. Without coordination, individuals and departments would lose sight of their roles within the organization. They would begin to pursue their own specialized interests, often at the expense of the larger organizational goals.
(Stoner, Collins, and Yaffon, 1985:327)

Having explored in some detail the *first major communication process* of high-speed management, namely *organizational integration* and its subprocesses—transformational leadership, corporate culture and corporate climate, and corporate teamwork—we are now in a position to direct our attention to the *second major communication process* of high-speed management, namely *organizational coordination* and three of its subprocesses—the R & D and marketing interface; the R & D, marketing, and manufacturing interface; and the R & D, marketing, manufacturing, and MIS interface.

Establishing and maintaining an effective coordination system in a volatile economic environment where an organization's primary and support activities are configured and dispersed throughout the world would be a next-to-impossible task were it not for the development of new information and communication technologies.

Communication and coordination costs are dropping sharply, driven by breathtaking advances in information systems and telecommunications technology. We have just seen the beginning of developments in this area which are spreading throughout the value chain. Boeing, for example, is employing computer-aided design technology to jointly design components on-line with foreign suppliers. Engineers in different countries are communicating via computer screens. Marketing systems and business practices continue to homogenize, facilitating the coordination of activities in different countries. The mobility of buyers and information is also growing rapidly, greasing the international spread of brand reputations and enhancing the importance of consistency in the way activities are performed worldwide. Increasing numbers of multinational and global firms are begetting globalization by their suppliers. There is also a sharp rise in the computerization of manufacturing as well as other activities in the value chain, which greatly facilitates coordination among dispersed sites. (Porter, 1986:36)

Such reciprocal coordination processes are at the core of effective high-speed management processes. They are essential for a product to be produced rapidly and in the hands of satisfied customers worldwide at low cost and with high quality and high value (DeMeyer, 1991).

Nowhere is this need for speed and coordination more apparent than in the R & D and marketing interface. Rapidly changing technology, quick market saturation, and unexpected global competition have led to the shortening of the new product life cycle. The shortened product life cycle has in turn placed increased pressure on firms to develop a more frequent and steady flow of new products which are appropriately targeted on specific market segments. At the center of such a new product development process is the rapid and effective coordination of the research and development and marketing interface.

Let us examine in some detail the information and communication activities involved in such a coordination process by (1) exploring the tools available for aligning the R & D and marketing units with their environment, (2) examining the dominant strategies employed in effecting such an alignment, (3) discussing the specific coordination activities required for effective alignment, and (4) investigating two examples of such coordination activities and alignment in order to locate the critical factors governing the R & D and marketing interface.

The Tools Available for Aligning the R & D and Marketing Units with Their Environment

The United States is in a period of economic challenge and organizational upheaval. There are myriad prescriptions for industrial and organizational renewal, and many of the factors linked to organizational success are being rediscovered today after a thirty-year hiatus. Our own analysis, however, indicates that these characteristics, while important, are merely manifestations of a more fundamental, dynamic process called fit—the search for an organization form that is both internally and externally consistent. We have argued that minimal fit is necessary for survival, tight fit is associated with corporate excellence, and early fit provides a competitive advantage that can lead to the organization Hall of Fame. Tomorrow's Hall of Fame companies are working on new organization forms today.
(Miles and Snow, 1984:27)

Today almost one-fourth of a firm's sales and one-third of a firm's profits come from products introduced into the marketplace in the last three years (Prescott, Kohl, and Venkatraman, 1986). What new products should a firm develop? How should these new products fit with a firm's product line? How must they fit with consumer taste? And what does this mean for the R & D and marketing interface? The answers to these questions and others depends in no small part on environmental constraints and on three information and communication tools for responding to these constraints: environmental assessment, product portfolio modeling, and structured innovation.

Environmental Assessment

In a volatile economic environment, successful organizations must keep one eye on their competitors and the other eye on their customers. Corporate strategy is effective when the internal organization of one's firm can create a more productive alignment between its organization and environment than one's competitors. Such an alignment may be *minimal or tight, fragile or anchored,* relative to one's competitors (Miles and Snow, 1984). Some type of minimal fit is required for corporate survival, while a tight fit generates optimal profits. Some fits are fragile in that they are easily disturbed by a change in either the organization's alignment between organizational activities or the alignment between products and the environment. On the other hand, some fits are anchored in that the fits between organizational activities and new products are interlocking and the interdependency leads to market domination. When an organization achieves a tight and anchored fit with its environment over an extended period of time, it becomes a model of corporate excellence.

In the rapidly changing computer environment, Kaypro has a minimal and fragile fit with its environment based on IBM compatibility and a small share of the portable computer market. Apple has a minimal anchored fit depending upon its domination of the educational personal computer and desktop publishing market. IBM has an extended, tight, and anchored fit with its environment grounded in domination of the personal, business, and mainframe computer market. However, all of these alignments are subject to change based on either market saturation, which ends one product's life cycle, or on unexpected competition, which arises when a technological change provides one firm with a competitive advantage over all others in an existing market or alternatively initiates a new product life cycle.

General Motors, Timex, Atari, and Texas Instruments—each one occupied an extended, tight, and anchored fit with its environment, a dominant position in the world auto, wristwatch, electronic games, and computer markets. However, as one product life cycle came to an end and no new products were introduced that provided a competitive advantage, these firms experienced low growth and shrinking markets as their products either saturated the market or were confronted by technological change that gave a competitive advantage to other firms. These once dominant firms watched their market positions erode as once extended, tight, and anchored fits with their environments began to change.

The key to strategic planning is a combination of analysis and intuition, keeping track of the unscheduled "strategic windows" at which market opportunities might occur and what strategies of the firm must be adjusted to capitalize on the opportunities. Those firms with a tight and anchored fit whose managers are competent in the areas of risk taking, management of innovation, and communication, and who foster in the organization a climate for monitoring technological and market windows when they occur will be the most successful. At the heart of environmental assessment aimed at establishing a tight and anchored fit between a firm and its environment are (a) competitive intelligence and (b) market analysis.

Competitive intelligence is the process of gathering and analyzing information about one's competitors' strengths and weaknesses. Competitive intelligence improves a firm's ability to predict its competitors' moves and proactively respond to them. However, to do this one must have accurate and reliable information on one's competitors. Several firms provide such information for a price. Corporate directory databases such as *D & B Dun's Market Identifiers* and *Trinet Establishment Data Base* identify firms by their specified markets. *Disclosure, Standard and Poors Corporate Descriptions,* and *Moody's Corporate Profiles* provide company background data and histories.

Once competitors have been identified, one needs to analyze and evaluate their finances, R & D capabilities, and personnel. *Disclosure, Media General Plus, Investment,* and *D & B Dun's Financial Records* provide financial data on over eleven thousand companies, indicating where they are investing, in what, and why. These same companies provide "competitive benchmark" measures between the financial performance of a firm and the leading firms in its industry. *PTS New Products* provides copies of all news released on new products, including the price, availability, use, and market strategy on these products. *Business Wire PR News* and *McGraw Hill News* provide a continuous flow of news releases on a company's strategic moves, product development, and acquisition strategies. In addition, *PTS Newsletter Data Base* provides key coverage and full text of industry and firm publications. To locate new advances in R & D, one can have a search made of new patents and specifications by *Dialog Patent Index;* of a firm's management and staff capabilities by *Trade and Industry ASAP;* and there are industrywide information service firms such as *Data Quest* in the computer industry, *Cole and Associates* in the automotive industry, and others. Similar competitive intelligence information is available in the European Economic Community and in the nations located on the Pacific Rim.

Information about one's customers is also required. Once again several sources exist for obtaining this information. Three firms— Burke Marketing, Information Resources Inc., and A. C. Nielson— have set up electronic cities. Burke Marketing has ADTEL, which consists of seven fixed market locations and twenty customer market locations across the United States. Information Resource Inc. has Behaviorscan, which consists of eight test market locations. A. C. Nielson has ERIM, which contains two test markets. The firms can determine consumer needs and pretest media advertising, product use, and satisfaction within a matter of days. They employ electronically controlled home TV sets in these communities, which permit remote control of ads on TV—modifying their time slots, wording, and visuals—and electronically monitored stores using bar codes to record each sale and the customer's name and address to accurately assess the relationship between advertising and sales. Shelf space comparisons are available in stores, as well as interactive TV for assessing product use and satisfaction (Russell, Adams, and Boundy, 1986). Again, similar interactive marketing analyses are available regarding customer preference in the EEC and the Pacific Rim.

In short, through environmental assessment, employing competitor intelligence and market analysis, data are available to guide an organization's new product development strategy.

Product Portfolio Modeling

Product portfolio modeling is a technique for mapping alternative scenarios for product life cycle change based upon an environmental assessment of consumer needs, alternative technological developments which influence product use, and anticipated product competition (Bennett and Cooper, 1984). Product portfolio modeling begins by assessing a product's rate of diffusion through a specified population. Six stages are involved: emergence, growth, dominance, maturity, product substitution, and decline. Three types of business intelligence based on environmental assessment are employed in order to develop alternate scenarios for change in the diffusion process.

First, one must examine market pull. Here one seeks to assess consumer needs which require new or modified product design based on existing technologies. Small business copiers, digital watches, laser disk information retrieval, video recorders, and user-friendly computers are all examples of such products. These products abruptly modified the rates of the diffusion of products in their respective life cycle by modifying existing products to new consumer demands. Three-fourths of all new products developed are of this type (Bennett and Cooper, 1984).

Second, one must assess technological push. A new technology can make possible new markets while eliminating old ones. New technologies make possible better, less costly products that satisfy specific customer needs, render existing products obsolete, and create entirely entirely new demands. Examples include handheld calculators, intelligent typewriters, videotext, and fiber-optic technologies. About one-fourth of all new products developed are of this type. Such products frequently lead to an early, tight, and anchored market fit.

Third, one must be aware of the market position of competitors. One firm's market position may either create or limit another firm's potential for market penetration. For example, the American automobile firms' focus on large and medium size cars created a large and uncontested market for small foreign cars. Conversely, IBM's positioning in the business computer market placed small upper limits on Apple's potential for market penetration.

The need for product portfolio modeling became apparent in the mid-1970s when several dominant firms failed to respond effectively to environmental change. Why was General Motors so slow in reacting to changing technologies in automotive design, engineering, and production? Why did Timex fail to enter the digital watch technology until they had lost their market position? Why didn't Atari anticipate the rapid saturation of the computer game market? Why did Texas Instruments, a company built on its innovative quality and flexible technical competence, fail to grasp the impact of the PC computer on the technical computer market? One answer to these questions is provided by Bennett and Cooper (1984), when they argue that frequently companies whose product portfolios are dominated by mature products develop a distinctive way of operating which militates against understanding environmental change and new product development. Utterback's (1981) study of fifty-eight significant product life cycle changes between 1930 and 1970 found that fifty-six of the fifty-eight dominant firms failed to make the transition to the new product life cycle. Only two firms in the sample—Pratt and Whitney and Waterman Pen—made the transition successfully from piston to jet engines and from fountain to ballpoint pens.

Product portfolio modeling is a high-speed management tool for anticipating and constructively responding to such problems. Such models for each of a firm's line of products allows for management planning, product development, investment patterns, and marketing in order to foster a range of market-oriented products at various stages in their respective life cycles. It also allows a firm to anticipate product dominance, competition, decline, and withdrawal. Environmental assessment studies, which are the basis for product portfolio modeling, are rapidly becoming an accepted tool for corporate planning. Klein and Linneman (1984) report that approximately 50 percent of the top 100 U.S. industrial, top 300 U.S. nonindustrial, and top 500 foreign industrial firms now employ some form of environmental assessment as part of the R & D and marketing interface in new product development.

Structured Innovation

All roads in a successful firm lead to the research and development unit. Corporate success depends upon the capacity of the R & D units to generate new and marketable products in a reasonably consistent pattern. How one achieves this structured pattern of innovations is a central concern of high-speed management. How can one create such a pattern? How should such an R & D unit be structured? What type of planning is involved? What type of control is most effective? What are the optimal strategies for such a unit? Let us explore the answers to each of these questions in turn.

There is a fundamental option available to managers of successful research and development units which has important implications for the appropriate selection of management styles. On the one hand, such a unit can choose to respond to the needs and changes in a given market. On the other hand, such a unit can choose to create and shape its market by innovative applications of technology to new product development.

The first option is a *market-driven orientation;* the second, *a technology-driven orientation.* Most firms position themselves somewhere in between the extremes of seeking technological and market dominance. Most successful organizations must deal effectively over time with both options. Research suggests that a firm's bias toward one or the other of these extremes has significant implications in regard to the type of coordination structure, planning, control, and strategy a successful R & D unit must employ in order to generate a structured pattern of innovative products.

Structure in a market-driven firm, it is argued, should be formal, hierarchical, and centralized with an efficiency orientation, while structure in a technology-driven firm should be informal, project oriented, functional, and adaptable in orientation.

Planning in a market-oriented firm should be centered on product life cycle, be tied to a market cost/benefit analysis, and involve a rigorous monitoring of competitors' actions with relatively short time horizons. Technology-oriented firms should be output centered, be flexible in resource allocation, and respond to perceptions of future payoff with relatively long time horizons.

Control for market-driven firms should be formal and written with well-specified objectives at the top of the hierarchy and functional tasks at the bottom and moderate technological competence at each level along with sophisticated market feedback (Williams, 1983; Shanklin and Ryans, 1984). Technology-driven firms should be informal and oral with explicitly articulated objectives and decision points that emphasize setting industrywide trends in cutting edge technology (Ansoff and Steward, 1967; Shanklin and Ryans, 1984).

Strategy for market-oriented firms should be grounded in market analysis that assigns research and development priorities, allocating resources with specific deadlines based on their competitors' market position, projected reductions in manufacturing costs, market size, and the potential for aggressive pricing policies. Technology-oriented firms should set R & D priorities, allocate resources, and fix deadlines based on the potential for market domination, high-end pricing, and the creation of patent-protected products (Shanklin and Ryans, 1984; Camillus, 1984).

Table 6.1 outlines what this means when translated into structure, style, and systems for market-driven and technology-driven orientations.

Corporate control over decision-making in both types of units tends to follow a similar pattern. The review committee for product development usually consists of the CEO, the head of R & D, the head of marketing, and the head of manufacturing. Product selection usually proceeds through the following incremental stages: idea generation, idea screening, product design, product testing, market forecasting, production plan, and business plan. Projects are recommended at each stage and evaluated against one another for potential success (Quinn, 1985; Shanklin and Ryans, 1984).

Using *Fortune's* list of the five hundred largest industrial and service companies as a base, business school professors, management consultants, and securities analysts were asked for nominations for the top masters of structured innovation in America. These eight firms were considered to be America's most innovative corporations: American Airlines, Apple Computer, Campbell Soup, General Electric, Intel, Merck, Minnesota Mining and Manufacturing, and Citicorp.

Intel is a classic instance of a *technology-driven* firm which has pursued technological dominance in product development, has protected its dominant position in various computer chip markets through patent rights, and has reaped high profits from high-end pricing of its products. General Electric is a classic instance of a *market-driven* firm in product development. GE pursues a strategy of product development based on a careful analysis of its competitors'

Table 6.1 ALTERNATIVES FOR STRUCTURE, STYLE, AND SYSTEMS IN MARKET-DRIVEN AND TECHNOLOGY-DRIVEN FIRMS

Market-Driven	Technology-Driven
Structure	
formal	informal
hierarchical structure	project oriented
centralized structure	function orientation
stress on efficiency in operations	stress on adaptability
focus on historical, financial, and cost measures	focus on future potential
rigorous monitoring of competition allocation	flexible resource
Style	
formal written communication managerial style	informal oral communication managerial style
unfamiliar with organizational objectives except at management level	articulation and sharing of objectives
moderate amount of technological competence	emphasis on leadership in competence
Systems	
deliberate approach to modifications and improvements based on customer suggestions and expressed needs/state-of-art	modifications and improvements essentially research related as are new products
mathematical marketing research methodologies	qualitative marketing research techniques

Source: Information for our chart was taken from Camillus, 1984, and King and Cushman, 1988.

market position and its own reduced manufacturing costs, size of market, and potential for aggressive pricing policies. IBM and 3M are examples of firms with R & D units vigorously pursuing *both market- and technology-driven* products (Camillus, 1984). The most difficult aspect of managing innovation in all of these firms is to ensure that risks and rewards are balanced in a way that prods employees toward prudent experimentation. Effective managers of innovation channel and control its main direction by manipulating R & D unit structures, planning, control, and strategies based on market and/or technology orientations. The choice of options is not free of environmental constraints. As indicated earlier, managerial choice influences product life cycles and manufacturing technology. In turn, managerial choices are constrained by the underlying focus which drives these life cycles and manufacturing technology systems.

Environmental assessment, product portfolio modeling, and structured innovation are essential information and communication tools for aligning an organization's R & D and marketing units with their environment. While these tools are essential, they are not sufficient for achieving an appropriate alignment. Organizations must add to these tools an appropriate strategy and a reciprocal coordination system.

The Dominant Strategies for Establishing an R & D and Marketing Interface

Because the state of technology and market conditions are continuously changing and competitive pressure to keep abreast is high, R & D not only needs to shine in its technical expertise, it also needs to excel in translating market needs into viable products and gearing for anticipated needs. Nimbleness and the ability to maintain a pragmatic balance between esoteric technological development and market needs are necessary.
(Gupta, Raj, and Wileman, 1985:289)

Environmental assessment, product portfolio modeling, and structured innovation are R & D and marketing tools which become effective only when guided by an appropriate product development strategy. Recently, practitioners and scholars alike have expressed renewed interest in technological innovation, product development, and new product marketing processes. Unfortunately much of this renewed interest has focused on tracing the success and failure of individual products without paying much attention to a firm's overall new product development strategies. One exception to this trend is Robert Cooper's (1985) study of the strategies employed by 122 industrial firms for aligning R & D and marketing units in new product development programs. This study explored each firm's development of new products over a ten-year period from 1970 to 1980 by investigating sixty-six individual strategy variables which explained 80 percent of the variation in six market outcome variables. The study reveals five main strategies for aligning the R & D and marketing units interface and for determining the frequency of occurrence of each strategy and the effectiveness of each strategy on market performance (Carter, Stearns, Reynolds, and Miller, 1994:21–41). Let us explore each in turn.

The Technology-Driven Strategy

The largest group of firms (26 percent) employed a strategy based on R & D domination of the new product development process. Such firms developed new products that were high-tech, complex, and employed sophisticated state-of-the-art production processes. These companies were proactive and offensive in their new product development programs, acquiring new development technologies, new product ideas, and new manufacturing processes. However, these technology-driven programs developed high-risk products which lacked product fit with the existing product line, had different end users, were targeted at low-growth or slow-growth markets, and lacked synergy with the firm's existing market resource base.

This lack of market orientation created new product programs which failed to meet corporate objectives, had a low success-high failure rate, a high program discontinuation rate, and the lowest new product profitability score of any of the strategies. However, the new product development program did have the highest impact on corporate sales (42 percent of the strategies employed). This technologically aggressive, high-impact program was plagued by product failures, cancellations, a lack of market orientation, poor market synergy, little product fit and focus, and a failure to target lucrative markets, which detracted from what might have been a strong and successful product innovation program (Cooper, 1985:189–190).

The Balanced Focus Strategy

The smallest group of firms (15.6 percent) employed a balanced alignment of R & D and marketing units based upon tight coordination and integration. This strategy consistently outperformed all other strategies by a large margin on each of the five market effectiveness measures. This strategy typically led to new products which closely fit with existing product lines and were targeted on consumer needs in high-growth, high-end pricing markets, which effectively utilized the existing market resources of the company.

A balanced focused strategy had the highest percentage of sales from new products in the last five years (47 percent), the highest success rate (72 percent), and was the most successful to employ against competitors, to generate the highest profits, to meet corporate goals more often, and the best to meet a performance objective for the product. From a consumer's point of view, this strategy was the only approach which yielded product differentiation based on high product quality and high customer value.

Cooper (1985:187) explains the basis of the success of this strategy:

> . . . because of this attention to the marketplace, the firm found itself in fairly attractive and familiar new product markets. First, their new product markets were high growth, high potential markets . . . these markets had a large potential, were rapidly growing, were large (dollar volume), and involved many customers (versus only a few). Second, firms targeted their new products at noncompetitive markets: markets lacking intense competition, price competitiveness, customers satisfied with competitor products, and a dominant competitor. Third, these firms avoided radically new markets to the firm . . . new product markets involved customers the firm already dealt with; no new competitors were encountered; the advertising and promotion methods required were familiar to the firm; and the salesforce and channel systems were not new to the company. Fourth, the customer needs served by Strategy B companies were familiar ones—needs the firm had served before.

Unfortunately, the smallest group of firms in this study employed this balanced focus strategy.

The Technologically Deficient Strategy

Firms in this group represented 16 percent of those sampled and pursued low-technology, low-risk, "me too" products, relying on mature technologies. Such firms were reactive to market competition, lacked a high-technology orientation, and tended to introduce products which had a poor fit with their existing product line and were positioned in low-growth markets.

Technologically deficient firms aimed their new products at customers they had served before expanding into new markets to the firm. The results were dismal: new products represented a low portion of corporate sales (30 percent), a low portion of corporate profits, and a high portion of product failures and cancellations. These firms were the smallest in the sample (mean sales totaled $38 million) and resided in low-tech markets with weak R & D and marketing units.

The Low-Budget, Conservative Strategy

This strategy was pursued by 24 percent of the firms employing relatively small R & D budgets with "me-too products" focused on existing markets and supplementing existing product lines. However, these firms were clever in that they balanced their small R & D programs with a conservative "stay at home" focus in marketing. They had the highest R & D, manufacturing, and marketing synergy. Their products were focused, closely related to existing product lines, targeted at high-growth markets, employed the firms' existing marketing base, and had a good fit with advertising and promotion, distribution, and sales forces.

Low-budget, conservative strategy firms had a high percentage of new product success and achieved the highest rate of new product profitability, but were low in growth and low in high-end pricing Such new product programs are safe, efficient, and profitable, with low impact on total corporate sales.

The High-Budget, Diverse Strategy

Firms employing this strategy represented 20 percent of the sample and had a high level of R & D spending which was poorly targeted on highly competitive new markets. However, in spite of the large budget, these firms lacked a technologically aggressive and sophisticated innovation program. The products developed were not proactive, high-tech, nor particularly complex. Most had unfocused new product programs and were diverse in terms of marketing strategies.

High-budget, diverse strategy firms tended to attack new markets with new products requiring new advertising and promotional and delivery networks but with noncompetitive products. They had a very poor performance record, high failure rate, low profit and sales rates, and a high program cancellation rate.

In summary, of the five strategies employed for linking R & D and marketing units in 122 industrial firms, only one achieved excellent results; two moderate results; and two poor results. *The Balanced*

Focus Strategy was by far the smallest and most successful group on virtually all the performance standards by targeting all new products in high-growth, high-end pricing markets. *The Low-Budget, Conservative Strategy* had moderate results with good new product success and profitability rates, but had low impact on the company performance due to the limited focus and number of new products placed in relatively mature markets. *The Technology-Driven Strategy* had modest results with new products being a high proportion of the firm's sales, but having low success, high failure, and low profitability due to poor market placement. *The Technologically Deficient Strategy* and the *High-Budget, Diverse Strategy* each had very poor results with poor performance on all market measures.

Once a firm has appropriately employed its environmental assessment, product portfolio modeling, and structured innovation tools to establish a balanced and focused strategy for aligning the R & D and marketing units, that firm must next check the coordination and integration of the alignment of these two units.

The Specific Coordination Activities Required for Effective Alignment

In essence, the capability to stretch technological developments to the fullest, but with the restraint of not imposing it on an unready market, is the key issue. In the process, marketing plays the key roles of communicator and facilitator. As communicator, marketing probes the market and conveys its impressions to R & D and in turn, tests potential product ideas in the market. Marketing cannot passively communicate information back and forth; it does not, at the same time, have the skill to be actively involved in technology development; it must, therefore, act as catalyst in facilitating the market led product development processes.
(Gupta, Raj, and Wileman, 1985:289).

Despite wide recognition of the importance of having tight reciprocal coordination between R & D and market units, most firms, as the last section indicates, frequently lack a systematic approach to such coordination. A typical new product development program proceeds through phases. Any systematic analysis of the coordination system required in aligning the R & D and marketing unit must begin by understanding the phases involved in new product development and then exploring the various linking activities required by development: a planning phase, a new product development phase, and a post-commercialization phase. Gupta, Raj, and Wileman (1985:293) undertook a careful review of the existing research literature on the necessary coordination inputs required in each phase and constructed a table listing the results (see table 6.2).

Next these authors surveyed 109 marketing and 107 R & D directories in the 167 high-technology firms in an effort to determine which of the above coordination processes were essential to successful new product development and which were not. Their results revealed that all nineteen areas were necessary and collectively sufficient for successful new product development. While all nineteen coordination

Table 6.2   AREAS REQUIRING R & D/MARKETING COORDINATION

A.   Marketing is involved with R & D in
1. Setting new product goals and priorities
2. Preparing R & D's budget proposals
3. Establishing product development schedules
4. Generating new product ideas
5. Screening new product ideas
6. Finding commercial applications of R & D's new product ideas/ technologies

B.   Marketing provides information to R & D on
7. Customer requirements of new products
8. Regulatory and legal restrictions on product performance and design
9. Test-marketing results
10. Feedback from customers regarding product performance on regular basis
11. Competitors' strategies

C.   R & D is involved with marketing in
12. Preparing marketing's budget proposal
13. Screening new product ideas
14. Modifying products according to the market's recommendations
15. Developing new products according to the market need
16. Designing communication strategies for the customers of new products
17. Designing user and service manuals
18. Training users of new products
19. Analyzing customer needs

activities were required, five of those activities were rated as more time-consuming than the others. Table 6.3 lists those rankings.

The firms who were most successful in developing and marketing new products achieved higher coordination than unsuccessful firms in each of the nineteen coordination areas listed in table 6.2 and spent more time in communication in the top five areas listed in table 6.3 than unsuccessful firms (Gupta, Raj, and Wileman, 1985:298).

Having examined in some detail the R & D and marketing interface by exploring the tools, strategies, and coordination activities involved in successful as opposed to unsuccessful firms, we are now in a position to investigate two examples of this interface in order to locate the critical factors involved.

Table 6.3   RELATIVE IMPORTANCE OF R & D/MARKETING COORDINATION PROCESSES

Top Five Coordination Areas

Marketing's Role	R & D's Role
1. Provide customer requirements to R & D	1. Get involved with marketing to develop products according to market needs
2. Provide customer feedback on product performance	2. Involve marketing in setting new product goals and priorities
3. Provide competitors' strategies to R & D	3. Involve marketing in screening new product ideas
4. Share test market results with R & D	4. Modify product according to market recommendations
5. Find commercial applications for new product ideas or technologies	5. Involve marketing in generating new product ideas

Abstracted from a chart by Gupta, Raj, and Wileman, 1985:295

Two Examples of the R & D/Marketing Interface

Dynamic interdependence is the basis of a transformational company—one that can think globally and act locally.
(Bartlett and Goshal, 1988:68)

The R & D and marketing interface, if it is to function effectively, requires the development of a complex reciprocal coordination process. The tools available to assist decision making include *environmental assessment* and its subcomponents—competitive intelligence and market analysis; *product portfolio modeling* and its subcomponents—market push, technology push, and the market position of one's competitors; and *structured innovation* and its subcomponents—the structure, planning, and control of market- and technology-driven new product development. The dominant strategies currently employed in aligning the R & D and marketing interface include the Technology-Driven, the Balanced Focus, the Technology-Deficient, the Low-Budget, Conservative, and the High-Budget, Diverse Strategies. Only one of these strategies, the Balanced Focus Strategy, can be said to work well, yet only 16 percent of the firms surveyed employed such an approach.

When such a strategy guides the R & D and marketing interface, a firm still must establish coordination linkages between R & D and marketing units at the planning, new product development and post-commercialization phases of new product development. In so doing, marketing must be involved with R & D in setting new product goals and products, preparing R & D budgets, establishing development schedules, generating new product ideas, screening ideas, and finding commercial applications for new products. Marketing provides information to R & D on consumer needs, regulatory and legal restrictions on product design and performance, test market results, customer feedback, and competitor strategies. R & D is involved with marketing in preparing marketing budgets, screening new product ideas, modifying products to meet customer needs, developing new products, designing customer communication strategies, designing user and service manuals, training users, and analyzing customer needs.

We are now in a position to examine the R & D and marketing interface in two very successful firms, Matsushita Electric Company of Japan and the General Electric Corporation of America, in order to locate critical factors governing this coordination process.

The R & D and Marketing Interface at Matsushita Electric Co.

Japan's Matsushita Electric Company occupies a global leadership position in consumer electronics based on its well-known Panasonic and National brands. Matsushita has a strong central control process governing its global operations (Schlendor, 1994:161). However, Matsushita is concerned that country marketing units have a strong say in their new product development program and have institutionalized a three-stage acess to the new product development program:

1. gaining subsidiary input into central management's new product planning process
2. ensuring that R & D and divisional marketing units are reciprocally coordinated in new product development processes
3. efficiently transferring new products from the development to manufacturing to marketing stages

Gaining Subsidiary Input into the Central Management Product Planning Process. Two major barriers face central management in succeeding in its new product development program. *First,* their new product development strategy may not be responsive to local market needs. *Second,* those workers required to implement the firm's new directions may not be committed to it. Matsushita is very conscious of these barriers and has established a multilevel coordination process between central management and local management aimed at removing these barriers. Such multiple linkages give central management a better understanding of and control over local performance. To illustrate how Matsushita's multilevel linkages work, let us examine the coordination process put in place to link central headquarters in Japan with the video division of MESA, the company's U.S. subsidiary (Schlendor, 1994:160).

The vice president, general manager, and assistant production manager of MESA are all former members of Matsushita's central headquarters and Japanese production units. The *vice president* began his career at Matsushita Electric Trading Company (METC), the unit in charge of overseas operations. While formally serving as vice president of U.S. operations, he continues to serve as a member of METC's senior management committee. He spends one-third of his time in Japan providing input into the central management planning process and the remainder of his time managing the U.S. operations. He is thus considered a full-time member of both units.

The *general manager* of MESA is a former member of Matsushita's product development team in Japan. He worked fourteen years in the video products division in Japan and maintains strong ties with that unit. He serves as their link with the U.S. operation and its unique marketing problems.

The *assistant product manager* of the video division is a U.S. citizen who spent five years working in Matsushita's video factory in

Japan. He handles the U.S. operation's day-to-day communications with that factory (Bartlett and Goshal, 1988:58).

These well-designed linkages between central headquarters in Japan and their video division operating in the United States guarantee that local management will have direct input into central headquarters, management development programs, and manufacturing, and that these units in turn will be able to obtain a serious commitment from those units that are located some distance from Japan.

R & D and Marketing Units Are Reciprocally Coordinated. At Matsushita, coordination between R & D and marketing begins with inputs at the three decision-making levels discussed above and continues throughout the product development process. Two examples will serve to illustrate these coordination processes; the first deals with new product research projects and the second with internal merchandising meetings.

Research projects undertaken by the Central Research Laboratories are developed in two different ways. *First,* there are long-term projects which cut across many different product divisions. These projects are proposed and decided upon jointly by the research laboratories, the various product divisions, and top management. These projects make up one-half of all the projects funded by corporate headquarters. The *second* type of research projects originates in specific divisions, meets local-level needs, and is put forward by the divisions involved. These projects make up one-half of the projects funded by corporate headquarters (Bartlett and Goshal, 1988:59). Each year both groups of proposals, those from the major R & D laboratories and those from local divisions, are submitted to an evaluation team made up of the engineering and development groups of the products divisions who select which projects are funded. Such an approach creates competition between technology-driven and market-driven interests, with each winning half of the R & D budget.

Matsushita Electric Company's new products development division holds an internal merchandising meeting each year which serves as a trade show. Senior marketing and sales people worldwide attract and see on display next year's proposed product line. The participants' feedback then is used to stop, redesign, or give a most favored position to specific products. The next year's product line is then selected and production begins. Such an approach to new product development allows marketing and sales people to have the final say on product development, design, manufacturing, and sales. It guarantees that R & D will be responsive to local marketing and sales interests (Bartlett and Goshal, 1988:59).

Managing the Transfer of New Products. The problem of managing the development of a new product through engineering, design, manufacturing, marketing, and sales is complex. Matsushita has developed a very creative system which relies on the transfer of people to assist in the solution of these coordination problems. To begin with, the careers of research engineers are structured so that most of them spend about five to eight years in the central research laboratories engaged in pure research, then spend another five to eight years in product divisions doing applied product and process development, and then spend the next five to eight years in direct operational functions, manufacturing, marketing, and elsewhere. Each engineer normally makes these transitions with the transfer of the major project on which he or she has been working (Bartlett and Goshal, 1988:60). In addition, wherever possible, the company tries to identify the manager who will head up production and marketing of a new product and make him or her a full-time member of the development team from its beginning. This injects production and marketing interests in product development at its earliest stages. This also serves to transfer product expertise from the laboratories at headquarters to its worldwide sales subsidiaries (Bartlett and Goshal, 1988:60).

Matsushita has institutionalized the coordination processes involved in the R & D and marketing interface at the planning, new product development, manufacturing, and marketing phases, and makes sure that coordination hits every level and function of the organization's activities.

The R & D and Marketing Interface at General Electric

The GE Research and Development Center is one of the world's largest and most diversified industrial laboratories. It is located in upstate New York and has four major components: the Chemical Research Center, the Electronics Research Center, the Engineering Physics Research Center, and the Materials Research Laboratory. At this corporate-level research facility, some 1,800 people work, including 475 men and women holding doctorates. GE also has major applied product development research facilities associated with each of its major businesses. The R & D Center employs only 5 percent of the twenty-two thousand scientists and engineers engaged in research at GE; it generates about 20 percent of the corporate patents, and annually contributes about five hundred articles to the world's technical literature. In the 1990s, GE's central and business-level R & D effort was approximately $4 billion (Gwynne, 1990:22).

The GE Research and Development Center's budget comes from two sources, a general assessment on each GE business operation and contracts undertaken for each business unit. In 1986, 75 percent of the funding came from the assessment and 25 percent from contracts. In 1987 CEO Jack Welch put together an internal task force to evaluate the operations of the Research and Development Center. At that time there was some talk of splitting up the center among GE's diverse business operations because it had become large and inefficient. This committee made several recommendations aimed at improving the laboratories responsiveness:

> "That the R & D center should continue to service the company and should not be split up among the businesses; that relevant exploratory work as opposed to development should be increased; and that the current method for funding the center needs re-examination." (Naj, 1990:1)

As a result of these recommendations, the R & D Center's funding changed. Now 25 percent comes from assessments and 75 percent must be sought from contracts from GE's internal businesses. Dr. Walter Robb, senior vice president of the center, said that such changes were a recognition that "GE's high-tech businesses have grown into multibillion dollar concerns that are now able to handle their own advanced engineering needs" (Robb, 1991:17). He also indicated that he was assigning a number of full-time liaison people from the central R & D Center to each of GE's major businesses who would spend 20 to 30 percent of their time as business representatives. In addition, the R & D Center cut 15 percent of its workforce and consolidated its operations.

The GE Research and Development Center has a project screening committee made up of the heads of each business, and they set the unit's priorities for the projects funded by assessment. The remaining central R & D Center research projects will be paid for by the specific businesses and thus undertaken at their request and under their specifications. Since that source of money could be used to fund projects at either the central R & D facility or at each of the business laboratories, projects are competitively funded.

Major new projects now being pursued by the R & D Center reflect these two diverse sources of funding. The R & D Center is pursuing long-term projects funded by assessments in artificial intelligence systems, parallel computer processing, and software development. They have developed a world-class effort in artificial systems—a technology which will ultimately affect all of GE's businesses. They have invented a new software tool called Gen-X which greatly simplifies the task of encoding expert systems, and they are exploring fifty applications within GE's businesses.

The central R & D Center is also pursuing specific projects for the various GE line businesses which the businesses fund. For GE Superabrasives, they are developing a revolutionary new way to make industrial diamonds. For GE Aircraft Engines, they are helping to pioneer a new method for making compressor and turbine rings. For GE Medical Systems, they are developing a clinical magnetic resonator. For GE Plastics, they are working on new composite plastics (Robb, 1991:21).

Coordination between GE's R & D and marketing units is obtained in two ways. *First,* each GE internal business has its own product development laboratory which is responsive to that business's market needs. *Second,* GE's central Research and Development Center depends for 75 percent of its funding on contracts from the various business divisions which will be given to it if and only if it can perform some research not doable by the divisions' own laboratories. Thus, financial incentives, or more precisely, the threat of a limited financial base creates a powerful motivational force for establishing the appropriate linkages for coordinating the marketing and R & D interface between specific businesses and the central R & D Center (GE R & D Center, 1991).

Critical Factors in the R & D and Marketing Interface

We began this chapter by exploring environmental assessment, product portfolio modeling, and structured innovation as essential tools for the R & D and marketing interface. Next we assessed five strategies guiding the R & D and marketing interface and found that only a Balanced Focus Strategy was effective. Then we explored the various coordination linkages essential in successfully carrying out such a Balanced Focus Strategy. Finally, we discussed two very successful examples of the R & D and marketing interface, one at the Matsushita Electric Company and one at General Electric, one motivated by an ingenious structural system of linkages and one motivated by the practical force of financial dependency. What then appear to be the critical factors governing the effective use of the R & D and marketing interface?

1. One must obtain precise and accurate information from appropriately employing environmental assessment, product portfolio modeling, and structured innovation.
2. One must pursue a balanced and focused coordination strategy.
3. One must establish the nineteen linkages essential for implementing an effective coordination strategy.
4. One must establish a structural and/or financial motivational system for motivating the successful use of the coordination system.

7

The R & D, Marketing, and Manufacturing Interface

Many companies have recently adapted programs of global manufacturing rationalization. Instead of multiproduct and multistage plants autonomously serving a national market on a local-for-local basis, it has become feasible and economically attractive to develop plants that manufacture only one product, or are involved in only a few stages of the production process, for the worldwide market. Firms that have embarked on such rationalization programs attempt to tap sources of efficiency through economies of scale and through capturing the comparative advantage of different countries.
(Mascarenhaus, 1984:91)

Coordinating a firm's primary and support activities has become a complex information and communication problem. This is due in part to each unit's need to be coordinated with all other units necessary for a given unit's effective functioning and in part because it raises the issue of which unit if any should occupy a controlling position in the coordination process. In recent years this latter issue has led to heated debate. A growing number of influential scholars have argued that Japan's phenomenal success as an international competitor has not been a result of culture nor a unique management system, but has been a result of a unique method for funding private sector economic development and Japan's tendency to allow manufacturing processes to exercise control over the coordination of R & D and marketing activities. No less a scholar of international competitiveness than Arno Penzias, the 1978 Nobel laureate physicist who runs one of the world's leading research institutes at AT&T's Bell Laboratories, made this claim in March of 1989 (Drucker, 1990:475). Why should manufacturing occupy such a central position in the coordination process? What effect does manufacturing have on R & D, marketing, and a firm's international competitive position? How do information technology and human communication processes fit into this coordination process? These and other questions can only be answered through a careful examination of the R & D, marketing, and manufacturing interface.

Our examination of this interface will be divided into four parts: (1) an examination of new manufacturing technologies; (2) an exploration of the strategies involved in effectively utilizing new manufacturing processes; (3) a discussion of the information and communication processes involved in coordinating the R & D, marketing, and manufacturing interface; and (4) a careful analysis of two examples of this interface in order to locate the critical factors governing the successful use of the coordination process.

The New Manufacturing Technologies

There are several important barriers to international rationalization. Host country interests, in their attempts to gain greater control over the environment, are increasingly trying to limit the autonomy of managerial decision making in multinational companies. Similarly geographic distances, differences in culture and time frames, varying local market conditions, the occurrence of particular situations arising in one subsidiary but not in others make international manufacturing integration difficult. In fact, many top executives feel that the major problem in conducting international business is how to coordinate and manage effectively the diversities inherent in international operations. Although many companies have adopted a global product division structure, it has been discovered that formal reorganizations in themselves do not guarantee effective integration of company resources. More attention should be paid to coordination processes used to achieve internal integration.
(Masarenhaus, 1984:92)

Manufacturing technologies management is more important to corporate success than most people realize. *First,* manufacturing systems typically represent the major share of a firm's human and financial assets. *Second,* manufacturing systems place upper parameters on product quality, complexity, and flexibility while determining productivity, required set-up time, work in progress, inventor needs, and machine utilization time. *Third,* manufacturing systems represent the largest time, financial, and personnel costs in increasing, decreasing, reorienting, or discontinuing products.

Four recent technological systems advances have created a revolution in manufacturing systems management: robots, integrated flexible systems, computer aided design and manufacturing, and computer-integrated manufacturing. These are high-speed management tools for manipulating manufacturing systems in order to provide a competitive advantage in product manufacturing (Jelinek and Goldhar, 1984).

Robots, which are small, inexpensive and flexible, are now available to manufacturers. A single such robot can be fitted with a variety of heads that enable it to perform a broad range of tasks such as picking up, repositioning, lubricating, drilling, welding, assembling, and painting. These robots have replaced very expensive, slow, and rigidly specific machines and very routine, boring, hazardous, and complex humanly performed tasks. More importantly, robots perform these tasks with speed, precision, and high quality control. A comparison of a conventional versus a robot production line within a Swedish household appliance firm indicates that the number of operators in a conventional line can be reduced from twenty-eight to six in a robot line; the floor space can be reduced from seventeen hundred meters to three hundred meters; the lead time for part design change from three or four weeks to four minutes; while investment costs increase from $450,000 to $850,000 (Jelinek and Goldhar, 1984). Savings of $900,000 were provided through shorter lead time, allowing the higher initial investment in the robot line to pay back its investment in one and a half years.

Many robots today are run by human laborers or function in conjunction with human laborers. Such coordination is a first step, but it limits production to human capacities. The next step beyond individual robots run by workers or in conjunction with workers is an integrated manufacturing system.

Integrated Flexible Systems (IFS) allow robots to work side by side with each other and with human beings to ensure maximum utilization of resources at lower costs by employing a computer to control material flow, operations, and sequencing of operations on a variety of products in order to optimize machine and personnel use. To be feasible for most industries, such systems must deal with frequent shifts from one product to another. Such systems normally consist of a group of machine tools integrated with materials handling systems, which perform a sequence of operations on a number of different products under computer control.

At Messerschmitt-Bolkow-Blohm in Augsburg, West Germany, a highly advanced flexible manufacturing system has been in full operation since 1980 to machine titanium and other materials into components for the Tornado fighter aircraft. Twenty-four machining stations fed by robot carts are controlled by one large computer that also manages the movement of tools, workpieces, and fixtures from machine to machine. The total system, which cost about $50 million, has reduced lead times by 26 percent, the number of machines by 44 percent, and overall annual costs by 24 percent. In productivity terms, the machines in this system are utilized 75 to 80 percent of the time, in contrast to typical stand-alone machines that are only utilized 15 to 30 percent of the time (Jelinek and Goldhar, 1984).

Computer-assisted design (CAD) and computer-aided manufacturing (CAM) systems represent a step beyond integrated manufacturing systems. Computer-assisted design allows an engineer on a monitoring screen to create and modify designs with a light pen. The computer can automatically provide alternative perspectives on the design and test the designs against performance and material criteria, as well as detect design flaws. When completed, the computer can print out multiple copies of the design plans. Since approximately 80 percent of the drafting work on projects normally consists in modifying designs, drafting productivity can be significantly increased. Computer-aided manufacturing allows for the generation of tapes from the design, which will guide numerically controlled production machines, order appropriate materials and parts, and set up production schedules with electronic speed and accuracy. General Motors used CAD/CAM to downsize the Cadillac Seville and design and produce their X car. Boeing used CAD/CAM to design and manufacture its 757 and 767 aircraft in one-third the time normally required (Mansfield, 1993).

Computer-integrated manufacturing systems (CIM) takes a giant step beyond robots, integrated flexible systems, computer-assisted design and computer-aided manufacturing. CIM is employed in controlling, sequencing, and optimizing a number of production processes with electronic speed and accuracy. CIM frequently achieves order-of-magnitude improvements in equipment utilization, personnel use, and capital productivity by integrating multiproduct manufacturing into a tight, responsive, and flexible coordination process. CIM encompasses everything in a plant from receiving a customer's order to shipping a finalized product. Elements of CIM include (CAD) computer-aided design; (CAM) computer-aided manufacturing; group technology (GT); computer-assisted planning processes (CAPP); material requirements planning (MRP); manufacturing resource planning (MRPI); automated storage and retrieval systems (ASIRS); database management systems (DBMS); office automation (OA); computer networks (CN); and expert systems (ES) capable of controlling the entire manufacturing process (Chen and Adams, 1991).

GE's large steam turbine generator plant in Schenectady employs CIM to routinely design turbines using computers to keep track of the 350,000 parts and their placement. Because the design constraints can be programmed, the engineer does not need to consciously keep track of them. GE's "blueprints," which are electronic, are automatically transmitted from engineering to materials procurement, to machine programming, and to the factory floor. There, shop loading and inventory scheduling and variances are automatically monitored, freeing supervisors to solve problems instead of tracking clerical work (Jelinek and Goldhar, 1984).

CIM is faster, more reliable, more accurate, and more predictable than nonautomated manufacturing processes, increases, decreases, modifications, and discontinuances of product lines involve lower material, inventory, production, and delivery costs in automated systems. The cycle time through the manufacturing process tends to be shorter and more manipulable. A continuous-flow manufacturing stands for minimization of waste, the reduction of time to flow the parts from launch to delivery to the customer (Feigenbaum, McCorduck, and Nii, 1988:55). Finally, at IBM's Burlington chip fabrication plant, a new expert system called the Logistic Management System or LMS is embedded in each of the computer-integrated manufacturing activities throughout the entire plant, automatically controlling the entire manufacturing process. LMS is viewed as a new kind of automated system.

> It's a community intelligence, born from the collective wisdom of various disciplines, experiences, and points of view, which dynamically disseminates the new intelligence around the same community that engendered it, solving problems that are "too tough for us humans to figure out." Burlington's LMS regulated the complex manufacturing tasks of an entire plant. It automatically picks up data and using the knowledge that has been given to it by scores of human experts, it reasons so thoroughly about manufacturing production, and makes corrections and changes

based on that reasoning so quickly, no individual or group of individuals can match its performance. (Feigenbaum, McCorduck, and Nii, 1988:63–64)

Organizations recognize that this increase in the speed with which a firm can respond to change and the decrease in cost of such a response can become an important source of competitive advantage. If a framework for understanding manufacturing technology as a driving force in corporate strategy can be developed and if an effective framework for coordinating the R & D, marketing, and manufacturing interface can be developed which preserves and/or increases the competitive advantage stemming from advances in manufacturing technologies, then new levels of corporate functioning and profitability appear achievable.

The Strategies Involved in Effectively Utilizing New Manufacturing Processes

The name of the game in manufacturing has become, not simply quality or low cost, but flexibility—the quest to give the customer his or her own personalized design, but with the cheapness and availability of mass-produced items. . . . In short, nothing less than a whole new style of manufacturing is in the process of being defined. As firms seek to add extra value by customizing their products, while managing somehow still to make them at affordable prices, the concept of "economy of scale" is being transformed into an idea best expressed as "economy of variety."
(*The Economist*, 1994:6)

The search for competitive advantage in a firm's manufacturing activities requires a careful analysis of a firm's market potential, competitive position, R & D capabilities, and manufacturing flexibility. Five strategies have emerged to guide a firm's focus in seeking competitive advantage: economies of sourcing, scale, focus, scope, and time. Each of these strategies may be used singly or in combination to achieve a *sustainable competitive advantage*. Let us explore each strategy in turn (Hayes and Pisano, 1994:78).

Economies of Sourcing

Competitive advantage can flow from economies of sourcing inputs into the manufacturing process. In recent years, the price of raw materials has remained relatively constant throughout the world, while the price of labor and money has been variable. For example, the cost of skilled labor in South Korea, Singapore, and Taiwan has remained low relative to the industrialized nations of the world. The cost of borrowing money in Japan and Korea has been low relative to the rest of the world. Many firms have attempted to capitalize on these economies of sourcing by manufacturing all or part of their products in these nations in order to obtain a competitive advantage. A firm's primary concern in regard to economies of sourcing has to be the projected stability of these labor and borrowing costs over time (Wheelwright and Hayes, 1985).

For example, the Hyundai Corporation manufactures cars in South Korea where they employ workers who perform the same tasks as their American counterparts at wages which are 70 percent lower per hour. In addition, the Hyundai Corporation is able to borrow money in Korea at an interest rate 40 percent less than their counterparts in America (*The Economist*, 1994:16). The net result is that Hyundai can manufacture a car for considerably less than their American counterparts, creating a low-price comparative advantage from economies of sourcing. However, labor costs in Korea are increasing at a rate 20 percent faster than in America, suggesting an erosion of competitive advantage over time.

Economies of Scale

Competitive advantage can follow from economies of scale—greater production volume is more economical in per unit cost than lesser production because the special purpose equipment which is justified by large-scale production can be amortized over a larger number of units. Scale-related costs decline as volume increases, falling 15 percent to 25 percent each time volume doubles. Normally such machines are faster, more accurate, and perform at higher quality levels than their human counterparts. Such machines are also more expensive and less flexible than human workers, thus requiring much larger runs of standardized products to offset their cost. A firm's primary concern in regard to economies of scale is market saturation and/or rapid product change based on innovation (McGrath and Hode, 1992).

For example, the Gillette Corporation employs economies of scale in manufacturing razor blades. Razor blades are limited in design, standardized, and disposable, creating a steady demand for the product over a long period of time. Razor blades are an ideal product for mass-producing machines that can achieve economies of scale. However, when product lines change, the old blade must be discontinued to make room for the new blade. Set-up time for retooling a machine is long, reducing the productivity of the equipment and requiring an increase in inventory as the old blade must be stored during the changeover in product lines. Gillette has experienced a small but continued growth in razor blade usage and has not experienced competition based on technological innovation.

Economies of Focus

Competitive advantage can follow from economies of focus when mass production techniques which achieve economies of scale are combined with a narrow product focus in a large and rapidly expanding market. "Factory costs are very sensitive to the variety of goods a plant produces. Reductions in product variety by half raises productivity by 30 percent, cuts costs 17 percent and substantially lowers the breakeven point. Cutting the product line in half again boosts productivity by 75 percent, slashes costs 30 percent, and drops the breakeven point below 50 percent" (Stalk, 1988:43). Economies of scale when combined with a highly focused, large and expanding market are very profitable. A firm's primary concerns in regard to economies of focus are market saturation and product line shift based on innovation, or a market demand for a broader range of products.

For example, the Japanese in the 1960s entered the ball bearing industry where competition was intense. The Japanese fielded product lines with one-half to one-fourth the variety of their competitors but which focused on the high-volume segment of the bearing industry—automobile applications. The Japanese used the low cost of their highly productive focused factories to undercut the price of Western competitors in capturing these markets (Stalk, 1988:43). The Japanese still exert control over this global market segment.

Economies of Scope

Competitive advantage based on economies of scope exists where multiple products can be more cheaply produced in combination than alone. In economies of scale, specialized equipment has the product *programmed into its hardware.* In economies of scope, the product is *programmed into computer software,* allowing many uses for the same equipment. Jelinek and Goldhar (1983:29) point out:

A computer-controlled machine tool does not "care" whether it works on a dozen units in succession of the same design or a dozen different product designs in random sequence. The change over time is almost negligible, since it involves simply reading a computer program. The machine "sets up" for each new design with electronic speed.

These new machines offer more than replicable accuracy and quality, they offer programmed flexibility. Economies of scope allow for custom-tailored products, just-in-time inventory, amortizations of factory costs over a variety of products, and greater knowledge of manufacturing processes. A firm's primary concerns in regard to economies of scale are a standardization in market taste, lack of knowledge regarding manufacturing, and lack of information technology software.

For example, Honda manufactures motorcycles employing economies of scope. In the late 1970s a Honda-Yamaha price war broke out over motorcycles. Both companies began the price war with sixty models. Honda opened a new flexible manufacturing plant and in the next eighteen months introduced 113 new models, effectively turning over its entire product line while developing custom-made models. Honda's new product scope devastated Yamaha in the marketplace while remaining price competitive (Stalk, 1988:45). Honda's change in manufacturing strategy had severely disrupted its own distribution and sales networks, which then required a change in coordination. Very simply, a flexible factory enjoys more variety with lower total cost than traditional factories, which must make a trade-off between economies of scope and scale.

Economies of Time

Competitive advantage based on economies of time exists when flexible manufacturing systems and rapid response systems expand variety and increase the frequency of innovation in a high-growth market. Economies of speed require that managers establish tight integration, coordination, and control processes within manufacturing activities and among R & D, marketing, and manufacturing in order to achieve a rapid response system. Stalk (1988:45) argues:

> Today's new-generation companies compete with flexible manufacturing and rapid-response systems, expanding variety and increasing innovation. A company that builds its strategy on this cycle is a more powerful competitor than one with a

traditional strategy based on low wages, scale, or focus. These older, cost-based strategies require managers to do whatever is necessary to drive down costs: move production to or source from a low-wage country; build new facilities or consolidate old plants to gain economies of scale; or focus operations down to the most economic subset of activities. These tactics reduce costs but at the expense of responsiveness.

In contrast, strategies based on the cycle of flexible manufacturing, rapid response, expanding variety, and increasing innovation are time based. Factories are close to the customers they serve. Organization structures enable fast responses rather than low costs and control. Companies concentrate on reducing if not eliminating the delays and using their response advantages to attract the most profitable customers.

Most manufacturing activities can be divided into three stages: the assembly stage, the subassembly stage and the components stage. In general at each stage there is a separate set of factories and businesses. Time-managed production must design products so speed of response can be achieved at each stage. CIM is required to tie all stages together into a rapid response system. This requires precise integration, coordination, and control. Flexible factories with tight integration, coordination, and control enjoy a big advantage in both productivity and time: "labor productivity in time based factories can be as much as 200% higher than in conventional plants; time based factories can respond eight to ten times faster than conventional factories" (Stalk, 1988:48).

Time-based manufacturing strategies vary along three important dimensions: length of product runs, organization of factory processes, and simplicity of scheduling procedures. Production runs tend to be short, frequently in lots of one. Two reasons motivate such small product runs. *First,* it is easier and faster to manufacture a product than to hold extras and place them in inventory. *Second,* flexible manufacturing seeks comparative advantage from product scope. The more often production changes, the greater the speed and variety of products available. Factory manufacturing processes are organized for both variety and continuous-flow production. Such a production sequence attempts to minimize time between operations in order to speed production, eliminating the need for parts inventory. Product scheduling is simple, frequently based on real-time merchandising. Orders for replacement products come from retail outlets at the end of each day. Materials are ordered during the night, the product is made the next morning and shipped that afternoon, appearing at the retail outlet later that day or the next day. A firm's primary concern in regard to economies of time is a breakdown in organizational integration, coordination, and control systems and/or a lack of market growth.

For example, Toyota was dissatisfied with the response time of one of its components suppliers. The supplier took fifteen days to produce a component after the arrival of the raw materials at the factory. Toyota sent its own engineers to the suppliers to help study and redesign the production process from a rapid response systems perspective. Toyota engineers cut lot size at the factory, reducing inventory and response time from fifteen days to six days. Next, they streamlined the factory floor organization and cut the number of inventory holding points, reducing response time from six to three days. Finally, Toyota engineers eliminated work-in-progress inventory, reducing response time from three days to one day. Installing a rapid response system in a supplier of components reduced Toyota's response time from fifteen days down to one day. This in turn made Toyota's subassembly and assembly processes more rapid and effective (Stalk, 1988:48). Increased effectiveness in coordination led to a decrease in rapid response time.

Economies of sourcing, scale, focus, scope, and time represent progressive increases in manufacturing variety and responsiveness to customer needs. Each of these economies in turn can become the source of competitive advantage. The combination of economies of scope or product variety and economies of time or speed of response is at the core of the linkage among manufacturing, high-speed management, and sustainable competitive advantage.

Coordinating the R & D, Marketing, and Manufacturing Interface

Because time flows throughout the system, focusing on time based competitive performance results in improvements across the board. Companies generally become time based competitors by first correcting their manufacturing techniques, then fixing sales and distribution, and finally adjusting their approach to innovation. Ultimately, it becomes the basis for a company's overall strategy.
(Stalk, 1988:47)

Coordination in manufacturing proceeds at three levels: within subunits, between similar units which are geographically separate, and between manufacturing and other units such as marketing and

R & D. Coordination in each case is premised on combining economies of scope and economies of time or the use of high-speed management to obtain a sustainable competitive advantage.

Subunit Coordination

Manufacturing includes three stages of subunit coordination: assembly, subassembly, and components. Economies of scope and time
affect each stage of production in different ways, so the failure to
establish effective coordination within and between each stage has
different costs. At the *assembly stage* it may or may not be a good
idea to invest heavily in CIM. The decision rests upon the frequency
of major product design changes and the length of the product life
cycle. According to Kempe and Bolwijn (1988:77), "managers still
cannot buy robots that are both flexible and inexpensive enough to
handle major design changes in end products, whose life cycles are
inherently short." If major design changes are frequent within a two-
year product life cycle or a product's life cycle drops below a year, it
normally is more cost effective in such cases for assembly processes
to be handled by self-managed or social-technical work teams. Such
work teams are more flexible than most machines, and workers if
properly trained and motivated can produce a high quality product.
  Kempe and Bolwijn (1988:77–78) elaborate:

> The key flexibility for assemblers in the longer run is the
> setup time required to move from one generation of products to
> the next. When delivering products quickly and reacting to chang-
> ing market demands by shortening product cycles, economies of
> scale are, of course, not worth pursuing. More important efficien-
> cies can be gained from reductions in work-in-progress invento-
> ries, stock inventories, through-put time, and transportation costs.
>   These considerations make it more attractive than ever to
> set up assembly factories close to end markets. They make the
> introduction of just-in-time operations necessary. As a matter of
> fact, industrial corporations add value (and realize high profit
> margins) less by refining the process of assembly than by mar-
> keting aggressively, distributing shrewdly, and backing up their
> retail customers with fast delivery, satisfactory service, and ap-
> pealing design.

The central problem in coordinating the assembly of a product is
flexibility, and the most flexible assembly system is the use of rather
simple machines, with people the most flexible of beings.

Most reductions in cost and improvements in quality in the last five years have come from the adoption of CIM by *subassembly* and *components manufacturing* processes. In all such cases products are redesigned so that fewer parts can be employed in a larger range of products, creating both simplicity and flexibility. At Philips, the world's largest manufacturer of compact disc players, they have reduced the number of subassemblies by 75 percent. IBM's manufacturing of proprinters not only reduced the number of subassemblies required by one-third but developed parts which snap together, allowing rapid CIM subassembly. Such a reduction in the number of subassemblies and snap together parts reduced the subassembly production time on Philips CTV from twelve and one-half hours in 1969 to sixty minutes in 1988 (Kempe and Bolwijn, 1988:79).

While the use of CIM equipment for assembly is expensive and, relatively speaking, inflexible, the use of CIM equipment for components involves smaller, less complex, more user-friendly, and much less expensive automated systems. CIM use at the components level was widespread, leading to very high-quality and low-cost parts. CIM components technologies have gone from high precision machines to ultra-high precision machines. They have progressed from micron to submicron technology and from plastic or metal parts to integrated plastic and metal parts.

Thus the degree of coordination within subunits between human beings and machines varies by stages, with the assembly stage containing more of a balance between man and machine and the subassembly and components stages being machine dominated.

Interunit Coordination

Coordination between manufacturing units situated in geographically distant locations has become an important, complex, and sophisticated process. Parthasarthy and Sethi (1993:532) undertook a careful study of several multinationals in various industries and found a significant cost savings from interunit coordination in several areas.

Manufacturing Support Activities
- Procurement
- Aggregate production planning
- Daily production planning and expediting
- Quality assurance
- Employee management and development
- Manufacturing engineering

Technology Support Activities
- Product design and improvement
- Process design and improvement
- New product and process introduction

In each area *within-function teams* were established to share information, discuss common problems, and develop workable solutions to problems. These within-function team meetings led to locating more cost-efficient vendors and establishing more effective materials flow, more efficient production planning and scheduling, and so on. In short, advances made in one plant diffused more rapidly to other plants, creating significant cost savings for the entire system.

Between-Unit Coordination with Marketing

At the heart of high-speed management is the relationship between marketing and manufacturing. Traditional manufacturing plants require a long lead time in order to obtain materials, resolve the conflicts between different equipment needs, schedule materials, and manufacture, assemble, ship, store, and sell a product. The long lead time in turn requires sales forecasts to guide planning. However, the longer the lead time required, the greater the error in the sales forecast. Such errors frequently lead to a balloon in inventory and/or a shortfall in the availability of the hottest selling products. This in turn leads to increased inventory cost and/or a loss of sales.

In 1970 Toyota could manufacture a car in two days. However, it took fifteen to twenty-six days for Toyota Sales to transmit the order to the factory, get the order schedule, ship the car, and deliver it to the customer. The sales and distribution function was generating 20 to 30 percent of the cost of a car. By 1988, Toyota had introduced real-time manufacturing, merchandising, and marketing, cutting product manufacture and delivery time to eight days and cutting product costs by 30 percent per unit. Better coordination between manufacturing and marketing made this difference (Stalk, 1988:49).

Between-Unit Coordination with R & D

A corporate strategy that allows firms to bring out new products three times faster than its competitors will enjoy a sustainable competitive advantage. Time-based coordination between R & D and manufacturing, according to Stalk (1988), provides just such an advantage. To achieve such a competitive advantage, time-based organizations have introduced a series of very specific coordination linkages (Messina and Tricomi, 1990).

First, time-based R & D-manufacturing linkages favor smaller, more frequent increments of improvement in existing products. This allows for incremental reprogramming of existing technology and rapid product evolution. *Second,* time-based R & D-manufacturing linkages use cross-functional teams in product development. This allows incremental change in products to be adjusted to manufacturing, marketing, and R & D requirements at the design phase, yielding more rapid and flexible manufacturing, marketing, and product improvement. *Third,* time-based R & D-manufacturing linkages schedule work based on local responsibility in setting and meeting deadlines. This allows for decentralization in planning and an increase in creativity (Stalk, 1988:49).

The effect of these time-based linkages is that the firms employing them have decreased the time required to produce an innovative change by as much as 300 percent. Mitsubishi Electric's residential air conditioner division introduced eleven incremental changes in its product between 1975 and 1985. These changes led to the total transformation of the product, decreasing cost and increasing reliability, quality, and serviceability. Mitsubishi's competitors by 1983 were only beginning to consider implementing changes over the next several years which would allow them to produce a similar product (Stalk, 1988:50).

Time-based comparative advantage in manufacturing requires close coordination in subunit, interunit, and between-unit activities to achieve a sustainable competitive advantage. *However, when such coordination is present, order-of-magnitude improvements occur in product cost, quality, and value as well as increased responsiveness to consumer taste.*

Two Examples of the Manufacturing, R & D, and Marketing Interface Aimed at Locating Critical Factors

By reducing time in every aspect of the business, these companies also reduce cost, improve quality and stay close to their customers.
(Stalk, 1988:46)

Attention is now directed to examining the manufacturing, R & D, and marketing interface in two firms—the Allen-Bradley Corporation and The Limited Company—in order to locate the critical factors governing this interface.

The Allen-Bradley Corporation

Gcnc Bylinsky (1986:64) visited the Allen-Bradley factory in Milwaukee, Wisconsin, and wrote the following report:

> It is 7:30 A.M. on the eighth floor of an 80-year-old Allen-Bradley Inc. building on Milwaukee's South Side. Two-and-a-half hours ago, an IBM mainframe computer at the company's nearby headquarters relayed yesterday's orders to a master scheduling computer. Now, at the scheduling computer's command, what may be the world's most advanced assembly line comes to life with pneumatic sighs and bird-like whistles. Lights flash. Without human intervention, plastic casings the size of pocket transistor radios start marching through 26 complex automated assembly stations.
>
> Bar code labels, computer-printed on the spot and pasted on each plastic casing by a mechanical arm, tell each station which of nearly 200 different parts to install in what combination. As the casings move along a conveyor belt, tiny mechanical fingers insert springs, another mechanical arm places covers over the casings, and automatic screwdrivers tighten the screws. At the end of the line a laser printer zaps detailed product information onto the side of each finished plastic box. The boxes arc then packaged, sorted into customer orders, and shunted into chutes ready for shipment—all automatically. The four technicians who stand by to unclog jams are rarely needed. Elapsed time per box from start to finish: 45 minutes.

Allen-Bradley produces contractors and relays that serve as electromechanical starters and controllers for electric motors. In April 1985 Allen-Bradley achieved a milestone in the development of computer-integrated manufacturing. Their assembly line can make lots as small as one or as large as six hundred at the same per unit cost. Currently, no other assembly line in the world can do that. Executives invested $15 million to develop and mount this line. A team of thirty engineers, technicians, accountants, and other specialists designed and built the line. Allen-Bradley built 60 percent of the machinery themselves with the remainder coming from outside suppliers. The engineers employed different bar codes to identify various contractors and relays, to track inventory, and to tell each machine on the assembly line what operations to perform. These bar codes allow the firm to make products in two sizes with 999 possible combinations of parts. Computer-controlled sensors perform 3,500 automatic inspection steps, helping to ensure quality control. "A laser gauge measures surfaces to keep them within toler-ances as small as one-sixth the diameter of a human hair" (Bylinsky, 1986:66).

This high-speed production system allows Allen-Bradley to main-tain zero inventory for its own components. It costs Allen-Bradley $6.42 to manufacture a product that sells for between $8.00 and $22.00 throughout the world, depending on what the market will sustain. While this firm was a latecomer to the market, it now holds a dominant share of the world's sales, achieving a sustainable com-petitive advantage over its competitors from economies of scope and time manufacturing.

The Limited Company

The Limited Company is a major manufacturer of women's apparel throughout the world. Each evening the store managers in 3,200 stores across the United States collect data regarding sales for that day—size, color, fashion number, and so on—through their elec-tronic point of sale computer system (EPOS). The cutting order in-formation is telecommunicated to The Limited's workshops in Hong Kong, Singapore, and Sri Lanka, and is translated into next-day manu-facturing orders. Within days these just-in-time inventory replace-ments are shipped to The Limited's Ohio distribution center on a Boeing 747 (Hochswender, 1990:5).

In addition to supplying replacement merchandise in a timely fashion, The Limited EPOS system can be used to monitor market-ing. It can track fashion design performance, pinpointing age groups, income level, and geographic locations where specific fashion de-signs sell well. Ultimately, EPOS could be used for ordering custom-ized designs by color, size, cut, and style with less than one week turnaround on delivery of orders. In the use of electronic point of sale merchandising for customized design, computer-integrated manufacturing for production, and just-in-time product delivery for marketing we see R & D, marketing, and manufacturing fused into a flexible, high-speed, reciprocally coordinated interface system.

The Critical Factors Governing the Manufacturing, R & D, and Marketing Interface

We began our analysis by exploring the basic tools central to the new manufacturing technology: robots, integrated flexible systems, computer-aided design and manufacturing, and computer-integrated manufacturing. Next we explored the basic strategies for achieving competitive advantage through manufacturing in economies of sourcing, scale, focus, scope, and time. Then we examined the coordination patterns involved in achieving economies of scope or flexibility and economies of time or rapid response systems by exploring subunit coordination in assembly, subassembly, and components; interunit coordination between geographically separate manufacturing units in regard to procurement, aggregate production planning, daily product planning, quality assurance, and so on; and between-unit coordination with manufacturing, marketing, and R & D. Finally, we examined two examples of the manufacturing, R & D, and marketing interface in the Allen-Bradley Corporation and The Limited Company, where we observed the functioning of the unique coordination systems involved in a flexible rapid response system.

We are now in a position to locate the critical factors central to an effective manufacturing, R & D, and marketing interface.

1. Manufacturing must be guided by the appropriate selection of a competitive advantage strategy. Today that strategy appears to be economies of scope and time, or flexible manufacturing and quick response systems.
2. Given an organization's product line, R & D, and marketing, the tools of the new manufacturing technologies must be ordered to achieve economies of scope and time.
3. Appropriate coordination systems must be established for subunit, interunit and between-unit functioning.
4. These coordination systems must continually be adapted to maintain and/or increase economies of scope and rapid response time.

"Superior overall manufacturing capability" is dependent upon a number of factors: (1) the coordination of human beings within the organization; (2) the coordination of units and subunits; (3) the coordination of manufacturing technologies; and (4) the coordination of planning and implementation of the administrative system.

Having explored in some detail coordination systems involved in the R & D and marketing interface and the manufacturing, R & D, and marketing interface, we are now in a position to explore the coordination systems involved in the R & D, marketing, manufacturing, and management information system interface.

8

The R & D, Marketing, Manufacturing, and Management Information System Interface

To work effectively in an organization requires an understanding of how the organization functions. An important way to achieve this understanding is by analyzing the organization's information flows, which requires an examination of its structures and activities and of the style of its managers.
(Scott, 1986:3)

A management information system, or MIS, has as its central responsibility the effective design, implementation, and use of computer systems within organizations. The management of MIS processes is a complex, diverse, pervasive, and rapidly changing activity. *First,* information management requires a working knowledge of various end-user environments, an organization's worldwide clustering of activities, the various power distributions within an organization, and an organization's environmental scanning activities. *Second,* information management requires a working knowledge of various types of computers; various networking and telecommunication technologies; various office, R & D, supplier, production, distribution, marketing, sales, and service technologies; and the computer languages, software programs, and artificial intelligence systems needed to support these activities. *Third,* information management requires knowledge of an organization's strategic planning and budgeting processes; its integration, coordination, and control processes; and its information technology vision and implementation and upgrading plan. In short, MIS management is too vast a job for one person; it requires an MIS team. It will be the purpose of this chapter to observe how an information management team functions by exploring the R & D, marketing, manufacturing, and MIS interface (Parker and Benson, 1987).

Our examination of this interface will be divided into four parts: (1) an exploration of the resources available for managing an organization's information system; (2) an investigation of the strategies available for effectively deploying these resources; (3) a discussion of the information and communication processes involved in coordinating the R & D, marketing, manufacturing, and MIS interface; and (4) a careful analysis of this interface in order to locate the critical factors governing the successful use of this coordination process.

The Resources Available for Managing Information Systems

The basic function of administration appears to be coalignment, not merely of people in coalition, but of institutionalized action—of technology and task environments into a viable domain, and of organizational design and structure appropriate to it. Administration, when it works well, keeps the organization at the nexus of several necessary streams of action.
(Zmud, Boynton, and Jacobs, 1986:17)

The primary resources available to assist in managing an organization's information system consist of the knowledge available to specific members of the information management team in regard to the current and future developments taking place in information technology and the specific current and future information needs of the organization. An information systems management team may vary in size from several to thousands depending upon an organization's size and MIS needs. Most Fortune 500 corporations consist of several hundred people distributed into a central headquarters staff and an MIS staff located in each functional division. Each staff normally includes an MIS director in charge of planning and budgeting; a database manager in charge of constructing and maintaining the unit's database; a telecommunications manager in charge of audio, visual, and data networking; an applications design and programming manager for each major organizational information process; and a systems support manager in charge of word processing, artificial intelligence, and decision support systems (Magnet, 1992); see figure 8.1.

Figure 8.1 **MIS ORGANIZATION CHART FOR A MEDIUM-SIZED BUSINESS**

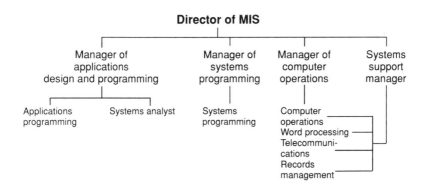

While it is not possible in this chapter to explore in detail the resources available from each member of the information management team, we will explore briefly the central issues confronted by database managers, telecommunication managers, and the applications programming and design managers.

Database Management

A database is a centrally maintained collection of interrelated and integrated records and other data items. A database that is distributed involves a central control database at corporate headquarters and operational databases located in each functional and/or small business unit. On a practical level a database consists of

- a database file;
- a database access;
- a security and operations system;
- a host language interface system;
- a natural language interface system;
- a data dictionary;
- an on-line access and update terminal;
- an output system or report generator.

The primary purpose of a database is to provide information for a variety of managerial purposes as well as organizational needs at the operations level. The most important factors influencing database *use* are accessibility, response time, and accuracy. It is the database manager's job to understand an organization's or unit's functioning in sufficient detail to construct and maintain a database which is easily accessible, has a quick response time, with high accuracy. Central to fulfilling this task is the appropriate development of a database file structure or logic. Currently four such logics are in use, each with different advantages and disadvantages. These include an inverted list logic, a hierarchical or tree logic, a network logic, and a relational logic (Charon, 1991:10–57).

The organization of a database logic includes the definition of each item and the definition of all relationships between and among data items. Central to the use of most database logics are *pointers*. A pointer is a special data item in a record that indicates which records to access next.

An *inverted list logic* maintains information in sequential order and, in addition, indexes that information with several smaller lists. Each list serves as a pointer in accessing the file. For example, a personnel record may sequentially report an employee's name, address, date of birth, sex, past experience, skills, etc. One pointer list may index the record by past experiences, another pointer list may index the employee's skills, etc. An inverted list logic accelerates file search and report construction through the use of topic-relevant lists.

A *hierarchical or tree logic* maintains information in sequential order based on hierarchical ordering. A pointer at the end of each level in the hierarchy refers the search to the next level. A problem with hierarchical or tree logic is that its schema cannot be easily altered once the original record structure is established.

A *network logic* maintains information sequentially but employs pointers to manifest the relationships of units to all other units. Whereas tree logics permit records to have only one relationship, a network logic allows each record to have multiple linkages. As the number of records increases arithmetically, the number of possible relationships increases geometrically; thus as a practical matter such structures require large capacity and may become cumbersome.

A *relational logic* differs from the inverted list, tree, and network logics in that there are no predefined data access pathways through the use of pointers. Instead, the file is in table form and associations between records are made on the basis of column or row intersects in the array. Relational databases require extensive computer processing because every search for data necessitates searching the entire database.

Easy access, rapid response, and high accuracy may require several decentralized databases, each based on a different logic. Payroll may want a relational logic; personnel an inverted list logic; manufacturing a hierarchical or tree logic; distribution and sales a network logic in order to have easy access, rapid response, and accurate records.

Telecommunications Management

Telecommunications is the interactive transmission of information at a distance in the form of signals (visual, voice, and/or data). A telecommunication system may employ one or more types of networks to transmit information. Information may be sent within a facility by local area networks (LAN) or private branch exchanges (PBX) and sent to other facilities via satellite, leased lines, or public facilities of local exchange carriers, long-distance carriers, and value-added network suppliers.

Telecommunications management is concerned with establishing, maintaining, and upgrading information flow in order to meet an organization's management and operations needs. Telecommunications management covers several functions: problem management, change management, configuration management, and performance and accounting management (Rose and Munn, 1988).

Problem management involves determination, diagnosis, bypass and recovery, resolution, and tracking and control. *Change management* involves the planning, control, and application of change to the organization's networks. *Configuration management* involves the planning, development, and operation of information systems capable of establishing necessary linkages between and within units. *Performance and accounting management* involves the process of quantifying, measuring, reporting, and controlling the usage, responsiveness, availability, and cost of networks.

Currently telecommunication managers are attempting to establish an open systems interconnect (OSI) for setting common standards in network products. OSI is in its early stages of development, but as time passes OSI promises the evolution of a common network architecture capable of total network integration. The integration, coordination, and control of the organizational processes necessary for high-speed management rests in the final analysis on establishing OSI (Rose and Munn, 1988).

Applications Programming and Design Management

Organizations are generally divided into a number of functional activities, such as R & D, marketing, and manufacturing. Computer applications and design are often similarly divided. A marketing information system, for example, supports the operations of the marketing department. Databases in other departments such as R & D and manufacturing must be drawn upon in order to support the effective operations of the marketing information system.

Applications programming and design managers must determine the most effective way to draw upon the organization's various databases and networks and what equipment and software are required in order to provide information and communication support for a given unit. For example, the major marketing information subsystems in a medium-sized organization include the following (Scott, 1986:413–414):

1. The sales information system:
   a. sales support
   b. sales analysis
   c. customer analysis
2. The marketing research and intelligence information systems:
   a. customer research
   b. market research
   c. competitor intelligence
3. The promotion and advertising information systems
4. The new product development system
5. The sales forecasting information system
6. The product planning information system
7. The product pricing information system
8. The expenditure control system

The overall objective of this integrated set of marketing subsystems is to improve the ability of marketing managers to:

- identity and evaluate profitable sales opportunities
- react rapidly to changes in market conditions
- establish profit-maximizing product prices
- control marketing costs
- deploy sales personnel effectively
- assist in allocating expenditures for marketing and funding
- integrate, coordinate, and control rapid response systems

Database managers, telecommunications managers, and applications and design managers are three important members of the

MIS management team. Their knowledge of information technologies and the organization's essential functions is the chief resource available to the MIS unit.

The MIS Strategies Available for Effectively Deploying an Organization's Information Resources

The field of Management Information Systems (MIS) has as its central concern the effective design, implementation, and use of computer-based systems in organizations. Recent research in MIS seeks to identify criteria by which effectiveness in systems design can be measured and to prescribe developments which lead to systems effectiveness.
(Markus and Robey, 1983:203)

Most organization information systems have developed in a piecemeal fashion. However, a point comes when the use of information technology in one area must be integrated and coordinated with another area. At that point the top MIS manager must consider how to evaluate overall MIS performance and develop a corporate MIS strategy. These validity and strategic issues are the chief concern of the organization's MIS management.

Evaluating Organizational MIS Performance

The validity of an information system rests on selecting an appropriate overall strategy for systems design, a strategy which will generate an appropriate fit between an organization's information systems and its organizational context of use. Four types of MIS fit can be employed to evaluate the appropriateness of the strategies being employed: user system fit, organization structure fit, power distribution fit, and environment fit (Markus and Robey, 1983).

User-system fit can be obtained in several ways. One can design the MIS system to fit the existing users, train users to fit the MIS system, or select new personnel to fit an MIS system. The relationship among a user's cognitive styles, the organization's corporate values, and MIS systems design is central to the effective development of user fit.

Organization structure-system fit can be obtained by understanding an organization's geographic dispersion of functions and the linking activities required between them. This relationship will reveal the degree of centralization, decentralization, or distributed structure to which the MIS system must be responsive in order to be effective.

Power distribution-system fit can be obtained by understanding the status and span of control issues involved in each of an organization's management positions. These issues govern from a power perspective who needs to know about organizational activities and thus how networks, message flow, and database information need to be routed and distributed.

Environment-system fit can be obtained by understanding the necessary environmental scanning activities of an organization. Monitoring one's industry, competitors, customers, investors, government regulators, potential acquisitions, and sources of raw materials requires a complex and interdependent environmental search.

MIS Organizational Strategy

Integrating the different demands of each of these validity sources for effective MIS functioning is at the heart of MIS management. Six basic strategies exist for integrating an MIS system: business systems planning, critical success factors, an applications portfolio, a stages approach, a value chain approach, and a high-speed management approach. Each of these may be used alone or in combination as a strategy for achieving MIS-organizational fit.

Business systems planning (BSP) is an MIS strategy developed in the 1970s by IBM for its own use and then made available to clients. The objective of BSP is to develop an understanding of all the data operations and flow which take place within a firm, so that the origins, use, and flow of information can be mapped onto the firm's organizational chart. The map is then simplified, rationalized, integrated, condensed, and controlled. Decisions then can be made regarding hardware, software, and expansion. BSP is a bottom-up strategy to MIS planning. It allows for the evolution of MIS development. However, it does not easily provide for overall organizational priorities, nor does it link an organization well with its outside environments.

Assessing *critical success factors (CSFs)* is an MIS strategy which tries to confront directly the link between corporate strategy and information strategy. It does so by asking top managers to specify their critical responsibilities and the data and equipment needed to perform those responsibilities in the most efficient way. These requirements then serve as necessary outputs for the MIS system. Matters of data availability, speed of reporting, networking, equipment, and reporting format are made explicit. By beginning with the question "what do general messages need?" rather than "how do data currently flow in the organization?," the CSF's approach attempts to build institutional linkages between corporate strategy and MIS strategy.

The applications portfolio (AP) is an MIS strategy which attempts to create a coordination system among existing organizational applications. It does so by creating a pyramid diagram of all functions carried out by the firm and indicating where information technologies applications are currently used. The advantage of this approach is that in a decentralized firm, the MIS head can keep track of the spread of MIS throughout the organization and influence its developments, improve its networking, and develop a central database to monitor decentralized purchasing.

The stages approach (SA) is an MIS strategy based on the assumption that most companies exhibit a relatively consistent planning and budgeting policy for MIS development. The stages involved in planning and budgeting are: (a) initiation, where data processing is introduced into the company; (b) contagion, where spending grows and many departments are clamoring for equipment; (c) control, when a central MIS order is imposed on the spread of data processing; (d) maturity, when MIS spending flattens out and grows in proportion to other expenditures in the firm; and (e) evaluations, the consistent monitoring of the system to improve integration, coordination, and control. The appeal of the SA approach is that it raises new questions at each stage of MIS development.

The value chain approach (VA) is an MIS strategy that uses a diagram of the corporation's value chain or how the flow of imports the firm buys is turned into finished outputs or products for customers. Then one explores the use of MIS at each stage of the value chain to isolate the need for new technologies, eliminate bottlenecks, and improve organizational integration, coordination, and control. The VA strategy has the great merit of focusing on the organization's needs rather than information technology availability.

The high-speed management approach (HSMA) is an MIS strategy based on using information technology to reduce the time required to produce a product in each stage of the value chain in order to get products to the consumer fast. Each operation in each stage of the value chain and each link between operations is examined for the possible adaptation of information technology to speed up the process. MIS units also have their own environmental scanning unit for new technology and an advocacy unit for selling new technology applications to various organizational units. This HSMA strategy is proactive. MIS strategy interacts with and sometimes controls corporate strategy.

MIS strategy must be constantly evaluated to determine its validity in meeting user, organizational structure, power, and environmental fit. Industry competition, organizational resources, and environmental constraints interact to determine which MIS strategy best fits organizational needs.

Having explored in some detail the resources available for the R & D, marketing, manufacturing, and MIS interface as well as the strategies available for establishing and maintaining a fit between information resource and organizational needs, we are now in a position to explore how MIS units function to coordinate such a fit.

The Information and Communication Processes Involved in Coordinating the R & D, Marketing, Manufacturing, and MIS Interface

Information technologies have the potential to link production systems together in ways that improve the performance of entire networks. These technologies can make it easier to serve large numbers of highly specialized markets. They make it possible to tie together computer networks of producers around the nation or around the world by forging tighter links between retail, wholesale, transportation, and manufacturing. . . . Fundamental changes in management practices are needed throughout business networks if the full potential of these new technologies are to be harnessed.
(Office of Technology Assessment, 1988.17)

To manage successfully an organization's information system, the MIS staff must not only understand an organization's total operation, it must also coalign all of an organization's information activities in order to develop a rapid response system. Such coordination requires the MIS staff to focus their attention on seven coordination activities and then apply the principles involved in these activities to each of a firm's information interfaces.

MIS Coordination Activities

Zmud, Boynton, and Jacobs (1986) argue that at the heart of all successful information systems coordination are the following seven activities: an information processing technology vision, a coalition architecture, a data architecture, a transportation architecture, a management process architecture, an investment architecture, and an applications map. Let us explore each in turn.

An information processing technology vision attempts to identify the future role of information technology in the organization. This vision can then serve as a guide for channeling the decisions of managers at various levels and in diverse units throughout the organization. A clear vision of the feasible and desirable role of MIS within a firm is an essential first step in coalignment of MIS activities.

A coalition architecture provides a forum in which various information technology users can address the critical issues involved in selecting, implementing, maintaining, and upgrading MIS within the organization. This architecture allows for the development of managerial support for various operationalizations of the information processing technology vision. There is strong evidence that coalitions of managers within an organization develop to represent their specific interests in policy decisions. The MIS staff needs to bring these coalitions out in the open so they can constructively assist in system design and functioning.

A data architecture ensures the free exchange of information, the integration of networks, and the establishment of security of an organization's collective knowledge. Policies must be established on database development placement, strategy, and control. Access to data is thus determined as well as data ownership and use.

A transportation architecture ensures sufficient information processing, data storage, and communication capacity to move information to where it is needed in time and in a form for its appropriate use. This architecture involves the type and location of processor units, the content and location of databases, and the type of network which links processor, database, and work stations together.

A management process architecture determines the complete set of generic management activities that must occur for the information technology to be operationalized. The MIS system must develop a plan with the appropriate managers for bringing on-line a given system. This involves strategic planning, in which business plans and information architecture definitions are integrated. It also involves tactical processes such as development, management service, and resource planning. Finally, it involves an operationalized level of maintenance resource and information service control.

An investment architecture establishes a market mechanism for determining the expansion and contraction of MIS services for the entire organization which is consistent with the information technology vision. Managers faced with information technology decisions need benchmark indicators for determining their share of costs and expenses.

An applications map creates an awareness of available application systems, information services, and data repositories throughout the organization. It reveals areas needing expansion, integration, and coordination.

Together these seven activities form the technical and managerial infrastructure for the successful functioning of an MIS unit.

However, this infrastructure requires specific organizational functions to give content to MIS activities.

The Coordination of a Firm's Major Information Interfaces

Coalignment depends on having some set of organizational functions and information activities to coordinate. In our treatment of the R & D and marketing interface and the R & D, marketing, and manufacturing interface, several necessary organizational functions and information activities were revealed. It is the task of MIS management to apply the seven MIS activities to these intersections in order to create a rapid response MIS system.

Table 8.1 reviews these necessary R & D and marketing coordination needs from chapters 6 and 7.

Table 8.1   AREAS REQUIRING R & D/MARKETING COORDINATION

A.   Marketing is involved with R & D in
1. Setting new product goals and priorities
2. Preparing R & D's budget proposals
3. Establishing product development schedules
4. Generating new product ideas
5. Screening new product ideas
6. Finding commercial applications of R & D's new product ideas/technologies

B.   Marketing provides information to R & D on
1. Customer requirements of new products
2. Regulatory and legal restrictions on product performance and design
3. Test-marketing results
4. Feedback from customers regarding product performance on a regular basis
5. Competitors' strategies

C.   R & D is involved with marketing in
1. Preparing marketing's budget proposal
2. Screening new product ideas
3. Modifying products according to marketing's recommendations
4. Developing new products according to the market need
5. Designing communication strategies for the customers of new products
6. Designing user and service manuals
7. Training users of new products
8. Analyzing customer needs

DeMeyer (1987:233) made a similar determination for the R & D, marketing, and manufacturing interface when he examined the ten most frequently matched pairs of databases employed in coordinating a large manufacturing firm's operations.

- Sales planning including forecasting with master production scheduling
- Process controls with quality reporting
- Inventory status with master production scheduling
- Design engineering (including CAD) with manufacturing engineering (including CAM)
- Sales planning (including forecasting) with inventory status
- Master production scheduling (MRP) with shop floor control
- Inventory status with purchasing
- Manufacturing engineering (including CAM) with process controls
- Master production scheduling (MRP) with order entry
- Master production scheduling (MRP) with purchasing

These two lists of necessary coordination points for the R & D and marketing and the R & D, marketing, and manufacturing interfaces are the raw materials out of which a rapid response information system is made. Then, by selecting an appropriate MIS strategy and applying the seven MIS activities to the analysis, development, and operationalization of the information systems needed, coalignment can be achieved.

In summary, we began our inquiry of MIS by observing that a management information system's chief resource is the knowledge its staff has regarding the current and future state of technology and how to adapt that technology to an organization's needs. We then explored briefly the knowledge base of these MIS staff members—a database manager's knowledge of file development, a telecommunications manager's knowledge base of network development, and an applications and design manager's knowledge base in specific applications implementation.

Since individual MIS staff members have different knowledge bases, a general MIS strategy is required to integrate these various knowledge bases into an effective MIS system. The term *organizational validity* refers to the specific criteria involved in evaluating the appropriateness of an MIS strategy in meeting organizational needs. Four such criteria were explored: user-systems fit, organization structure-systems fit, power-systems fit, and environment-systems fit. Then six general MIS strategies were explored for achieving a tight fit:

business systems planning, critical success factors, an applications portfolio, a stages approach, a value chain approach, and a high-speed management approach.

Next we explored the application of these strategies in operationalizing an MIS system. Such an operationalization involves developing an information technology vision, a coalition architecture, a data architecture, a transport architecture, an information systems architecture, an investment architecture, and an applications map. We then discussed the applications of an MIS strategy and its implementation process to coordinating the necessary linkages among R & D, marketing, manufacturing, and MIS.

We are now in a position to explore an example of the R & D, marketing, manufacturing, and MIS interface in order to locate the critical factors governing the effective functioning of this coordination process.

The Location of Critical Factors in the R & D, Marketing, Manufacturing, and MIS Interface

An MIS is a comprehensive and coordinated set of information subsystems which are rationally integrated and which transform data into information in a variety of ways to enhance productivity in conformance with managers' styles and characteristics on the basis of established quality criteria.
(Scott, 1986:97)

New technologies and quick response systems are revolutionizing the everyday practices of most organizations. Traditional retailing firms in the women's clothing industry like Sears, Macy's, Lerners, Casual Corner, and Loehmann's plan their product lines twelve to eighteen months in advance. In the last chapter we commented on the speed of response in The Limited Corporation's rapid response merchandising systems. We now want to explore that system in greater detail from an MIS perspective. Figure 8.2 contains a more detailed layout of the overall quick response system at The Limited.

The root cause for spending twelve to eighteen months in all the phases of retailing sales in the women's fashion industry is the general lack of coordination between segments of the soft-goods chain. At every level, high-speed management practice at The Limited reduced the time required to perform the various functions by

Figure 8.2 REAL TIME MERCHANDISING

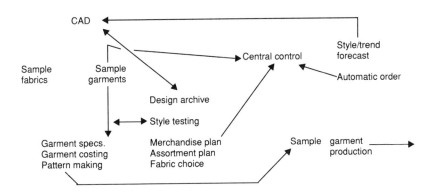

introducing information technology and effective communication to reduce response time. Short-cycle manufacturing, faster transmission of more information, and drastically shortened logistics make it possible to reduce time and work closer to the customer.

The *rapid time merchandising (RTM)* at The Limited involves five key information technologies: computer-aided design systems; consumer style-testing systems; merchandising analysis systems; advanced inventory to replenish systems; production planning systems; and new organizational structures for merchandising. Brown (1989:20) explains the overall system:

Computer Aided Design

CAD systems substantially reduce the time required to create a prototype garment and a cost sheet. Linking them directly to automatic marker making and cutting permits prototype samples to be produced within hours. CAD technology can also be adapted for consumer style testing. Renderings in true colors of proposed new styles can be shown to consumers to gauge their preference before styles are put into a line and produced.

Consumer Style Testing

Today's progressive merchandisers routinely test new products with target customers as part of product development. Significant improvements in style forecasting can be made through testing as close to the retail selling period as possible. Testing fall 1989 merchandise in December 1988 yields tangible improvements, but under RTM, such testing would occur in June and July of 1989—and be even more accurate.

Merchandising Analysis Systems

Advanced merchandising systems incorporating artificial intelligence support the analysis of sales data, consumer style testing, and fabric and production capacity. Most major retailers are now able to send their suppliers weekly data on levels of transactions, so real time merchandisers need support systems to aid decision making. Otherwise such information will go unread.

Inventory Replenishment and Production Planning

The merchandising planning horizon is shorter and closer under RTM. Inventory replenishment in a speeded up environment must be faster and more accurate but it still will outstrip the capacity of merchandisers and buyers to deal personally with all the numbers and make the right decision on time. New technology has created "decision explosions" and real time merchandising is needed to control them.

Organization Structure and Relationships

Under RTM, the roles and interactions of buyers and merchandisers change. To get started, companies need to create an action plan.

This organization-wide RTM system crosses departmental lines linking R & D, marketing, manufacturing, and MIS. From the RTM system's point of view these functional groupings are necessary but do not delineate information systems boundaries well.

Figure 8.3 shows how the RTM system looks from a marketing information systems perspective. Note that the various functions performed by marketing overlap with various aspects of the RTM system while other functions are more explicit than the RTM system. Marketing and RTM are subsystems of the overall organization which sometimes shares information and network links and sometimes does not.

Now consider the addition of a factory production MIS subsystem (see figure 8.4). Again note how this subsystem sometimes overlaps with the RTM and marketing system and sometimes does not. It overlaps at points where coordination is required as indicated in our previous discussion and it does not on unique features of its own system.

Here, then, are the critical factors governing the coordination of the R & D, marketing, manufacturing, and MIS interface:

Figure 8.3 MARKETING INFORMATION SYSTEMS PERSPECTIVE

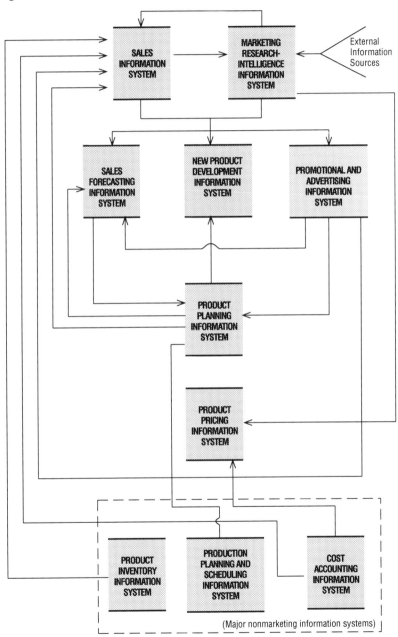

(Adapted from Scott, George M. (1986). *Principles of Management Information Systems*. New York: McGraw-Hill Book Company, 414.)

Figure 8.4   THE PRODUCTION PROCESSES AND INFORMATION SYSTEMS

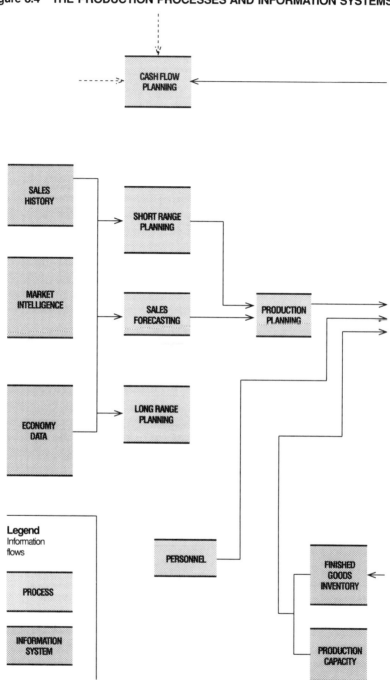

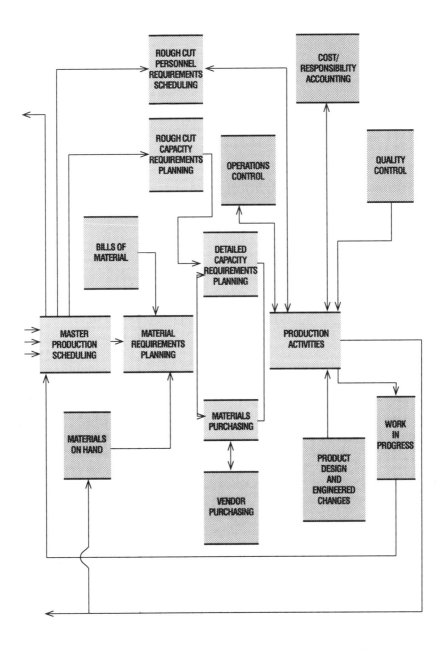

(Adapted from Scott, George M. (1986) *Principles of Management Information Systems*. New York: McGraw-Hill Book Company, 430.

tion, and management process architecture, along with an applications map.

3. An MIS system must put in place a rapid response system that coordinates R & D, marketing, manufacturing, and MIS at their necessary coordination points.

4. All of the above listed factors must meet the tests of the user, organization structure, power, and environmental fit, thus achieving MIS validity.

Summary of Organizational Coordination Processes

The elimination of bottlenecks, delays, errors, and overbloated inventories is at the heart of a firm's coordination system. To make such improvements, employees must examine carefully all of a firm's linkages and map carefully its information and communication flow. Once this is done specific tools, strategies, and topics for sharing information exist that allow one to maximize a firm's speed-to-market with a product. In exploring the R & D and marketing interface, we examined the coordination tools of environmental assessment, product portfolio modeling, and structured innovation to evaluate a firm's information and communication flow. Then a firm's coordination strategies were assessed in order to move to a balanced R & D and market-driven pattern. Finally, we assessed the topics discussed in coordinating units and institutionalizing the coordination process.

When a firm employs the R & D, marketing, and manufacturing linkages, its tools for coordination are robots, integrated flexible systems, computer-aided design and manufacturing systems, and computer-integrated systems. Then a firm's strategies of economies of scale, sourcing, focus, scope, and time were assessed as optimal coordination patterns. The topics to be discussed in institutionalizing the most effective coordination patterns were illustrated. Finally, the R & D, marketing, manufacturing, and MIS linkages were assessed. The tools for coordination are database, telecom, applications, and design of management systems. The strategies for optimizing coordination are critical success factors, applications portfolio, stages, value chain, and high-speed management approaches. The coordination topics for institutionalizing the coordination processes were illustrated in an example.

Having explored in some detail how high-speed management must function in a firm's integration and coordination processes, we will now examine a firm's control processes.

PART III

Organizational Control Processes

High-speed management leaders exact organizational control not through the formal organizational chart, but by monitoring the performance of every level of a firm. . . . The task of management then becomes to manage the cycle times and to seek out, by eliciting feedback from employees, new ways of reducing cycle time.
(Turner, 1989:6)

At the heart of a high-speed management organizational control system is the need to audit information and communication flow processes and then to continuously improve a firm's performance by seeking feedback from the stakeholders involved. This involves a two-stage process, auditing and modifying a firm's linkages so as to improve high-speed performance.

Auditing a firm's high-speed management performance is the subject of chapter 9. Three types of information and communication are discussed, and they lead to three types of management audits. *First,* one employs cross-functional teams to map and locate the critical success factors in various organizational functional and business processes. *Second,* environmental scanning and benchmarking teams are employed to map competitors' and world-class firms' use of these same processes. *Third,* one needs to audit the skills, training programs, and time required to upgrade one's own organizational processes. Two examples are provided of such audits.

Finally, the strategies available to guide an organizational linking program aimed at improving organizational performance are

215

discussed. Five strategies are explored and illustrated: (1) confront, (2) focus, (3) circumvent, (4) join, and (5) withdraw. These strategies are then explored in terms of their ability to enhance a firm's core capabilities. Toyota, Ford, Mazda, and The Limited serve as exemplars of the appropriate use of linking strategies to improve core capabilities.

An organization's integration, coordination, and control processes are the underlying communication processes which make a high-speed management firm work.

9

Auditing the Speed of a Firm's Information and Communication Flow

Fast-cycle companies map a firm's information and communication flow so as to identify major interfaces, bottlenecks, and behavior patterns. . . . They study competitors and superior performances in other industries for helpful ideas. . . . They know just where in the system compressing time will add the most value to the customers. Not surprisingly, these are the activities they attack first and upgrade continuously. . . . To compress time and gain the benefits, a company has to work in and manage through relatively small, self-managed teams made up from different parts of the organization.
(Bower and Hout, 1988:113)

It is an old and valid adage in organizations that what you measure is what you get. Organizational leaders understand that the performance targets a firm establishes strongly affects the behaviors of managers and employees. Leaders have long realized that financial measures alone fail to capture the necessary performance standards for organizational success. Academic researchers have attempted to remedy the inadequacies of financial performance measures being employed alone by adding measures from a customer perspective to the financial measures—an internal speed of information and communication flow perspective, and a world class innovation and learning or benchmarking perspective. This balanced scorecard approach (Kaplan and Norton 1992) provides high-speed managers with a monitoring system capable of generating appropriate goals and setting performance targets which yield success.

It has been a major discovery of the 1980s that an organization must find a way to unleash the creative minds and passionate

217

energy of its employees. Five core values appear to underlay such an unleashing—

* *People support what they help create:* Involving cross functional teams in the innovation process ultimately yields cross functional support resulting in concrete company-wide action;

* *A credible process yields credible outcomes:* Understanding and embracing the innovation process results in ownership and dedication to the outcomes of innovation;

* *You can't do things differently until you see things differently:* Creating an environment for innovative thought fosters new insights and ideas which leads to inspired implementation;

* *You must step into your future before you can create your future:* Developing a vision of the future is the elementary foundation of the process that creates the future;

* *Visionary strategies cannot be created by companies that only talk to themselves:* Expert perspectives from outside the organization provide strategic insights to the people inside the organization. (IdeaScope Associates 1994:1)

These two groups of insights—(1) that a firm's performance targets must be financial, customer, internal speed, learning, and innovative oriented and (2) that people support what they help create, a credible process yields credible outcomes, you can't do things differently until you see things differently, you must step into your future before you can create that future, and visioning strategies cannot be created by companies that only talk to themselves—have transformed organizational communication auditing from a static external process into a dynamic internal and external process.

In order to understand this transformation, we will (1) explore the operational nature of this transformation, (2) examine how a firm audits its basic internal business functions and processes, (3) investigate how a firm employs external audits, (4) understand a firm's and an individual's learning potential and training timeline; and (5) analyze how high-speed management audits work at Toyota and GE.

Operationalizing the Transformation

The companies that find a way to engage every mind— harness every volt of passionate energy—bring excitement to the lives of their people—and break every artificial barrier between

people—will be the companies that win in the 90s and beyond. We intend to be the biggest and best of those companies.
(Welch, CEO, GE, 1993:4)

Let us explore in turn each of the transformations in this measurement system in order to observe the new motivational, educational, and operational base of its operation.

A Customer Perspective. Under the *old* approach, focus groups were held to identify the need for and reaction to new products. These focus groups audited customer preference in a passive manner. Under the *new* approach, customers are made members, along with workers, and managers of self-managed, cross-functional, benchmarking or outside linking teams. Such teams then attempt to collectively resolve the following set of issues: (1) What product or attributes do customers want in a product and what is the pentup demand for the product? (2) Which of these products and/or attributes of the product are associated with our firm and which are associated with a competitor's firm? (3) How can our firm's value chain be reengineered to assure that such products and/or attributes are associated primarily with our firm? This active and creative role for all stakeholders attempts to operationalize the four values discussed above in the auditing and implementation process of a firm's continuous improvement program. It invites customers to participate in creating a firm's future and invites a firm's employees to look outside the firm at its customers' preferences and competitors' core competencies as part of the reengineering process in improving a firm's own core competencies.

An Internal Speed of Information and Communication Flow Perspective. Under the *old* approach, a consultant would be hired who specialized in information, communication flow, and time management. This consultant would then conduct a survey and do a participant observation. The survey would ask employees if they had enough information to carry out their jobs and if they could interact with ease with their supervisors. The participant observation would involve measuring the time it takes to perform each organizational function and business process. A report would be submitted to management along with recommendations for change. Under the *new* approach, a consultant or facilitator is brought in to provide a one-hour lecture on speed-to-market diagnostics and skills. The consultant then answers questions on the lecture. Next the consultant leads a cross-functional, benchmarking, or outside linking team which process maps the most time consuming and costly business process. The consultant then leads the team's effort at reengineering the business process and readjusts that effort until it meets some world class benchmark in performance. The consultant and team members each creatively participate in the audit and development of a firm's future world class business processes. They also learn the skills required to employ that process or processes.

A World Class Innovation or Learning Perspective. Under the *old* system, managers would locate some outdated or ineffective business process and identify the new skills involved in changing that process. Next, management would send the workers to school to learn the new technologies and skills. Equipment would be purchased and installed and workers would return and use the equipment. Under the *new* system workers would audit the performance of their existing business processes. Then they would visit some firm which already had implemented a world class business process and they would observe and audit its performance. Next they would form a team to reengineer their own system in such a way as to exceed the performance criteria of the observed benchmark. Then the members of the world class benchmark would visit the newly reengineered firm and audit its performance to see if it really exceeded their system. Then fine tunings would be made based on that audit. Again teamwork facilitates motivation, creative input, participation in the future system, and on the job learning.

A Financial Perspective. Under the *old* system, cost, margins, quality, productivity, and return on assets would be measured by a firm's accountant and compared with the industry standards. If they fall below industrial averages on these performance criteria, a consultant would be called in to audit the firm and recommend an intervention aimed at correcting the problem. If management considers the intervention cost-effective, the consultant would be hired to implement the suggestions. Under the *new* approach, each business unit keeps certain financial information on itself, its competitors, and world class benchmarks. Then they ask their workers and suppliers to improve their present performance between 5 and 10 percent per year. Finally, they calculate each worker's and unit's value added contribution to the business process. If these figures for sales, productivity, costs, quality, turn around time, and speed of response do not exceed the competitors', then the firm sets up a cross-functional, benchmarking, or outside linking team to improve the process to world class standards. Training and reeducation are provided for the individual and units which fall below these standards.

In this way, organizational audits have been transformed from a static external to a dynamic internal and external monitoring system. This transformation makes customers, workers, suppliers, managers and stockholders active participants in operationalizing the diagnostic and in implementing the intervention, creating motivation, innovation, learning, and high performance standards.

Auditing a Firm's Basic Internal Business Functions and Processes

One result of cross-function teams, process mapping sessions, and the changes these sessions stimulated is that continuous flow manufacturing was brought online at all 15 IBM Europe facilities with the following effects: cycle time and inventory levels improved, costs dropped, quality rose, and the company became more flexible in meeting customer demands. That may not be the end of the rainbow, but it's not bad from a two day audit session.
(Hardaker and Ward, 1987:113)

Organizational audits frequently employ information technologies such as computers, infrared scanners, artificial intelligence systems, and decision support systems to monitor ongoing organizational activities. However, most time compression programs rely primarily on a management and stakeholder team to analyze and reengineer current organizational interaction patterns in order to obtain a significant competitive advantage. This is true because three separate types of audits or information are required to make such a constructive intervention aimed at improving organizational performances.

First, one needs an audit or map of a firm's existing organizational functions and business processes which describes the content, flow, and timing of information, communication, and materials, and their current timeline for each loop in these activities. *Second,* one needs to audit or benchmark one's chief competitors or another firm not in one's industry who is a top performer on the functions or busines processes under examination. They can serve as a benchmarking and learning program for function and process improvement. *Third,* one needs an audit of the overall ability of a firm to learn and continuously improve, and some measure of the current level of workers skills, the type of training needed to improve, and the expected timeline for making a firm operational in the improvement. It is the purpose of this chapter to indicate how to audit a firm in order to obtain this information and to provide two examples. Let us explore how each of these three types of audits function.

Any attempt to map and improve an organization's functions or business processes is confronted at the outset with three issues. *First,* such a map can be constructed reliably by utilizing employees who have first hand knowledge of that process. *Second,* any attempt to simplify or improve such functions for business processes requires a representative from the units involved who can influence the members of those units to modify their behavior. *Third,* such a representative from each unit must be able to accurately and articulately represent the interests, concerns, and contributions of each unit member so an effective coalignment process aimed at improving performance can be formed.

The central mechanism for mapping and improving these organizational functions and business processes is cross-functional teamwork. Such a team if it is to meet the above mentioned criteria, must select unit heads and process leaders from the organizational units involved. To this group we must add a teamwork facilitator. Then, in line with the cross-functional teamwork process described in chapter five, the team must perform the following team functions and proceed through the following stages of analysis.

Team Functions: Process Map Simplification

1. Take a business or organizational process and map its interaction in the form of information exchange, decision making, and materials flow with a functional business unit.
2. Simplify map to meet productivity, quality, and response time targets.
3. Implement changes in process map.
4. Monitor implementation.

Team Functions: Critical Success Factors for Reengineering

1. Develop mission statement.
2. Outline critical success factors or targets.
3. Evaluate organizational function or business processes.

4. Develop plan to reengineer and set targets.
5. Implement plan.
6. Monitor implementation.

The Mapping Process. Cross-functional teamwork involves an intense one- or two-day teamwork session that proceeds through a three-step problem-solving process:

1. Develop a clear understanding of the team's mission.
2. Identify the necessary and sufficient critical success factors for fulfilling the mission.
3. Identify and evaluate the business processes essential to meeting the critical success factors. (See chapter 5 for details of steps 1, 2, and 3 of this mapping process.)

Finally, each member of the cross-functional team helps those leaders representing the low performing organizational function or business process reengineer their map so as to improve performance. This brings the best knowledge and experience of a firm and the social pressures of needing help from one's peers to bear on upgrading a firm's performance.

Now the team must decide on the best way to obtain follow-through on improvements needed and relevant measures for demonstrating that things are improving. This is achieved normally by reconvening the team at agreed upon times to review the Process Quality Management process and examine the implementation results. Particularly important in such a review is to realize that while the mission statement and critical success factors remain constant, the quality ratings of the organizational processes hopefully change, creating a subsequent change in the priorities graph, that is, a change in what organizational processes are in Zones 1, 2, and 3.

External Audits Through "Best Practices" Teamwork

Benchmarking's benefits as a strategic planning method are that it identifies the key to success for each area studied, provides specific quantitative targets to shoot for, creates an awareness of state-of-the-art approaches, and helps companies cultivate a culture where change, adaptation, and continuous improvement are actively sought out.
(Altany, 1990:14)

Any attempt to improve the performance of one's own firm is only meaningful in the context of one's competitors. If they are improving faster than you are, your efforts will fail to affect the bottom line. This means that at the same time one maps the organizational and/or business processes of one's own firm, one must map also a top-performing competitor or world-class firm in another industry. This form of mapping is termed *world-class benchmarking*. Let us explore a benchmarking audit's focus, process, and techniques.

Benchmarking Focus

Most theorists distinguish three types of benchmarking—strategic, process, and customer.

1. *Strategic benchmarking* compares the success of different companies to one another in creating long-term value for shareholders with that of industrial peers. This is accomplished by measuring such factors as total shareholder return on assets, the ratio of a company's market value to book value, the positive spread in a firm's return on capital and its cost of capital and the value added productivity per employee, etc. Each of these measures provides some overall estimate of a firm's effectiveness in creating increased stockholder value given its general corporate strategy and allows a comparison among similar firms which employ differing strategies. For example, Ernst and Young, classified over 500 firms as novice, journeyman, and master based on their respective return on assets (ROA) and value added per employee (VAE).

Firms classified as *novice* have less than 2 percent (ROA) and less than $47,000 (VAE). Firms classified as *journeyman* had 2–6 percent (ROA) and $47,000 to $73,000 (VAE). Firms viewed as *masters* (Port, et al., 1992:47), i.e. firms worthy of benchmarking, had 7 percent or higher (ROA) and $74,000 (VAE).

2. *Process benchmarking*, on the other hand, seeks to isolate one or more of a firm's primary business processes, i.e., product development, billing and collection, integrated manufacturing, customer service, etc. and benchmark that process against a world-class competitor in regard to process and product cost, quality, speed-to-market. For example, Robert Camp, the manager of benchmarking competency at the Xerox Corporation, indicates that his firm operates in more than one hundred countries and performs benchmarking in each. Over the past ten years, the firms Xerox has process-benchmarked against have grown. Camp reports that they include

the names of some of America's largest corporations, including American Express Co. (billing and collection); American Hospital Supply Co. (automated inventory control); Ford Motor Co. (manufacturing floor layout); General Electric Co. (robotics); and L. L. Bean, Hershey Foods, and Mary Kay Cosmetics (warehouse and distribution), etc.

3. *Customer benchmarking* involves surveying customers regarding what qualities of one's own and one's competitors' product attributes are considered the most important in influencing purchases. Given this attribute list, a firm then benchmarks those attributes in competing firms' products in order to add them to their own product. Customer benchmarking is a four-step process:

   a. Identify the attributes that influence customer value perceptions.
   b. Assess corporate performance.
   c. Analyze competitors' performance and standing.
   d. Close gaps between current performance and customer expectations.

For example, the Chrysler Corporation recently designed its new LH auto series by benchmarking the best attributes of other automobiles in the world. Chrysler took more than two hundred dream attributes by customers of their ideal car and benchmarked them. They studied the Accura Legend and Nissan Maxima for suspension systems, the BMW for ventilation and heating, and so on, and then designed a car with the best combination of these features available for its price range: The emergent design is aimed at recapturing Chrysler's lost market shares in the mid-price range auto market.

Customer benchmarking has been listed by such firms as Xerox, Motorola, and GM as key strategies for regaining lost market shares in their respective competitive markets.

Benchmarking Process

The actual processes involved in implementing a best practices program are varied. Xerox, one of the earliest firms to systematically utilize benchmarking, employs a ten-step, four-stage process (see table 9.1).

Underlying this ten-step, four-stage process are several well-developed fundamental activities.

Table 9.1   THE BENCHMARKING PROCESS

Planning	1. Identify what is to be benchmarked
	2. Identify comparative companies
Analysis	3. Determine data collection method and collect data
	4. Determine current performance levels
Integration	5. Project future performance levels
	6. Communicate benchmark findings and gain acceptance
Action	7. Establish functional goals
	8. Develop action plans
	9. Implement specific actions and monitor progress
	10. Recalibrate benchmarks

(Adapted from Camp, 1992:4)

First, know your own operation and carefully assess its strengths and weaknesses.

Second, locate world-class leaders and competitors to benchmark against.

Third, carefully measure productivity, quality, and speed-to-market.

Fourth, carefully analyze how and why the benchmark is different from yours.

Fifth, incorporate and improve on the best practices to gain superiority.

Sixth, continuously update benchmarking of your organization's central competitive processes.

Seventh, remember, in the final analysis, the customer is the best judge of how good you are.

When unsuccessful, this benchmarking audit process normally fails at the measurement phase, the analysis of difference phase, and in the cost of the benchmarking process given its benefits to the firm.

Benchmark Auditing Techniques

Throughout the United States international benchmarking institutes have been established which serve as clearinghouses for data on world-class performances (see table 9.2). These data banks, combined with a site visit, provide the materials necessary for such an audit. Table 9.2 is one database selection of world-class performers for benchmarking by organizational function and/or business processes.

Table 9.2   THE CREME DE LA CREME (EXAMPLES OF WORLD-CLASS BENCHMARKING CANDIDATES)

Automated inventory control	Westinghouse, Apple Computer, Federal Express
Billing and collection	American Express, MCI
Customer service	Xerox, Nordstrom, L.L. Bean
Environmental management	3M, Ben & Jerry's, Dow Chemical
Manufacturing operations management	Hewlett-Packard, Corning Glass, Philip Morris
Marketing	Helene Curtis, The Limited, Microsoft
Product development	Motorola, Digitial Equipment, Sony, 3M
Purchasing	Honda, Zerox, NCR
Quality process	Westinghouse, Florida Power, Xerox
Robotics	General Electric
Sales management	IBM, Procter & Gamble, Merck
Warehousing and distribution	L.L. Bean, Hershey Foods, Mary Kay Cosmetics

Let us take a look at the clearing house data on one such benchmark—improving procurement (table 9.3). Over half or 50 percent of overall production costs are usually purchased parts and materials. For this reason world-class companies make every attempt to manage this area of production efficiently.

Such benchmarks then become critical success factors or targets for reengineering a firm's functions and/or business processes.

Auditing a Firm's and/or Individual's Learning Potential and Training Time Line

A Learning Organization is an organization skilled at creating, acquiring, and transferring knowledge, and at modifying its behavior to reflect new knowledge and insights.
(Garvin, 1993:78)

Once we have the output generated by our first two audits, we know what we are now doing, how long it takes and at what cost,

Table 9.3 BENCHMARKING AT WORK: IMPROVING PROCUREMENT

	Typical Company	World-Class Company
COST FACTORS		
Suppliers per purchasing agent	3.4	5
Agents per $100 million of purchasing	5.4	2.2
Purchasing costs as a % of purchases made	3.3%	0.8%
TIME FACTORS		
Supplier evaluations (weeks)	3	0.4
Supplier lead times (weeks)	150	8
Time spent placing an order (weeks)	6	0.001
QUALITY OF DELIVERIES		
Late	33%	2%
Rejected	1.5%	0.0001%
Materials shortages (# of instances per year)	400	4

(Adapted from Port, Cary, Kelly, and Forest, 1992:76)

and what a world-class benchmark does with that same function or business process and how long it takes and at what cost. We are then in a position to audit our own firm's learning potential and our workers' skills, training required, and estimated time line for making our continuous improvement operational. These last three tasks are the focus of our learning audit. Let us explore each of them in turn.

Measuring a Firm's Learning Potential

It is a true but not very useful insight that all organizations are interdependent systems of units and subunits held together by organizational communications. Our discussion of value chain theory in chapter 2 attempted to refine this insight by mapping the functional units and business processes of a firm and indicating where they were coaligned by an organization's information and communication processes. We attempted to make such a claim more useful by arguing that the value-added contributions of each functional unit or business process could be added to or cancelled out by the performances of a firm's other functional units and/or business processes.

Next we divided a firm's information and communication into three processes—integration, coordination, and control systems—specifying the focus, structure, and functioning of each subsystem. We indicated that a firm's integration system employed communication to develop goals, a set of targets for reaching these goals, and the structures and functions involved in reaching those targets such as leadership, corporate climate, and corporate teamwork. Further utility was given to our analysis of information and communication processes when we outlined the styles, strategies, and techniques of various types of leaders and indicated where they might appropriately and inappropriately be employed for undertaking continuous and discontinuous change. We then provided an in-depth analysis of corporate climate and corporate teamwork and their appropriate functioning.

In Part 2 of our inquiry we explored the information and communication tools, strategies, message content, and techniques for appropriately coordinating a firm's R & D, marketing, manufacturing, and MIS interfaces. In this chapter, we have just explored how three types of organizational audits can provide the information necessary to determine how to continue to improve a firm's speed-to-market directly and profits, sales, productivity, and quality indirectly. In the next chapter, we shall see how to take the information provided by these three types of audits and select a strategy and continuous improvement program that will provide a firm with a world-class information and communication system.

The complexity of all this boggles the mind. Thus we are in need of some overall organizational auditing tool for telling us how much of this we have correct, and how much we do not have correct and thus must learn. In addition, we need some overall estimate of our ability to employ the various parts of a continuous improvement program to change the firm to a world-class performer. Such a measure, if valid, would be a direct measure of a firm's total learning capability and be an invaluable aid to planning a change and estimating its chances for success or failure.

Fortunately, between 1988 and 1992, the consulting firm of Ernst and Young, in conjunction with Michigan State University, developed just such an auditing tool. They explored 945 continuous improvement practices in over 580 organizations in four industries on three continents (Stumple, 1992:3). This study correlated various continuous improvement practices with various organizational performances. The results of this study are contained in table 9.4.

Table 9.4   CONTINUOUS IMPROVEMENT TEAMS BY LEARNING LEVELS

	Novice	Journeyman	Master
Profitability	Less than 2% (ROA)	2%–6.9% (ROA)	7% or higher (ROA)
Production	Less than $47,000 (VAE)	$47,000–73,000 (VAE)	$74,000 or higher (VAE)
Type of Work Team	Self-managed Cross-functional	Self-managed Cross-functional Internal Benchmarking	Self-managed Cross-functional External Banchmarking Outside Linking

This research divides firms into three groups—novice, journeyman, and master—based on the firm's annual return on assets (ROA) and value added per employee (VAE). Then it indicates which types of continuous improvement program each has the skill to employ and seven continuous improvement activities that each category of firm must learn in order to move the firm's performance to the next level. If firms attempt to jump levels and employ the continuous improvement tools for that level before the performance level outcomes are reached, then the overall performance of the firm, its systems performance, tends to cancel out the effective use of that tool.

Thus, by auditing a firm's overall performance on such outcome measures as return on assets (ROA) and value added per employee (VAE), one can estimate its overall organizational learning levels and what continuous improvement can and cannot be undertaken successfully.

Measuring a Firm's and Individual's Learning to Operationalize Time Line

Once we know a firm's learning potential we are in need of some measure of its workers' skills and the availability of and length of time it takes a training program to teach and make operational the use of those skills. The location of such tests for skills, internal and external training programs, and length of time required to make the skills operational are a local matter. They vary by types of skills, schedules of internal and external training programs, and the job training periods.

Having discussed in some detail how to conduct these three types of audits, let us explore two firms' use of these auditing processes.

High-Speed Management Audits at Toyota and General Electric

The numbers are really incredible. General Electric used to take three weeks after an order to deliver a custom-made industrial circuit breaker box. Now it takes three days. AT&T used to need two years to design a new phone. Now it can do the job in one. Motorola used to turn out electric pagers three weeks after the factory got the order. Now it takes two hours.

Speed is catching on fast. A recent survey of 50 major U.S. firms found that practically all put their base strategies, as the new approach is called, at the top of their priority lists. Why? Because speed kills the competition.
(Dumaine, 1989:54)

Whenever high-speed management firms are planning a major change in the firm's strategy, structure, and/or performance, they normally audit themselves and their competitors in order to gauge the probable and potential success of their proposed change. Let us explore two such changes at world-class performing firms.

Toyota Motors' High-Speed Management Audits

In late 1987, the Toyota Motor Company was considering updating its automobile production strategy. Table 9.5 discusses the unique features of its current system while table 9.6 provides data from Toyota's cross-functional teams process mapping of its own and three Detroit firms—GM, Ford, and Chrysler. In all four business processes that were mapped—new product development, production, plant schedules, and dealer ordering—Toyota led its competitors and was the world-class benchmark (Bower and Hout, 1988:112–113).

The results by 1990 were that Toyota held 43 percent of the Japanese market, held 6 percent of the U.S. market, was fourth in rank behind the big three U.S. automakers, and was scheduled to bring out another six new redesigned models in the next year. In addition, it ranked top in quality (Taylor, 1990:66). It therefore decided to improve its corporate culture by providing a nine-month training program for all of its new white-collar workers (Taylor,

Table 9.5   TOYOTA PERFORMS CRITICAL OPERATIONS FASTER

	Toyota
New Product Development	Self-organizing development teams and early supplier involvement speed up the appearance of new products
Plant Schedule	A full-mix daily schedule and orders that flow directly to suppliers multiply inventory turns
Production	JIT lot sizes and flexible cells create rapid flow through the plant
Dealer Ordering	Limited option packages and an on-line order entry system means orders can be scheduled almost at once
Customer	Places Order

(Adapted from Bower and Hout, 1988)

Table 9.6   HIGH-SPEED MANAGEMENT AT TOYOTA

	GM, Ford, and Chrysler Motors	Toyota
New Product Development	8 years	3 years
Plant Schedule	8 times/year	16 times/year
Production	5 days	2 days
Dealer Ordering	5 days	1 day
Customer	Places order	Places order

(Adapted from Bower and Hout, 1988)

1990:66). Toyota's management believed such a training program would contribute most to its current success by generating uniform high performance and incremental improvements in existing world-class benchmarked processes (Sasaki, 1991:15–25).

General Electric's High-Speed Management Audits

By early 1990, Gary Rogers, the forty-five-year-old head of GE's appliance division, was seeking to put his mark on the development of that division and position himself as a potential successor to the aging CEO Jack Welch. To accomplish this goal he undertook a divisionwide attempt to compress cycle time on all the products in the division. Employing cross-functional teams he mapped, simplified, and benchmarked all production processes (Feder, 1992:C3).

Rogers made his mark on GE's appliance operation between 1990 and 1992 by pushing to reduce the time between receipt of orders and product delivery. For GE electric ranges made in Louisville, Kentucky, and refrigerators made in Decatur, Illinois, the cycle time was cut from sixteen weeks to six days and the average production cycle for all appliances was reduced by 70 percent. These time compression processes cut inventories by 50 percent for an annual savings of $300 million (Feder, 1992:C3).

In January of 1992, Jack Welch, the fifty-six-year-old CEO of General Electric, called Rogers "one of the great young leaders of the company" and announced Rogers's promotion to head of GE Plastics division, making him one of two top candidates for becoming CEO when Welch retires (Feder, 1992:C3).

Summary

Having discussed how to employ cross-functional teams to map one's own organizational functions and business processes, benchmarked a world-class performer in the same area, obtained an overall estimate of a firm's learning potential and an estimate of the length of time and training required to make a given continuous improvement operational, we are now in a position to employ this information to develop an information and communication strategic linking program and select the appropriate type of intervention to improve a firm's performance. This will be discussed in the following, final chapter of this book.

10

Information and Communication in a Strategic Linking Program

There is currently a convergence of attention and concern among managers and management scholars across the basic issues of organizational success and failure. . . . Successful organizations achieve strategic fit with their environment and support their strategies with appropriately designed structures and management processes; less successful organizations typically exhibit poor fit externally and/or internally.
(Miles and Snow, 1984:10–11)

A rationale is provided for these claims based upon four distinctions which characterize an organization's capacity to negotiate an appropriate coalignment or linking strategy with its customers and then orders its organizational structures and processes in a manner appropriate to operationalizing its strategic fit.

- *Minimal fit* among strategy, structure, and process is essential to all organizations operating in competitive environments. If a misfit occurs for a prolonged period, the result usually is failure.
- *Tight fit,* both internally and externally, is associated with excellence. Tight fit is the underlying causal dynamic producing sustained, excellent performance and a strong corporate culture.
- *Early fit,* the discovery and articulation of a new pattern of strategy, structure, and process, frequently results in performance records which in sporting circles would merit Hall of Fame status. The invention or early application of a new organization form may provide a more powerful competitive advantage than a market or technological breakthrough.

235

- *Fragile fit* involves vulnerability to both shifting external con-
ditions and to inadvertent internal unraveling. Even Hall of
Fame organization may become victims of deteriorating fit.
(Miles and Snow, 1984:10–11)

The bottom line claim of the first nine chapters of this book
has been that *reduced cycle time in getting a product to market can
generate a sustainable competitive advantage.* Reduced cycle time in
turn depends upon the appropriate use of environmental scanning
theory, value chain theory, and continuous improvement theory. The
appropriate use of these three theories in turn requires that a firm's
leadership team and management system correctly establish a *tight*
fit between a firm's internal and external resources and its customers' pentup demand.

Up until now little attention has been paid to explicating the
important strategies which govern and guide the successful
coalignment of these processes. It will be the purpose of this chapter to explicate, illustrate, and evaluate this bottom line strategic
process. More specifically, we shall provide (1) an analysis of the
strategies involved in coaligning a firm's internal and external resources with its customers' pentup demand for a product in order
to establish a tight linking fit; (2) an analysis of the long-term strategies involved in coaligning a firm's value chain and continuous improvement program in order to sustain a tight linking fit; (3) an
overtime data based evaluation of high-speed management as a strategic system for establishing a tight environmental fit; and (4) a brief
summary and conclusion to our discussion of high-speed management. Let us address each of these issues in turn.

The Strategies for Establishing a Tight Linking Fit between a Firm and Its Customers

Understanding the what of competitiveness is a prerequisite
for catching up. Understanding the why of competitiveness is a
prerequisite for getting out front.
(Hamal and Prahalad, 1993:76)

A careful analysis of the successful coalignment between a firm's
internal and external resources and its customers' pentup demand
involves a three step analysis.

First, a firm must understand the competitive dynamic governing its customer's desired attributes in a product. *Second,* a firm

must understand which of those desired attributes the customer associates with its core competencies and which with its competitors' core competencies. *Third,* a firm must know how long it takes for it to get a product with those desired attributes to market and how long it takes each of its competitors. Once this information is known, a firm has a strategic outline of potential sources of competitive advantage for the industry. When this analysis is complete, a firm is in a position to select an appropriate strategy for dealing with each of its competitors and for *establishing* a tight fit with its customers. Five such strategies appear evident: (1) confront, (2) focus, (3) circumvent, (4) join, and (5) withdraw. (See table 10.1.)

Confront: When a firm's customers identify their desired attributes in a product with the core competencies of the firm and not with its competitors and the firm has a speed-to-market time quicker than its competitors, then confrontation is the strategy employed. Toyota chose to confront Mercedes and BMW in the luxury car market with its Lexus car. Toyota believed it could obtain sustainable competitive advantage in styling, price, and quality from each of its internal and external business processes while obtaining greater compressed cycle time than its two competitors. The results were dramatic. Toyota grabbed 23 percent of the market at the expense of Mercedes and BMW while ranking lowest in customer complaints with 47 per 1000 cars, while Mercedes had 99 per 100 and BMW had 141 per 100 (*USA Today,* June 2, 1991, B3).

Focus: When a customer's desired attributes and a competitor's value chain comparison reveals an insignificant competitive advantage at both the customer attribute and speed-to-market level between a firm's own value chain and its competitors except in one area of important concern to the customer, then a firm can focus upon manifesting a competitive advantage in that area. VISA Credit Card company developed an artificial intelligence system for electronically approving credit card purchases within sixty seconds. This electronic system cut down the average store owner non-payment of purchase slips by 82 percent per year. This saves both VISA and the stores it services billions of U.S. dollars per year. By focusing on this aspect of its value chain, VISA has been able to dramatically increase its market share while decreasing its bad debts (Feigenbaum, McCorduck, and Nii, 1988).

Circumvent: When a customer's desired attributes and a competitor's value chain comparison reveals a substantial competitive advantage from circumventing some aspect of a competitor's value chain which gives a firm a customer attribute and reduced cycle time advantage, then this firm can circumvent a competitor. Perrigo is a private drug firm which manufactures any liquid, pill, or capsule which is a large seller and which is off patent. It contacts major sales outlets and produces a product in the same size, shape, colored package, and content as a well known brand product. However, where the brand name normally would appear, Perrigo places the name of the chain store selling the product. Since Perrigo has no R & D costs and no advertising costs, it can market its products at a much lower cost than its brand name and get to market faster than its competitors. When the product is put on the shelf of a chain store near the brand name product, most customers cannot tell the difference in package and content. The customer may pick up the less expensive product, thus providing large savings to the customer and larger profits to the chain and Perrigo than does its brand name competitors. Perrigo, by circumventing the R & D and advertising costs of its competitors' value chain, has created a sustainable competitive advantage.

Join: When a customer's desired attributes and a competitor's value chain comparison reveals a substantial competitive advantage for a firm's competitor to some aspect of its product or all of its product and in time to market, then a firm can form whatever type of alliance is appropriate to obtain the use of that aspect or product and equalize its speed-to-market by joining with its competitor. General Motors found that the Japanese automakers could produce a compact car for less money, $500 per car, and in less time than GM could. GM formed a joint venture with Toyota and Mitsubishi to produce cars under the GEO brand name and sell them as its own. As a result of GM negotiating a linking arrangement with Toyota and Mitsubishi, today the GEO series of cars, one of GM's largest selling autos, is produced in the same way as Toyota.

Withdraw: When a customer's desired attributes and a competitor's value chain comparison reveals a substantial competitive advantage for a firm's competitor for some aspect of a product or the total product and the competitor's time to market; when the competitor will not join with its rival firm in any way; when that aspect or product or customer advantage cannot be circumvented—then a firm may withdraw its product from the market in order to preserve its own reputation for other products in the market. This withdrawal may be temporary or permanent, and partial or total. Between 1985 and 1993 on at least three occasions, IBM was prepared to bring out a new product in both the workstation and PC market when its chief competitors Sun and Compaq brought out new products faster, just weeks ahead of IBM, that were so clearly superior in performance that IBM chose to cannibalize its own product rather than weaken its reputation. IBM thus took the loss in R & D and manufacturing investment, rather than place a significantly inferior product on the market. In each case, their withdrawal was temporary until they could develop a better product (Bryan, 1990).

Table 10.1   STRATEGIES FOR ESTABLISHING A TIGHT FIT WITH CUSTOMERS AND COMPETITORS

Strategy	Customer Attribute Advantage	Speed Advantage	Model Firm
CONFRONT	Own firm	Own firm	Toyota
FOCUS	Competitors excel in all but one area	Competitors excel in all but one area	VISA
CIRCUMVENT	Own firm by shortening value chain	Own firm by shortening value chain	Perrigo
JOIN	Friendly competitors	Friendly competitors	GM
WITHDRAW	Unfriendly competitors	Unfriendly competitors	IBM

Establishing a tight linking fit between a firm and its customers pentup demand requires an appropriate and thus successful linking strategy. A customer, competitor, and own firm value chain analysis should suggest which strategy or strategies are most appropriate—confrontation, focus, circumvention, joining, and/or withdrawal.

However, as we have seen in the case of General Motors, IBM, and Sears, establishing a tight fit at one point in time and sustaining a tight fit overtime can be two entirely different matters.

The Strategies Involved in Sustaining Coalignment between a Firm and Its Customers

There are two basic approaches to garnering greater productivity, whether these reasons be capital or human. This first is downsizing, cutting investment and head count in hopes of

*becoming lean and mean—in essence, reducing the buck paid for
the bang. The second approach, resource leveraging, seeks to get
the most out of the resources one has—to get a much bigger bang
for the buck. Resource leveraging is essentially energizing, while
downsizing is essentially demoralizing.*
(Hamal and Prahalad, 1993:78)

Sustainable competitive advantage exists when, according to
Coyne (1986:26), "customers perceive a consistent differentiation on
important attributes between a producer's product or service and
those of his competitors and that difference is the direct consequence of a capability gap between the producer and his competitors and both the difference in important attributes and the capability
gap can be expected to endure over time." A capability, according to
Stalk, Evans and Shulman (1992:62) "is a set of business processes
strategically understood. Every company has business processes
that deliver value to the customer. But few think of them as the
primary object of strategy."

Capability-based competitors review their value chain in comparison to their competitors, locate those functional and business
processes in which they have competitive advantage and then try to
link or coalign those functions and processes in some systematic
way so as to set an industry benchmark which will yield a sustainable competitive advantage. We believe there are three separate and
yet combinable theoretic means for converting value-added organizational functions and business processes into strategic capabilities
which can establish a world-class benchmark and generate a sustainable competitive advantage. Those are knowledge-based
coalignment, alliance-based coalignment, and technology-based
coalignment of value-added functions and business processes. Let
us explore each in turn.

Knowledge-Based Capabilities. In comparing a firm's value chain
with the value chain of all of the firm's competitors, one may locate
some single or combination of value-added organizational function(s)
and/or business process(es) in which one excels in comparison to
one's competitors. The question will then arise as to how the firm
should strategically link and configure those value-added activities
with its customers in order to obtain a sustainable competitive advantage. In such cases, it is one's own firm's unique knowledge in
the form of value-added activities which when grouped into capabilities in linking with the customers, yields a competitive advantage.
Then, through the judicious use of a firm's continuous improvement

program, these capabilities are focused, linked, and improved in such a manner as to create a sustainable competitive advantage and new world-class benchmark.

The Toyota Production System (TPS), sometimes called lean production management, illustrates the development of such an internal knowledge-based capability. Kiichiro Toyoda and Taiichi Ohno led the development of this knowledge-based capability. In the 1960s, Toyota took the skills of its automotive craftspeople and the standardization and mass production techniques used by Ford Motor Corporation and asked their workers to form into small self-managed and cross-functional teams and integrate these two processes. The goal was to combine the quality of a craftsperson with the standardization of mass production. Kiichiro Toyoda also felt that each worker on this new line should be trained in several areas: production tasks, maintenance, recordkeeping, quality control, and so on (Taylor, 1990).

Management delegated to workers both the right and responsibility to continuously improve the process. Next, Toyota formed small cross-functional teams between factory workers and suppliers in order to improve the quality and inventory levels of parts. In what must be considered a breakthrough in creative thinking, these continuous improvement teams came up with the Kanban system. Parts were to be inspected at the manufacturer's plants and then shipped to Toyota just in time for use. This substantially reduced the capital tied up in inventory, in turn substantially reducing costs, increasing the turnover ratio on capital, and improving product quality (Womack, Jones, and Roos, 1990).

In the 1980s, Toyota attempted to develop a continuous flow manufacturing system for turning out small numbers of different cars at a low price. The central problem in achieving this goal was the tooling cost and time for custom-designed dies needed to stamp out parts for a car. The tools and machines needed for this stamping process form up to 73 percent of the total cost of a new car. The process itself accounts for two-thirds of the time needed to build a car. Cross-functional teams and self-managed teams were set up and, employing an international benchmarking against the U.S. auto industry, in just three years were able to cut the cost and time of designing and manufacturing with these dies by between one-half to two-thirds when compared to the U.S. automakers.

Production processes were simplified and redesigned and the quality improved. Next Toyota saw the need to reorganize its management system and become more responsible by cutting out two layers of middle management or about one thousand executives. Finally, Toyota divided its product development teams into three groups: small front-wheel-drive cars, big rear-wheel-drive cars, and trucks. In a creative breakthrough aimed at correctly targeting its specific auto models within the three divisions on narrow customer niches, each model was given a chief engineer who headed a cross-functional team made up of representatives from each functional unit and business process in the value chain. This group scans the customers, competitors, and general economic trends in order to appropriately design, manufacture, and market a new car for its customer niche (Consumano, 1988).

After forty years of focused continuous improvement programs by employing self-managed and cross-functional teams, benchmarking and breakthroughs, Toyota's lean manufacturing system has become a model for sequencing the value-added aspects of a firm's value chain to form a knowledge-based strategic capability that has created a sustainable competitive advantage. Today, Toyota builds cars and trucks on average faster, with higher quality and more unique features, and at a lower cost than any of its competitors. Customers have responded to this knowledge-based capability by increasing Toyota's market shares, ranking these cars top in quality, and demanding that other producers provide similar standard features (Womack, Jones, and Roos, 1990).

Whereas knowledge-based capabilities reside totally in the linkages within the firm, as does the effective use of continuous improvement programs, alliance-based capabilities reside in the negotiated linkages between firms, as does the effective use of continuous improvement programs.

Alliance-Based Capabilities. In comparing a firm's value chain with the firm's competitors, one may find that while aspects of a firm's value chain can produce value-added activities, some portions of the firm's value chain of most concern to the customer are not present or not functioning at an appropriate level. Under such conditions, an organization may choose to form one or more linking arrangements with other firms who are performing well in these customer-sensitive areas in order to obtain sustainable competitive advantage.

The knowledge necessary to do this resides in an alliance-based strategic capability. Such linkages may take the form of mergers, acquisitions, equity partnerships, consortia, joint ventures, development agreements, supply agreements, and/or marketing agreements (Nohria and Garcia-Pont, 1991:105). However, in all cases, continuous improvement programs are needed to set up the inside, outside, and between-organization linkages and to upgrade their collective performance to create a world-class benchmark.

Successful strategic alliances are few and far between because of the difficult problems involved in a firm's having an important part of its value chain residing either partially or completely within another organization. The Ford Motor Corporation's thirteen-year joint venture with the Mazda Corporation, however, did establish world-class benchmarks for both organizations in two different areas and as such warrants our close attention.

In 1979, Ford and Mazda formed a joint venture to cooperate on the development of new vehicles and to share valuable expertise. Ford was to share product design, international marketing, and finance expertise with Mazda, while Mazda was to share product development and manufacturing expertise with Ford. Both firms were to remain totally autonomous in this joint venture. They were to undertake only those cooperative projects which had mutual benefits. This was to be judged on a project-by-project basis. Early on, the need for a set of operating rules, a set of coordination rules, and an impartial outside arbitrator for disputes became evident. Mazda president Wadra and Ford president Bouton outlined those operating rules.

1. Keep top management involved: The boss must set a tone for the relationship. Otherwise middle managers will resist ceding partial control of a project to a partner.
2. Meet often, and often informally: Meetings should be at all levels and should include time for socializing. Trust can't be built solely around a boardroom table.
3. Use a matchmaker: A third party can mediate disputes, suggest new ways of approaching the partner, and offer an independent sounding board.
4. Maintain your independence: Independence helps both parties hone the areas of expertise that made them desirable partners in the first place.
5. Allow no "sacrifice" deals: Every project must be viable for each partner. It is up to senior management to see that an overall balance is maintained.
6. Appoint a monitor: Someone must take primary responsibility for monitoring all aspects of the alliance.
7. Anticipate cultural differences: They may be corporate, or national. Stay flexible, and try to place culturally sensitive executives in key posts. (Treece, Miller, and Melcher, 1992:104)

A four-person monitoring group was then set up and established the following coordination rules. Members of this group are in daily contact with each other by computer and must meet face to face at least once every eight months. Four months after this group's face-to-face meeting, Ford and Mazda's chairmen and staff meet to review the progress of ongoing projects. In addition, twice a year the heads of each firm's product development and manufacturing units meet; self-managed, cross-functional, and international benchmarking teams for each project work together daily (Treece, Miller, and Melcher, 1992:104).

Finally, a member of the Sumitomo Bank of Japan was selected as the impartial arbitrator for unresolvable disputes. Such disputes arose frequently in the early years of the joint venture and then disappeared entirely (Treece, Miller, and Melcher, 1992:103). Ford and Mazda's joint venture has helped each firm establish world-class organizational capabilities in previously weak areas of their respective value chains. For example, today one in every four Ford cars sold in the United States benefited from some degree of Mazda's help, while two of every five Mazdas have some Ford help. In addition, Ford obtained access to Mazda's distribution capabilities in Japan and became the largest seller there—72,000 U.S. cars last year—and modeled its super efficient Hermosilla, Mexico plant on the design of a Mazda plant in Japan (Treece, Miller, and Melcher, 1992:103). Today, Ford's Mexico manufacturing plant, thanks to Mazda, is outpacing all other U.S. and Japanese corporations in reducing product cost and increasing product quality (Lohr, 1992:D2). Today, Mazda's auto designs, marketing, and finance, with the help of Ford, have led to a dramatic increase in Mazda's auto market shares (Treece, Miller, and Melcher, 1992:104).

Technology-Based Capabilities. In comparing a firm's value chain with the firm's competitors, one may find that while some aspects of a firm's value chain can produce value-added activities, some portions of a firm's value chain of most concern to the customers cannot, without the addition of some new state-of-the-art technology. Under such conditions, the firm's entire value chain may be in need of modification in order to reap the benefits of the addition of this new technology.

The knowledge necessary to obtain this value-added advantage resides in the innovative and appropriate use of these new technologies. In all cases, continuous improvement programs are necessary to implement the new technologies and to appropriately adjust the value chain to the technology so as not to lose other value-added gains. The list of corporations that have attempted to leapfrog their competition but failed are legion and include GM, IBM, and AT&T. However, one such attempt which has led to dramatic success is that of The Limited.

The Limited Company is a major manufacturer of women's apparel throughout the world. Each evening the store managers in 3,200 stores across the United States collect data regarding sales for that day—size, color, fashion, number, and so on—through their electronic point of sale computer system (EPOS). The cutting order information is telecommunicated to The Limited's workshops in Hong Kong, Singapore, and Sri Lanka, and is translated into next-day manufacturing orders. Within days these just-in-time inventory replacements are shipped to The Limited's Ohio distribution center on a Boeing 747 (Hochswender 1990).

In addition to supplying replacement merchandise in a timely fashion, The Limited's EPOS system can be used to monitor marketing. It can track fashion design performance, pinpointing age groups, income level, and geographic locations where specific fashion designs sell well. Ultimately, EPOS could be used for ordering customized designs by color, size, cut, and style with less than one week turnaround on delivery of orders. In the use of electronic point of sale merchandising for customized design, computer-integrated manufacturing for production, and just-in-time product delivery for marketing, we see R & D, marketing, and manufacturing fused into a flexible, high-speed, reciprocally coordinated interface system (Phillips and Denkin, 1989:192).

The Limited diversified its business in 1990 by acquiring Lerner, Victoria's Secret, Lane Bryant, and opening The Limited Express. In each of these chains, EPOS has been employed as a value-added tool for successfully dominating their respective market niches (Phillips and Denkin, 1989:199).

Finally, "The Limited's mass merchandisers can take the newest trends from Paris or New York and place cheaper versions in its stores weeks before the original designs are produced" (Hochswender, 1990:5). This provides The Limited with a technology-based capability for dominating its respective markets.

Capability-based competitors review their value chain in comparison to their competitors and locate those functional and business processes in which they have competitive advantage. They try to link or coalign those functions or processes in some systematic way so as to set world-class benchmarks which will yield sustainable competitive advantage through knowledge-based, alliance-based, and/or technology-based coalignment. Continuous improvement programs are then employed to generate and maintain this sustainable competitive advantage. Toyota, Ford, and The Limited each in turn successfully employed capabilities analysis as outlined previously to obtain a recognizable, sustainable competitive advantage from its knowledge-based, alliance-based, and technology-based capabilities.

We began this chapter by noting that a firm's strategic fit with its environment was the key to corporate success in the 1990s. We noted that tight fit led to sustained excellent performance. We now see that knowledge-based, alliance-based, and technology-based capabilities generate a tight fit, creating the underlying dynamic necessary for producing excellence in negotiated linking processes.

Summary of an Organization's Control Processes

Effective organizational control involves auditing a firm's high-speed management performance by benchmarking it against the best in the world and then modifying the information and communication linkages in order to move closer to or surpass the benchmark. Auditing can be undertaken by tracking three types of information—functional units and business process flow, environmental scanning and benchmarking flow, and skills and training development flow. Two examples were provided of such audits and how they were used to fine-tune a firm's high-speed management performance.

Once we understand where a firm's problems with speed-to-market exist and the performance levels of competitors and desires of customers, then five strategies exist for controlling a firm's response: confront, focus, circumvent, join, and withdraw. The appropriate strategy then guides the upgrading of a firm's performance by improving its core capabilities in knowledge, technology, or networking. Several examples were explored of how to institutionalize such a change.

We are now at the end of our journey aimed at developing an organizational communication theory of integration, coordination, and control of a firm's performance through high-speed management. Our task has been to locate a pent-up demand for a product, then to modify a firm's internal and external information and communication linkages so as to reduce a firm's cycle time more than its competitors in providing a high-quality product. In so doing, we aim to improve a firm's market shares and profits. Thus, we develop a sustainable competitive advantage through the improved integration, coordination, and control of a firm's information and communication systems.

If high-speed management is an inductively derived theory based on the practices of high performance world class firms, then it is appropriate to end this book by inquiring into the empirical generalizations which can be derived from all of these firms in general and at least one specific example of such a firm overtime.

An Overtime Data Based Evaluation of High-Speed Management Strategies

It's not a matter of getting it right the first time: it's a matter of continuously changing to keep it right.
(Berling, 1993:25)

Two sets of data illustrate the effectiveness of high-speed management's competitive and continuous improvement strategies overtime. *First,* there are some very informative studies undertaken between the mid 1980s and today regarding the effectiveness and sources of ineffectiveness in the implementation of various types of continuous improvement programs. Second, there is data available regarding the 1992 competition between eight firms in the electrotechnology industry which includes one high-speed management firm, General Electric, a U.S. firm, and several European and Japanese firms. Let us explore each of these data bases in turn.

Studies of Continuous Improvement Programs

Many organizations throughout the world have undertaken various teamwork, cycle time reduction, and reengineering programs over the last decade aimed at improving organizational performance. Several recent studies which assess this effort have been published which report that between 60 and 70 percent of all such efforts fail and that the 30 percent which do succeed have certain unique management characteristics which foster success.

First, a group of studies undertaken by Arthur D. Little, A. T. Kearney, Rath and Strong, and Ernst and Young, which surveyed over 1,200 firms across industries in the Americas, Europe, and Asia, report that between 60 and 70 percent of all TQM, cycle time reduction, and reengineering efforts aimed at improving a firm's performance fail to meet management's expectations for success and were discontinued within two years (Titzel, 1992:12; Fuchsberg, 1991:B1; *The Economist,* 1992:67).

Second, Venkatraman and Prescott, in their 1990 study of 2,000 strategic business units, found that productivity and quality increases which required significant investment increase product cost, cut market shares and profits in product markets that were export, service, emerging, mature, and/or declining oriented. *Thus reorganizational efforts which led to productivity and quality improvements and product cost reductions were the only changes which increased sales profits and market shares* (Venkatraman and Prescott, 1990:1–19).

Third, several studies of over 200 firms which attempted to reduce cycle time in getting products to market revealed that reduced cycle time tended to increase productivity, quality, sales, and profits between 30 and 50 percent while allowing for a reduction in product price. Improved cycle time reduction led to process simplification and standardization which in turn yielded increased productivity and quality and more rapid adjustment to changes in customer demand (Spanner, Nuna, and Chandra, 1993:90–101; Mascarenhaus, 1992:499–510; Vesey, 1991:23–33).

Fourth, in 1992 Ernst and Young reported the results of their survey of over 500 firms undertaking reorganization in the Americas, Europe, and Asia. They found that only the highest performing firms had the learning potential and skills as a firm to successfully undertake major reorganizations. These high performance firms had a 7 percent or better return on assets and a value added per employee of $74,000 or better. *This suggests that only the highest performing firms had the organizational capability to change significantly and rapidly without failure* (Port, Cary, Kelly, and Forrest, 1992:66–74).

Finally, in 1994 the Deutsche Bank Research arm reported the results of their study of the efforts of 300 high performance global firms at organizational improvement through TQM, cycle time reduction, and reengineering programs. They found that high performance U.S. firms had improved the value added output of their firms by 56 percent, Japanese firms by –11.7 percent, and European firms by 36 percent over the last five years. Japan's decline was due in part to the 50 percent appreciation in the yen. The top improvements in productivity by a firm as measured by value-added per employee were:

Boeing	US	214.3%
Deutsche Babcock	Germany	153.5%
KHD	Germany	98.4%
Mannesmann	Germany	95.8%
Ebara	Japan	78.8%
Mitsubishi Heavy Ind	Japan	77.7%

(Gibson 1994:22).

The top improvements in productivity by country as measured by value added per employee were:

USA	Change 89–95	56.6%	1995 absolute	$59,590
Japan		–11.7%		$53,835
Europe		36.9%		$24,170

and the total added in total assets were:

USA	2.1%	17.0%
Japan	–20.7%	7.2%
Europe	–2.4%	13.1%

(Gibson 1994:22).

Collectively, these studies argue that only firms with certain specific management characteristics can succeed on a continuing basis at improving their performances. They must (1) hold prices constant or reduce prices while improving productivity and quality; (2) focus on reducing a firm's cycle time in order to obtain large 30 to 50 percent improvements in sales, profits, and market shares; and (3) have a proven record of aggregate learning ability, 7 percent ROA, $74,000+ value added per employee. Currently, high performance U.S. firms on average are the most successful +56 percent at increasing productivity over the last five years.

Studies of Competition in the Electrotechnical Industry

The electrotechnical industry consists of six major multinational firms. These are General Electric, Hitachi, Siemans, Toshiba, ABB, and Mitsubishi Electric. These firms compete based on the power generation, power transmission, power distribution, motors and drives, and automation markets. Each firm also has other diversified interests such as railway infrastructure, financial services, jet engines, and others. For descriptive financial data see tables 10.2 and 10.3.

Table 10.2 1992 ELECTROTECHNICAL INDUSTRY

	Sales billion US $	Employees 000s	Sales per Employees 000s	Operating Profits 000s	Market Capitalization Billions	Market Value per Employee 000s
General Electric	61.9*	276	224	7.7*	79.3*	269*
Hitachi	60.4	328	184	2.0	25.8	60
Siemens	49.7	418*	119	1.2	21.7	47,
Toshiba	37.1	171	218	0.6	21.3	88
ABB	27.8	214	130	2.0	10.7	43
Mitsubishi Electric	26.1	100	261*	1.0	11.6	83

*Leader

(Constructed from Annual Reports)

Table 10.3   1984–1992 ELECTROTECHNICAL INDUSTRY

	8 Year Average Annual Growth in Revenues	8 Year Average Annual Growth in Employees	8 Year Average Annual Return on Sales Margin
GE	10%*	–2%	13%*
Hitachi	6%	9%	9%
Siemans	7%	4%	2%
Toshiba	5%	6%	N/A
ABB	7%	7%	N/A
Mitsubishi	7%	5%	N/A

*Leader

(Constructed from Annual Reports)

GE's performance is in most respects exemplary. In 1992 GE lead the industry in sales, profits, market capitalization, market value per employee, eight year average annual growth in revenues, least growth in employees, and average return on sales. What is most telling is that GE's profits in 1992 were greater than the next five firms combined, its market value per employee was four times higher than its next closest competitor, and its market capitalization was three times greater than its next closest competitor. All this with an average annual sales growth over eight years of 10 percent and an average annual growth in employees of –2 percent.

In 1993, ABB commissioned its benchmarking unit to discover why GE led the industry. They reported back that *it was not due to such economic variables* as its selection of businesses, its acquisition strategy, its between business synergy, its aggressive globalization, or the use of low cost foreign labor.

It was due to such management communication variables as:

1. a vision that is credibly communicated and lived;
2. very tough targets set from the top;
3. rapid decision-making;
4. rapid implementation by empowered employees;
5. a continuous push for improvement;
6. short feedback;
7. learning time; and
8. the delegation and ownership to the action level.

(Harnischfeger, Wense, and Hagan, 1993).

Jack Welch, the CEO of GE, summarized what our data based analysis of a high-speed management firm in the Electrotechnology Industry has taught him and GE when he states:

> People overestimate how complex business is. We've chosen one of the world's more simple professions. (1993b:92)
>
> If you can't sell a top-quality product at the world's least price, you're going to be out of the game. (1993b:82)
>
> We have seen what wins in our marketplace around the globe: speed, speed, and more speed. (1993a:2)
>
> Trust is enormously powerful in a corporation. People won't give their best unless they believe they'll be treated fairly. . . . The only way I know to create that kind of trust is by laying out your values and then walking the talk. (1993b:92)
>
> Another thing I've learned is the value of stretching the organization by setting the bar higher than people think they can go. The standard of performance we use is be as good as the best in the world. Invariably people find a way to get there or most of the way. They dream, they reach, they search. (1993b:88)
>
> Winning will depend not on big deals—acquisitions or depositions—but on a million smaller victories won by men and women who all came to work every day excited about finding a better way of doing things. (1990:4)
>
> The companies that find a way to engage every mind—harness every volt of passionate energy—bring excitement to the lives of their people—and break every artificial barrier between people—will be the companies that win in the 1990s and beyond. We intend to be the biggest and best of them. (1993b:1)

A Brief Summary and Conclusion to The Book

High-speed management is a set of communication and management principles designed to buffer a firm against environmental volatility by allowing for rapid adaptation to changing environmental conditions.
(King, 1994:2)

Our rather detailed inquiry into the nature, function, and scope of high-speed management has come to an end. We have observed large firms such as General Electric and small firms like the Bumper

Works attempt to cope with the global economy and the rather dramatic and volatile forces that such a system has unleashed. We have witnessed the volatility of unexpected competition, quick market saturation, and technological breakthroughs on the organizations in our communities and on our lives.

This book has tried to outline one constructive response to this uncertainty—high-speed management—a set of communication principles and practices for increasing the speed with which an organization can respond to environmental volatility and maintain its integrity. High-speed management, as we have seen, transforms the traditional role which communication and management play in the integration, coordination, and control of organizational processes.

This transformation features a shift from incremental change and learning processes to discontinuous change and learning processes, a change which emphasizes the use of creativity, clear targets, rapid learning, and team empowerment. High-speed management faces the challenge of discontinuous change by betting not on acquisitions, capital accumulation, or the use of advanced technology, but on the human ability to learn, to work in teams, and to continuously improve what human beings have created. In that sense it presents an optimistic view of human beings and of a firm's capacity to respond intelligently to rapid change.

However, to meet the challenge of discontinuous change through the use of high-speed management, we must sharpen our communication skills—our integration, coordination, and control communication processes.

That this can be done we have observed through the lens of this book and the firms we have examined. We now have to learn the skills, apply the principles, and continuously improve their use. This book, in short, is an invitation to change and improve yourself, your firm, and the global environment in which we live. It is a critical and yet constructive response.

References

Chapter 1: The Economic Environment Which Gave Rise to High-Speed Management

Baig, E. (January 19, 1987). America's most admired corporations. *Fortune.* 18–31.

Ballen, K. (February 10, 1992). America's most admired corporations. *Fortune.* 40–72.

Bartlett, C., and Goshal, S. (September/October, 1993). What is a global manager? *Harvard Business Review.* 124–132.

Bartmess, A., and Cerny, K. (Winter 1993). Building competitive advantage through a global network capability. *California Management Review.* 78–103.

Brown, W. and Karagozoglu, N. (1993). Leading the way to faster new product development. *Academy of Management Executive* 3:36–47.

Business Week. (1993). The productivity pacesetters. June 14:79.

Castells, Manuel. (1986). High technology, world development, and the structured transformation: The trends and debate. *Alternatives.* 11:297–342.

Clark, E. (November/December, 1989). What strategy can do for technology. *Harvard Business Review.* 94–98.

Cohen, S., and Zysman, J. (November 1984). Competitiveness: Presidential commission on industrial competitiveness (BRIE Working Power 8, Berkeley *Roundtable on International Economy.* University of California, Berkeley).

Cushman, Donald P., and King, Sarah S. (1989). The role of communication in high technology organizations: The emergence of high-speed management. In S. S. King (ed.), *Human Communication as a Field of Study.* Albany: State University of New York Press.

Cushman, Donald P., and King, Sarah S. (1988). The role of mass media in world community. *Informatologia Yugoslavia* 20:131–151.

Cushman, D. P., and King, S. S. (1993). A comparative study of communication within multinational organizations in the United States and Western Europe. In R. Shuter (ed.), *Annual of International and Intercultural Communication* 18. Beverly Hills, Calif.: Sage.

Davenport, Carol. (January 6, 1989). America's most admired corporations. *Fortune.* 16–27.

Department of Commerce (1992). *Facts on the Pacific Rim 1992.* Sacramento, CA.

Dent, Harry. (May, 1990). Corporation of the future. *Small Business Reports.* 55–63.

Directory of On Line Data Bases (1992). New York: Elsevier.

Dumaine, B. (February 13, 1989). How managers can succeed through speed. *Fortune.* 54–59.

Dumaine, B. (July 16, 1990). Turnaround champs. *Fortune.* 36–44.

The Economist. (January 15, 1994). Ready to take on the world. 65–66.

Feigenbaum, Edward, McCorduck, Pamela and Nii, Penny. (1988). *The Rise of the Expert Company.* New York: Times Books.

Fornham, A. (February 7, 1994). America's most admired company. *Fortune.* 50–70.

Fraker, Sue. (March 5, 1984). High-speed management for the high-tech age. *Fortune,* pp. 62–68.

Gluck, F. (Spring 1983). Global competition in the 1980s. *The Journal of Business Strategy* 3:4; 22–27.

Gold, B. (1987). Approaches to accelerating product and process development. *Production Innovation Management* 4:81–88.

Gupta, A., and Wilemon, D. (Winter 1990). Accelerating the development of technology-based new products. *California Management Review* 32:24–45.

Henderson, J., and Scott, A. J. (1986). Global restructuring and the informalization of the American semiconductor industry. In M. Birchemy and R. McQuizidled (eds.). *The Development of the High Technology Industry: An International Survey.* London: Croom Helm.

Hillkirk, John. (January 12, 1989). It could be trade boom or bust. *USA Today.* B4B.

Hutton, C. (January 18, 1988). America's most admired corporations. *Fortune.* 32–52.

King, S. S., and Cushman, D. P. (eds.) (1994). *High-Speed Management: Organizational Communication in the 1990s: A Reader.* Albany: State University of New York Press.

McDonough, E., and Barczak, G. (1991). Speeding up new product development: The effects of leadership style and sources of technology. *Journal of Product Innovation Management* 8:203–228.

Makin, C. E. (January 10, 1983). Ranking corporate reputations. *Fortune.* 33–44.

Millson, M., Raj, S. and Wilemon, D. (1992). A survey of major approaches for accelerating new product development. *Journal of Product Innovation Management* 9:53–69.

Nayak, R. (November/December 1990) Planning speeds technology development. *Planning Review.* 14–20.

New York Times. (January 3, 1992). Longtime executives are promoted by G.E. 63.

Naj, A. K. (June 14, 1990). GE's latest invention. *New York Times.* A1.

Perry, N. (January 1985). America's best run companies. *Fortune.* 17–29.

Perry, N. (February 10, 1992). What's powering Mexico's success. *Fortune.* 109–115.

Port, Otis. (June 16, 1986). High tech to the rescue. *Business Week.* 100–108.

Porter, M., and Miller, V. (July-August 1985). How information gives you competitive advantage. *Harvard Business Review.* 149–160.

Pura, R. (January 28, 1992). ASIAN leaders see need to create united market to avoid loss of trade. *Wall Street Journal.* A10.

Rapoport, C. (April 20, 1992). Getting in touch with the Japanese. *Fortune.* 149–155.

Rebello, K. (December 9, 1988). Super chip puts mainframe on desktop. *USA Today.* B1.

Reese, J. (February 8, 1993). America's most admired corporations. *Fortune.* 49–72.

Russell, E., Adams, A., and Boundy, B. (Winter 1986). High-technology test marketing Campbell Soup Company. *The Journal of Consumer Marketing* 3:1:71–80.

Sawers, J., and Tabb, W. K. (1984). *Sunbelt/Snowbelt: Urban Development and Regional Restructuring.* New York: Oxford University Press.

Scheen, E. (January 18, 1988). America's most admired corporations. *Fortune.* 32–52.

Sellers, P. (January 7, 1985). America's most admired corporations. *Fortune.* 17–29.

Smith, S. (January 24, 1990). America's most admired corporations. *Fortune.* 58–89.

Sprout, A. (February 11, 1991). America's most admired corporations. *Fortune.* 52–79.

Ulrich, D., and Wiersema, N. (1989). Organizational capability as competitive advantage. *Human Resources Planning* 10:112–149.

Vesey, J. (1991). The new competitors: They think in terms of speed
to market. *Academy of Management Executives* 5:23–33.

Wall Street Journal. (August 11, 1992). The wealth of nations. A10.

Walton, J. (1985). The I.M.F. riot. Paper delivered at the I.S.A. Conference on the Urban Impact of the New International Division of
Labor, Hong Kong.

Wilke, J. (February 13, 1992). Analysts believe new chip from Digital
may give market advantage to company. *Wall Street Journal.* A2.

Young, John. (Spring 1990). An American giant rethinks globalization.
Information Strategy. 5–10.

Chapter 2: High-Speed Management: A Theoretic and Practical Communication Framework

Automotive News. (1993). 1980–1993 A Compilation.

Borrus, A. (May 7, 1990) Japanese streak ahead in Asia. *Business
Week* 31:54–55.

Carnevale, A. (1992). *America and the Economy.* Washington, D.C.:
U.S. Department of Labor.

Coyne, K. (January 1986). The anatomy of sustainable competitive
advantage. *Business Horizons* 29:46–62.

Cushman, D. P., and King, S. S. (1989). The role of communication
in high-technology organizations: The emergence of high-speed
management. In S. S. King (ed.), *Human Communication As a
Field of Study.* Albany: State University of New York Press.

Cushman, D., and King, S. S. (1992). High-speed management: A revolution in organizational communication in the 1990s. In S. Deetz
(ed.), *Communication Yearbook 16.* 1993.

Cvar, M. (1986). Case studies in global competition: Patterns of success and failure. In M. Porter (ed.), *Competition in Global Industry.* Boston: Harvard Business School Press. 483–517.

Lohr, S. (June 18, 1992). Ford and Chrysler outpace Japanese in
reducing costs. *New York Times.* D1.

Mockler, Robert. (1972). *The Management Control Process.* Englewood,
N.J.: Prentice-Hall.

Ourusoff, A. (August 22, 1989). Car wars. *Financial World.* 40–41.

Poling, H. (November 20, 1989). Interview. *Automobile News.* E7.

Porter, M. E. (Winter 1986). Changing patterns of international competition. *California Management Review* 27.2: 9–39.

Porter, M., and Millar, V. (July-August 1985). How information gives competitive advantage. *Harvard Business Review.* 149–160.

Robinson, R. (Spring/Summer 1981). Background concepts and philosophy on international business from World War II to the present. *Journal of International Business Studies* 1321.

Rockart, J., and Short, J. (Winter 1989). ITT in the 1990s: Managing organizational interdependence. *Sloan Management Review* 30: 7–17.

Smith, K., Grimm, C., Chen, M., and Gannon, M. (1989). Predictors of response time to competitive strategic action: Preliminary theory and evidence. *Journal of Business Research* 8:245–258.

Stalk, G. (July/August 1988). Time: The next source of competitive advantage. *Harvard Business Review.* 41–51.

Stalk, G., Evans, P., and Shulman, L. (March-April 1992). Competing on capabilities: The new rules of corporate strategy. *Harvard Business Review.* 57–69.

Taylor, A. (February 26, 1990a). Can American cars come back? *Fortune.* 62–65.

Taylor, A. (November 19, 1990b). Why Toyota keeps getting better. *Fortune.* 121:66–79.

Templin, N. (May 28, 1993). Toyota is stand out once again. In J. D. Powers, Quality survey. *Wall Street Journal.* B1.

Thompson, J. D. (1967). *Organizations in Action: Social Science Bases of Administration Theory.* New York: McGraw Hill.

Tichy, N., and Charan, R. (September/October 1989). Speed, simplicity, self-confidence: An interview with Jack Welch. *Harvard Business Review.* 112–120.

Treece, J., and Howr, J. (August 14, 1989). Shaking up Detroit. *Business Week.* 74–80.

Vesey, J. (1991). The new competitors: They think in terms of "speed to market." *Academy of Management Executives* 2:23–33.

White, J. (September 9, 1991). Japanese auto makers help U.S. suppliers become more efficient. *Wall Street Journal.* A1, A7.

Woods, W. (October 4, 1993). The world's top automobiles change lanes. *Fortune.* 73–76.

Part I: Organizational Integration Processes

Drucker, P. (September/October, 1988). Management and the world's work. *Harvard Business Review.* 65–76.

Chapter 3: High-Speed Management Leadership: A Global Perspective

Andrews, E. (August 17, 1993a). AT&T paying $12.6 billion for McGaw Cellular. *New York Times.* A1.

Andrews, E. (August 8, 1993b). AT&T reaches out and grabs everyone. *New York Times.* 3-1.

Bartmess, A., and Cerney, K. (Winter 1993). Building competitive advantage through a global network of capabilities. *California Management Review.* 78–103.

Bartlett, C., and Goshal, S. (October/September 1993). What is a global manager? *Harvard Business Review.* 124–132.

Barton, D. (1992). Core capabilities and core rigidities: A paradox in managing new product development. *Strategic Management Journal* 13:111–128.

Blake, Robert, and Mouton, Jane. (1978). *The New Management Grid.* Houston: Gulf Publishing.

Bray, D. W., Campbell, R. J., and Grant, D. L. (1974). *Formative Years in Business: A Long-Term AT&T Study of Managerial Lives.* New York: Wiley.

Burdett, J. (1993). Managing in the age of discontinuity. *Management Decisions* 31:10–17.

Byrd, Richard. (1987). Corporate leadership skill: "A new synthesis." *Organizational Dynamics.* 34–43.

Cohn, R. (March 2, 1992). The very model of efficiency. *New York Times.* D1–D8.

Cushman, D., and King, S. (1995). Leading organizational change: A high-speed management perspective. In D. Cushman and S. S. King (eds.), *Communicating Change: A Management Perspective.* Albany: State University of New York Press.

Cushman, D., and King, S. (eds.) (1994b). *High-Speed Management and Organizational Communication in the 1990s: A Reader.* Albany: State University of New York Press.

Cushman, D., and King, S. (1994a). A comparative study of communication within multinational organizations in the U.S. and Europe. In R. Wiseman and R. Shuter (eds.), *Communication in Multinational Organizations: Annual of International and Intercultural Organizations* 18. Beverly Hills, Calif.: Sage. 94–117.

Cushman, D., and King, S. (1993). High-speed management: A revolution in organizational communication in the 1990s. In S. Deetz (ed.), *Communication Yearbook* 16. Newbury Park, Calif.: Sage. 209–236.

Cushman, D., and King, S. S. (1992). High-speed management: A revolution in organizational communication in the 1990s. In H. Cross and W. Commons (eds.), *The Proceedings of the Fifth Conference on Corporate Communication.* Madison, N.J.: Fairleigh Dickinson University. 99–113.

Drucker, P. (September/October 1988). Management and the world's work. *Harvard Business Review* 65:76.

Dumaine, B. (February 22, 1993). The new non-manager managers. *Fortune.* 36–112.

Fortune. (April 8, 1991). General Electric as CEO boot camp. 12.

Fortune. (April 9, 1993). The Fortune 500. 185.

French, J., and Raven, B. (1959). The bases of social power. In D. Cartwright (ed.), *Studies of Social Power.* Ann Arbor, Mich.: Institute of Social Research. 150–167.

Harris, G. (May/June 1993). The post-capitalist executive: An interview with Peter Drucker. *Harvard Business Review.* 115–122.

Hersey, P., and Blanchard, K. H. (1977). *Management of Organizational Behavior.* Englewood, NJ: Prentice Hall.

Hunsicker, J. Quincy. (1985). Vision, leadership and Europe's business future. *European Management Journal* 3.3: 22–38.

Jacob, R. (1992). The search for the organization of tomorrow. *Fortune.* 2:91–98.

Kantor, R. (November/December 1989). The new managerial work. *Harvard Business Review.* 85–92.

Kerr, S., and Jarmier, J. M. (1978). Substitutes for leadership: Their meaning and measurement. *Organizational Behavior and Human Performance* 22:375–403.

Kirkpatrick, D. (May 17, 1993). Could AT&T rule the world? *Fortune.* 55–64.

Levin, D. (July 12, 1992). New L/H as in last hope. *New York Times.* 3-1, C1.

Lewyn, M. (August 30, 1992). AT&T's bold bet. *Business Week.* 27–32.

Liberson, S., and O'Conner, J. F. (1972). Leadership and organizational performance: A study of large corporations. *American Sociological Review* 37:117–130.

Likert, Rensis. (1961). *New Patterns of Management.* New York: McGraw Hill.

Miner, J. B. (1978). Twenty years of research on role motivation theory of managerial effectiveness. *Personnel Psychology* 31:739–760.

Mintzberg, H. (1973). *The Nature of Management Work.* New York: Harper and Row.

New York Times (March 9, 1992). GE top managers make excellent CEOs. D1.

Nohria, N., and Garcia-Pont, C. (1991). Global strategies, linkages, and industrial structure. *Strategic Management* 6:105–124.

Obloj, K., Cushman, D. P., and Kozminski, A. (1994). *Winning: Continuous Improvement Theory in High Performance Organizations.* Albany: State University of New York Press.

Ostroff, F., and Smith, D. (1992). Redesigning the corporation: The horizontal organization. *The McKinsey Quarterly* 1:148–168.

Prahalad, C. K., and Hamal, G. (May/June 1990). The core competencies of the corporation. *Harvard Business Review.* 74–91.

Prokesch, Steven. (January 25, 1987). Remaking the American C.E.O. *New York Times.* C1, 8.

Schonfeld, E. (September 7, 1992). Acacia, Lee's parting shot. *Fortune.* 56–57.

Seller, S. (June 6, 1988). How IBM teaches techies to sell, *Fortune.* 71–73.

Sherman, D. (March 27, 1989). The mind of Jack Welch. *Fortune.* 39–50.

Smart, T. (1993). Jack Welch on the art of thinking small. *Business Week.* 212–216.

Smart, T., Engardio, P., and Smith, G. A. (November 8, 1993). GE's brave new world. *Business Week.* 64–70.

Snow, C., Miles, R., and Coleman, H. (1993). Managing 21st century network organizations. *Organizational Dynamics.* 5 19.

Stalk, G., Evans, P., and Schulman, L. (March/April 1992). Competing on capabilities: The new rules of corporate strategy. *Harvard Business Review.* 57–69.

Stewart, T. (August 12, 1991). GE keeps those ideas coming. *Fortune.* 118–122.

Stewart, T. (May 18, 1992). The firm of tomorrow. *Fortune.* 93–98.

Stewart, T. (August 23, 1993). Reengineering: The hot new managing tool. *Fortune.* 41–48.

Stogdill, R. M. (1974). *Handbook of Leadership: A Survey of Theory and Research.* New York: Free Press.

Taylor, A. (July 27, 1992). Chrysler's next boss speaks. *Fortune.* 82–83.

Taylor, W. (March/April 1991). The logic of global business: An interview with ABB's Percy Barnevick. *Harvard Business Review.* 105.

Thompson, J. D. (1967). *Organizations in Action: Social Science Bases of Administration Theory.* New York: McGraw-Hill.

Tichy, N. M. (1989). GE's Crotonville: A staging ground for corporate revolution. *Academy of Management Executive* 3:99–106.

Tichy, N. M., and Charon, P. (September/October 1989). Speed, simplicity, and self-confidence: An interview with Jack Welch. *Harvard Business Review.* 112–120.

Tichy, N. M., and Devanno, M. (July 1986). The transformational leader. *Training and Development Journal* 40.7:27–32.

Tichy, N. M., and Ulrich, D. (Fall 1984). SMR Forum: The leadership challenge: A call for the transformational leaders. *Sloan Management Review.* 59–68.

Tushman, M. L., Newman, W. H. and Romanelli, E. (Fall 1986). Convergence and upheaval: Managing the unsteady pace of organizational evolution. *California Management Review* 29.1:29–44.

Welch, J. (April 27, 1988). Managing for the nineties. *GE Speech Reprint.*

Womack, J., Jones, D., and Roos, M. (September 23, 1990). How lean production can change the world. *New York Times Magazine.* 22–37.

Workout, September 1991.

Yukl, G. 1989). *Leadership in Organizations.* Englewood Cliffs, N.J.: Prentice-Hall.

Zaleznick, A. (May/June 1977). Managers and leaders: Are they different? *Harvard Business Review.* 67–78.

Chapter 4: High-Speed Management Corporate Climate

Arnst, C., and Verity, J. (August 9, 1993). IBM: A work in progress. *Business Week.* 24–25.

Buck, F. (1986). In Rogers, F. C., *The IBM Way.* Holmes, Pa.: Random House.

Calori, R., and Sarnin, P. (1991). Corporate culture and economic performance: A French study. *Organizational Studies.* 48–74.

Cushman, D., King, S. S., and Smith, T. (1988). The rules perspective on organizational communication. In G. Goldhaber and G. Barnett (eds.), *Handbook of Organizational Communication.* Norwood, N.J.: Ablex. 55–94.

Davis, L. J. (March, 1988). They call him Neutron. *Business Month.* 25–29.

Dobrzynski, J. (August 2, 1993). These board members aren't IBM compatible. *Business Week.* 23.

The Economist (January 14, 1993). The toughest job in America business. 23–35.

Farnham, A. (February 7, 1994). America's most admired company, *Fortune.* 50–53.

Fortune. (November 30, 1992). News and trends, 16.

Gutknecht, D. (Winter 1982). Conceptualizing culture in organizational theory. *California Sociologist.* 68–87.

Hansell, S. (April 9, 1994). Kidder, Peabody jolted by phantom bond trades. *Wall Street Journal.* D8.

Hays, L. (February 23, 1994a). Three more IBM directors are leaving, including John Ropel, ex-chairman. *Wall Street Journal.* B9.

Hays, L. (May 13, 1994b). Gerstner is struggling as he tries to change ingrained IBM culture. *Wall Street Journal.* A1, A8.

Hofstede, G. (1993). Cultural constraints in management themes. *Academy of Management Executives* 7/8:81–94.

Hutton, C. (January 7, 1986). America's most admired corporations. *Fortune.* 16–27.

IBM (December 1983). IBM's goals for the 1980s. *Think.* 11–23.

IBM (1984). *Annual Report: IBM.* Armonk, N.Y.

IBM (1985a). *IBM Management Development Center,* Armonk, N.Y.: IBM.

IBM (1985b). *Marketing and Systems Engineering Careers.* Armonk, N.Y.: International Business Machines Corp.

IBM (1985c). *National Accounts Division Entry Marketing Education Program.* White Plains, N.Y.: International Business Machines Corp.

IBM (1985d). *On Managing: A Selection of Management Briefing Letters from IBM's Chief Executives.* Armonk, N.Y.: ISG Business Systems.

Larsen, P. (1994). Corporate culture and morality: Durkheim inspired reflections on the limits of corporate culture. *Journal of Management Studies* 31.1:1–18.

Lewis, D. (May 1985). Interview with Dick Lewis, account executive in national accounts division, IBM, Atlanta, Georgia. Quoted by Scott Blaney. Training program for IBM marketing department. (unpublished paper).

Lohr, S. (June 26, 1994). On the road with chairman Lou. *New York Times,* C1–5.

Luciana, L. (November 11, 1985). Seeing the future work at IBM. *Fortune.* 165.

McMenamin, B. (March 14, 1994). What kind of duck are you? *Forbes.* 124–128.

Mitchell, K., and Dobrzynak, J. (December 14, 1987). Jack Welch: How good a manager? *Business Week.* 92–103.

New York Times. (February 12, 1986). The I.B.M. in G.N.P. E61.

Pascale, R. (Winter 1985). The paradox of "corporate culture": Reconciling ourselves to socialization. *California Management Review* 27:26–41.

Petre, P. (January 5, 1989). The man who brought GE to life. *Fortune.* 76–77.

Philipsen, G. (1981). The prospect for cultural communication. Paper presented at the *Seminar on Communication Theory from*

Eastern and Western Perspectives, East-West Communication Institute, East-West Center, Honolulu, Hawaii.

Porter, B. and Parker, W. (Spring/Summer 1993). Cultural change. *Human Resources Management.* 31:45–67.

Posner, B., Koyzes, J., and Schmidt, W. (Fall 1985). Shared values make a difference: An empirical test of corporate culture. *Human Resource Management* 4:243–309.

Quann, B. G. (1985). How IBM assesses its business-to-business advertising. *Business Marketing,* 106, 108–111, 112.

Quick, J. (1988). Crafting an organizational culture: Herb's hand at Southwest Airlines. *Organizational Dynamics.* 45–46.

Reimann, B. and Weiner, Y. (March/April, 1988). Corporate culture avoiding the Elisit Trap. *Business Horizon.* 31–44.

Robotham, J. (January 18, 1994). Big Blue leaves others in its wake. *The Australian.* 25.

Schein, E. (Winter 1984). Coming to a new awareness of organizational culture. *Sloan Management Review.* 3–16.

Seller, S. (June 6, 1988). How IBM teaches techics to sell, *Fortune,* 71–73.

Sellers, P. (January 1985). America's most admired corporations. *Fortune.* 17–29.

Teitelbaum, R. (April 18, 1994). *The Fortune 500.* 220.

Tichy, N., and Charon, (September/October 1989). Speed, simplicity, and self-confidence: An interview with Jack Welch. *Harvard Business Review.* 112–189.

Watson, T. J. (1963). *A Business and Its Beliefs: The Ideas That Helped Build IBM.* New York: McGraw-Hill.

Weaver, R. (1964). *Visions of Order: The Cultural Crises of Our Time.* Baton Rouge, LA: Louisiana University Press.

Welsh, T. (February 17, 1994). Best and worst corporate reputations. *Fortune.* 58–65.

Chapter 5: High-Speed Management Teamwork

Barrett, F. (Winter 1987). Teamwork: How to expand its power and punch. *Business Quarterly.* 24–31.

Bohman, L., and Deal, T. (1993). What makes a team work? *Organizational Dynamics.* 34–44.

Blattberg, R. C.. and Deighton, J. (Fall 1991). Interactive marketing: Exploiting the age of addressability. *Sloan Management Review.* 5–14.

Cohen, B., and Zhou, X. (April 1991). Status process in enduring group groups. *American Sociological Review* 56:179–188.

Cohn, S., and Ledford, G. (1994). The effectiveness of self-managed teams: A quasi-experiment. *Human Relations* 47:13–43.

Cushman, D. (1993). When is teamwork a good and when is it a bad solution to organizational problems? In M. Cross and W. Cummins (eds.), *Approaching 2000: The Proceedings of the Sixth Conference on Communication.* Madison, N.J.: Fairleigh Dickinson University. 83–93.

Denton, D. (October, 1992). Building a team. *Quality Process.* 87–91.

The Economist. (April 18, 1992). The cracks in quality. 68–69.

Fiorelli, J. (1988). Power in work games: Team member perspectives. *Human Relations* 41:1–12.

Flynn, J., and Care, F. (1994). High-speed management and continuous improvement: Teamwork applications at General Electric. In S. S. King and D. P. Cushman (eds.), *High-Speed Management and Organizational Communication in the 1990s.* Albany: State University of New York Press. 233–261.

Flynn, R., McCombs, T., and Ellery, D. (1987). Staffing the self-managed work teams. *Journal of Leadership and Organizational Development* 11:26–31.

Hardaker, M., and Ward, B. (November/December 1987). Getting things done: How to make a team work. *Harvard Business Review.* 112–117.

Henke, J., Krackenberg, R., and Lyons, T. (1993). Perspective: Cross-functional teams: Good concept, poor implementation. *Journal of Product Innovation and Management* 10:216–229.

Hershock, R., Cowman, C., and Peters, D. (1994). From experience: Action teams that work. *Journal of Product Innovation and Management* 11:94–109.

Holusha, J. (January 29, 1989). No utopia, but to workers, it's a job. *New York Times.* C1.

Ju, Y., and Cushman, D. P. (1994). *Teamwork Within a High-Speed Management Perspective.* Albany: State University of New York Press.

Katzenback, J., and Smith, D. (March/April 1993). The discipline of teams. *Harvard Business Review.* 111–120.

Kelly, R. (November/December 1988). In praise of followers. *Harvard Business Review.* 142–148.

Lefton, R., and Buzzotta, V. (Winter, 1987–88). Teams and teamwork: A study of executive level teams. *National Productivity Review.* 11–21.

Manz, C. (1992). Self-leading work teams: Moving beyond the self-management myth. *Human Relations* 45:13–15.

Obloj, K., Cushman, D., and Kozminski, A. (1995). *Winning: Continuous Improvement Theory in High Performance Organizations.* Albany: State University of New York Press.

Pinto, M., and Pinto, K. (1990). Project team communication and cross-functional cooperation in new program development. *Journal of Product Innovation and Management* 7:200–212.

Port, O., Cary, J., Kelly, K., and Forest, S. (November 30, 1992). *Quarterly Business.* 66–71.

Slovacek, C., and Cushman, D. P. (February 1993). Measuring the success of TQM depends on the circumstances. *Washington Business Review.* 19–25.

Walter, R. (November 1992). Benchmarking for beginners. *Sales and Marketing and Management Journal.* 59–64.

Part II: Organizational Coordination Processes

Turner, I. (Spring, 1989). Management update. *Journal of General Management.* 14:1–9.

Chapter 6: The R & D and Marketing Interface

Ansoff, H. and Stewart, J. (1967). Strategies for a techology based business. *Harvard Business Review* 45:31–82.

Bartlett, C., and Goshal, B. (Fall 1988). Organizing for world wide effectiveness: The transnational solution. *California Management Review.* 54–74.

Bennett, R., and Cooper, R. (September/October 1984). The product life cycle trap. *Business Horizons* 27:7–16.

Blattburg, R., and Deighton, J. (Fall 1994). Inactive marketing: Exploiting the age of addressability. *Sloan Management Review.* 5–14.

Camillus, J. (1984). Technology-driven and market-driven life cycles: Implications for multinational corporate strategy. *Columbia Journal of World Business* 14:56–60.

Carter, N., Stearns, T., Reynolds, P., and Miller, B. (1994). New venture strategies: Theory development with an empirical base. *Strategic Management Journal* 15:21–41.

Cooper, R. (1985). Overall corporate strategies for new product programs. *Industrial Marketing Management* 14:179–193.

DeMeyer, A. (Spring 1991). Tech talk: How managers are stimulating global R & D communication. *Sloan Management Review* 49:49–58.

GE Research and Development Center. (1991). *Facts.* Schenectady, N.Y. 9.

Gupta, A., Raj, S., and Wileman, D. (1985). R & D and marketing dialogue in high-tech firms. *Industrial Marketing and Management* 14:289–300.

Gwynne, P. (1990). The changing role of corporate R & D. *Monogram.* 22–33.

King, S. S., and Cushman, D. P. (1988). Technology and market forces: Their application in the information marketplace. *Informatologia Yugoslavia* 20:142–157.

Klein, H., and Linneman, R. (1984). Environmental assessment: An international study of corporate practice. *Journal of Business Strategy* 5:66–75.

Miles, R., and Snow, C. (1984). Fit, failure, and the hall of fame. *California Management Review.* 10–27.

Naj, A. (June 14, 1992). GE's latest innovation: A way to move ideas from lab to market. *Wall Street Journal.* 1.

Porter, M. (Spring 1986). The strategic role of international marketing. *Journal of Consumer Marketing* 3:17–21.

Prescott, J., Kohl, A. J., and Venkatraman, P. (1986). The market share-profitability relationship: An empirical assessment of major assertions and contradictions. *Strategic Management Journal* 7:377–394.

Quinn, J. (May/June 1985). Managing innovation: Controlled chaos. *Harvard Business Review.* 73–84.

Robb, W. (March/April 1991). How good is our research? *Research and Technology Management.* 16–21.

Robertson, T. (Fall 1993). How to reduce market penetration cycle time. *Sloan Management Review.* 87–95.

Russell, E., Adams, J., and Boundy, B. (Winter 1986). High tech test marketing at Campbell Soup Company. *Journal of Consumer Marketing* 3:71–80.

Schlendor, B. (July 11, 1994). Matsushita shows how to go global. *Fortune.* 159–166.

Shanklin, W., and Ryans, J. (November/December 1984). Organizing for high tech marketing. *Harvard Business Review.* 164–171.

Stoner, J., Collins, R., and Yaffon, P. (1985). *Management for Australia.* Sydney, Australia: Prentice-Hall.

Turner, I. (Spring 1989). Management update. *Journal of General Management* 14:5.

Utterback, J. (1981). In the innovative process: Evolution vs. revolution. Proceedings of a Symposium for Senior Executives, MIT.

Williams, J. (1983). Technological evaluation and competitive response. *Strategic Management Journal* 4:55:65.

Chapter 7: The R & D, Marketing, and Manufacturing Interface

Bylinsky, G. (May 26, 1986). A breakthrough in automating the assembly line. *Fortune.* 64–66.

Chen, Y., and Adams, E. (February 1991). The impact of flexible manufacturing systems on production and quality. *IEEE Transactions on Engineering Management* 35:33–45.

Drucker, P. (May/June 1990). The emerging theory of manufacturing. *Harvard Business Review.* 94–102.

The Economist. (March 5, 1994). Manufacturing technology. 1–17.

Feigenbaum, E., McCorduck, P., and Nii, H. (1988). *The Rise of the Expert Company.* New York: Times Books.

Hayes, R., and Pisano, G. (January/February 1994). Beyond world class: The new manufacturing structure. *Harvard Business Review.* 77–86.

Hochswender, W. (May 13, 1990). How fashions spread round the world at the speed of light. 5.

Jelinek, M., and Goldhar, J. (Spring 1983) The interface between strategy and manufacturing technology. *Columbia Journal of World Business.* 26–36.

Jelinek, M., and Goldhar, J. (Summer 1984). The strategic implications of the factory of the future. *Sloan Management Review.* 29–37.

Kempe, T., and Bolwijn, P. (March/April 1988). Manufacturing: the case for vertical integration. *Harvard Business Review.* 75–81.

McGrath, M., and Hode, R. (May/June 1992). Manufacturing's new economies of scale. *Harvard Business Review.* 94–102.

Macarenhaus, B. (Winter 1984). The coordination of manufacturing in multinational companies. *Journal of International Business Studies.* 91–106.

Mansfield, E. (February 1993). The diffusion of flexible manufacturing systems in Japan, Europe, and the United States. *Management Science.* 149–159.

Messina, G., and Tricomi, G. (1990). Manufacturing communication architectures computers. *Industry* 13:285–293.

Parthasarthy, R., and Sethi, P. (1993). Relation of strategy to flexible automation: A test of fit and performance implications. *Strategic Management Journal* 14:529–569.

Scott, G. (1986). *Principles of Management Information Systems.* New York: McGraw Hill.

Stalk, G. (July/August 1988). Time: The next source of competitive advantage. *Harvard Business Review.* 41–51.

Wheelwright, S., and Hayes, K. (January/February ??). Competing through manufacturing. *Harvard Business Review.* 99–109.

Chapter 8: The R & D, Marketing, Manufacturing, and Management Information System Interface

Brown, P. (February/March 1989). Fashions quickening pulse. *Retailing Techology and Operations.* 16–22.

Charon, R. (September/October 1991). How networks reshape organizations—for results. *Harvard Business Review.* 104–115.

DeMeyer, A. (1987). The integration of information systems in manufacturing. *OMEGA: International Journal of Management Science* 5:229–338.

Magnet, M. (November 30, 1992). Who's winning the information revolution? *Fortune.* 110–117.

Markus D., and Robey, C. (1983). In Dick, J. *Computer Systems in Business.* Boston: PWS Computer Science.

Office of Technology Assessment. (1988). *Technology and the American Economic Transition: Choices for the Future.* Washington, D.C.: Government Printing Office.

Parker, M., and Benson, R. (December 1991). Information economics: An introduction. *Datamation.* 86–91.

Rose, E., and Munn, (1988). SNA network management directions. *IBM Systems Journal* 27:3–14.

Scott, G. (1986). *Principles of Management Information Systems.* New York: McGraw Hill.

Zmud, R., Boynton, A., and Jacobs, G. (Summer 1986). The information economy: A new perspective for effective management. *Data Base,* 17–23.

Part III: Organizational Control Processes

Turner, I. (Spring 1989). Management update. *Journal of General Management* 5:1–9.

Chapter 9: Auditing the Speed of a Firm's Information and Communication Flow

Altany, D. (February 1992). Benchmarkers unite. *Industry Week* 24:1–8.

Altany, D. (November 5, 1990). Copycats. *Industry Week.* 11–18.

Bower, J., and Hout, T. (November-December 1988). Fast-cycle capability for competitive power. *Harvard Business Review.* 110–118.

Camp, R. (July 1992). Learning from the best leads to superior performance. *Journal of Business Strategy.* 3–5.

Dumaine, B. (February 12, 1989). How managers can succeed through speed. *Fortune.* 54–59.

Feder, B. (January 3, 1992). Longtime executives are promoted by GE. *New York Times.* C3.

Garvin, D. (July/August 1993). Building a learning organization. *Harvard Business Review.* 78–91.

Garvin, D. (December 1989). Competing on the eight dimensions of quality. *Harvard Business Review.* 101–109.

Hardaker, M., and Ward, B. (November/December 1987). Getting things done. *Harvard Business Review.* 112–118.

Port, O., Cary, J., Kelly, K., and Forest, R. (November 30, 1992). Quality. *Business Week.* 64.

Sasaki, T. (1991). How the Japanese accelerated new car development. *Journal of Long Range Planning* 24:15–25.

Stumple, R. (1992). *Best Practices Resort.* Ernest and Young and Associates. Quality Foundation.

Taylor, A. (November 19, 1990). Why Toyota keeps getting better and better and better. *Fortune.* 66–79.

Turner, I. (1989). Management update. *Journal of General Management* 14:1–9.

Chapter 10: Information and Communication in a Strategic Linking Program

Berling, R. (July/August 1993). The emerging approach to business strategy: Building a relationship adventure. *Business Horizons.* 16–24.

Bryan, E. (November/December 1990). The world turned upside down? IBM in the 1990s. *Business Horizons.* 39–47.

Coyne, K. (January, February 1986). The anatomy of sustainable competitive advantage. *Business Horizons.* 211–218.

Consumano, M. (Fall 1988). Manufacturing innovation: Lessons from the Japanese auto industry. *Sloan Management Review.* 29–39.

The Economist (April 18, 1992). The cracks in quality. 67–68.

Feigenbaum, E., McCorduck, P., and Nii, P. (1988). *The Rise of the Export Company.* New York: Times Books.

Fuchsberg, G. (May 14, 1991). Quality programs show shoddy results. *Wall Street Journal.* B1.

Gibson, M. (July 14, 1994). Deutsche takes a long hard look at company stakeholders. *The European,* 22.

Hamal, G. and Prahalad, C. (March/April, 1993, 75–84). Strategy as stretch and leverage. *Harvard Business Review.* 75–84.

Harnischfeger, F., Wense, G., and Hagen, T. (November 1, 1993), General Electric: A company for ABB to learn from? *Mannheim,* 1–63.

Hochswender, W. (May 13, 1991). How fashion spreads around the world at the speed of light. *New York Times.* E5.

King, S. S. (1994). High-speed management and organizational communication: A road map. In S. S. King and D. P. Cushman (eds.). *High-Speed Management and Organizational Communication in the 1990s: A Reader.* Albany: State University of New York Press, 1–5.

Lohr, S. (June 18, 1992). Ford and Chrysler outpace Japanese in reducing costs. *New York Times.* D2.

Mascarenhas, B. (1992). Order of entry and preference in international markets. *Strategic Management* 13:429–510.

Miles, R. and Snow, C. (Spring 1984). Fit, failure and the Hall of Fame *California Management Review* 24:10–38.

Nohria, N. and Garcia-Pont, C. (1991). Global strategic linkages and industrial structure. *Strategic Management Journal* 12:105–124.

Obloj, K., Cushman, D. P., and Kozminski, A. (1994). *Winning: Continuous Improvement in High Performance Organizations.* Albany: State University of New York Press.

Phillips, S. and Denkin, A. (November 8, 1989). Is there no limit to the Limited's growth. *Business Week.* 192–199.

Port, O., Cary, J., Kelly, K., and Forest, S. (November 30, 1992). Quality, 66–74.

Powell, T. (1992). Organizational alignment as competitive advantage. *Strategic Management Journal* 13:119–134.

Saski, T. (1991). How the Japanese accelerated new car development. *Long Range Planning* 24:15–25.

Spanner, G. Nuna, J., and Chandra, G. (1993). Time-based strategies: Theory and Practice. *Long Term Planning.* 26:90–101.

Stalk, G., Evans, P., and Shulman, L. (March/April 1992). Competing on capabilities: The new role of corporate strategy. *Harvard Business Review.* 57–69.

Taylor, A. (November 19, 1990). Why Toyota keeps getting better and better and better. *Fortune.* 66–79.

Tichy, N. and Charon, R. (September/October 1989). Speed, simplicity, and self-confidence: An interview with Jack Welch. *Harvard Business Review.* 112–120.

Titzeli, R. (May 18, 1992). Making quality more than a fad. *Fortune.* 12–13.

Treece, J. (March 26, 1990). How Ford and Mazda shared the driver's seat. *Business Week.* 94–95.

Treece, J., Miller, L., and Melcher, R. (February 10, 1992). The Partners. *Business Week.* 102–107.

USA Today (June 2, 1991). B3.

USA Today (June 3, 1993). U.S. car brands improve quality. B3.

Ventkatraman, N. and Prescott, J. (1990). Environment strategy coalignment: An empirical test of its performance implications. *Strategic Management Journal* 11:1–23.

Vesey, J. (1991). Speed-to-market distinguishes the new competitors. *Academy of Management Executives.* 23–33.

Welch, J. (January 25, 1993a). Jack Welch's lessons for success. *Fortune.* 86–93.

Welch, J. (April 28, 1993b). The speed and spirit of a boundaryless company. *GE Speech Reprints.* 1–4.

Welch, J. (April 24, 1991). In pursuit of speed. *GE Speech Reprints.* 1–4.

Welch, J. (April 25, 1990). A boundary-less company in a decade of change. *GE Speech Reprints.* 1–5.

Womack, J., Jones, D., and Roos, D. (199). *The Machine That Changed the World.* New York: Macmillan.

Index

ABB, 249
Allen-Bradley Corporation, 192–93
American Airlines, 39–40, 161
Arthur D. Little, 123, 247–48
A. T. Kearney, 123, 247–48
AT&T, 58, 61, 66, 74, 231

benchmarking (*see* high-speed management, best practices)
BMW, 39–40, 237

change
    incremental change, 47–48, 64, 103, 118, 253
    discontinuous change, 47–48, 64–74, 103–18, 253
    framebreaking change (*see* discontinuous change)
Chrysler, 30, 73–74, 225, 232
coalignment, 24, 39–47
communication, definition of, 37–39, 129
communication processes, 17, 36, 229
    organizational integration, 47–49, 53–150
        climate, 48, 53, 89–118, 150
        leadership, 47, 53, 55–68, 150
            power perspectives, 57–58
            trait perspectives, 58
            behavioral perspectives, 58–61
            situational perspectives, 61–63
            coalignment broker, 70–71
            managing discontinuous change, 71–74

            network leader, 68–70
            transformational leader, 65–68
            transformational leadership
              skills: anticipatory, 65; visionary, 65–66; value-congruence, 66; empowering, 66; self-understanding, 66
        teamwork, 48, 53
        Workout, 81–82
    organizational coordination, 49–50, 151–216
        communication and information technology
            R & D and Marketing, 49, 151–52, 154, 214
              tools: environmental assessment, 155–58; product portfolio modeling, 158–60; structural innovation, 160–63
              strategies, 163–67
              alignment activities, 167–76
            R & D, Marketing, and Manufacturing, 49–50, 152
              tools: robots, 179; integrated flexible systems, 179–80; CAD/CAM, 180; CIS, 180–82
              strategies, 182–87
              alignment activities, 187–94
            R & D, Marketing, Manufacturing, and MIS, 50, 152, 195–214
              resources, 194–201
              strategies, 201–04
              alignment activities, 204–14

environmental scanning (see high-
    speed management)
organizational control, 50–51, 215–33,
    235–52
    audit, 217, 246–47
    process mapping, 51, 83, 140–49,
        222, 223
    information and communication
        planning and linking, 51, 227–33,
        235–47
competitive advantage, 28–29, 41
    low product cost, 21, 28–29, 30
    product differentiation, 21, 29–30
    scope competitive advantage, 29–30,
        184–85
    time competitive advantage, 21–22, 29,
        30, 151, 185, 236
    economies of sourcing, scale, and
        focus, 183–85
core competencies, 68–70
    knowledge-based, 69
    alliance-based, 69
    technology-based, 69–70
culture, 89
    myth, ritual, and social drama, 90–91,
        101–04, 114–15
critical success factors (CSPs), 142–49,
    175–76, 193–94, 223

Danville, Illinois Bumper Works, 44–45

embeddedness, 124
economic trends, 3–7
Ernst and Young, 126, 229–30, 247–48

Ford, 29, 32–35, 73–74, 232, 243–44

GE (General Electric), 17, 18, 40, 66, 75–
    87, 91, 105, 161, 173–75, 233, 249–52
General Motors, 32–35, 135, 156, 159, 180,
    231, 239

high-speed management
    definition, 2, 16, 18–19, 37, 252–53
    philosophic perspective, 36
    theoretic perspective, 41–45

evaluation, 247–53
continuous improvement, 16, 23, 36–
    45, 121–50, 230, 235–53
    teamwork, 119–50, 219–21
        self-managed teamwork, 41, 42, 44,
            122, 128–39, 148–49
        New England Town Meeting,
            129–39
        cross-functional teamwork, 41, 43,
            44, 83, 122, 139–49, 222–23
        best practices teamwork, 41, 43–
            45, 122, 224–28
        negotiated linking, 41–122, 235–52
            strategic fit, 235–36
    environmental scanning, 16, 23–27, 35, 46
    value chain theory, 16, 23, 27–32, 35,
        46, 60–70, 121, 140, 228
Honda, 29, 185

information, definition of, 37–39
IBM, 18, 40, 91–105, 143–48, 156–62, 181,
    189, 239
Intel, 161
international competition
    multidomestic approach, 28, 32
    global approach, 28, 30

Kaiser and Associates, 18

Limited Company, The, 193, 208–14, 245

McKinsey & Company, 17, 67–68
MasterCard, 40
Matsushita Electric Company, 170–73,
    191, 249–52
Mazda, 243–44
Motorola, 17, 74, 231

NUMMI, 137–39

Rath and Strong, 123, 247–48
revolution in information and communi-
    cation technologies, 4–5, 151–216

Sears, 40, 239
socialization, 95–104

speed of response (*see* competitive
  advantage)

TQM, 123, 247–48
Toyota, 29, 32–35, 44–49, 73–74, 135, 187,
  190, 231–33, 237, 241–42

Visa, 40, 238

Welch, Jack, 26, 75–87, 252
Western Union, 40

Xerox, 141, 224–26